LINGUISTICS:
AN INTRODUCTION
TO LANGUAGE AND
COMMUNICATION

LINGUISTICS: AN INTRODUCTION TO LANGUAGE AND COMMUNICATION

Adrian Akmajian
Richard A. Demers
Robert M. Harnish

The MIT Press
Cambridge, Massachusetts,
and London, England

Second printing, September 1979
Copyright © 1979 by
The Massachusetts Institute of Technology

This book was set in VIP Times Roman by Grafacon, Inc., printed and bound by The Alpine Press Inc., in the United States of America.

Library of Congress Cataloging in Publication Data

Akmajian, Adrian
  Linguistics, an introduction to language and communication.

  Bibliography: p.
  Includes index.
  1. Linguistics. 2. Animal communication.
I. Demers, Richard A., joint author. II. Harnish, Robert M., joint author. III. Title.
P121.A4384   410   79-4079
ISBN 0-262-05058-5 (hard)
ISBN 0-262-51019-7 (paper)

To Melina and Rachel
Kathryn
and the memory of Robert S. Adams

CONTENTS

Contents

Contents

Contents ix

ACKNOWLEDGMENTS

This textbook is the product of many years of collaboration among the authors, but that collaboration alone could not have allowed us to complete this project. Valuable comments and criticisms came to us from Morris Halle, Kenneth Hale, Joan Bresnan, Eloise Jelinek, Gary Foulke, Adrienne Lehrer, Kerry Demers, and Penny Akmajian, to whom we remain grateful for examining different portions of the manuscript. The authors alone, however, are responsible for the contents of this book.

We owe a deep debt of gratitude to Kathryn Bayles; not only has she been our consultant on language and the brain, she is the author of chapter 13 on that topic.

Many thanks to Tom Larson, who bravely tackled the job of indexing the text, and to Paul Akmajian, our artist, whose drawings appear in figures 2.1–2.4 and 2.6, 6.2 and 6.3, 10.2 and 10.3, and in all figures in chapter 13.

The outstanding work and tireless dedication of Dorothy Shank, our preliminary editor and typist, resulted in a manuscript of sterling form.

Finally, we must express our gratitude and appreciation to all those students who have over the years taught us how to teach linguistics.

NOTE TO
THE TEACHER

This book grew directly out of our experiences in collaborating on teaching introductory linguistics courses at the University of Arizona, and it is intended to reflect our serious concern with pedagogical soundness as much as factual and theoretical soundness. Part I of the text deals with animal communication systems, a subject matter that is not traditionally thought to be part of an introductory linguistics course. However, this field is not only attracting an ever wider range of interest on the part of language-oriented scholars from diverse disciplines, but we have also discovered that it is an excellent way to stimulate interest in the field of linguistics on the part of beginning students. By beginning our course with this topic, we already have some background in communication systems by the time we begin studying human language, thus allowing the great contrast between animal systems and human language to throw into greater relief the interesting properties of human language. Chapters 2 through 4 stand as fairly independent chapters, providing basic facts about bee, bird, and primate communication. In chapter 5 we summarize and tie together the material in chapters 2–4, at the same time looking ahead by comparing the animal systems to human language.

Part II deals with the study of human language and communciation, and here we include traditional (and not so traditional) subdisciplines of linguistics. The chapters in this section are by no means uniform in their approach, scope, or content, reflecting the fact that at the present writing the various subdisciplines of linguistics are simply not at the same stage of development. For example, chapter 6, on phonology, presents reasonably well-established, detailed results; in contrast, chapter 8, on syntax, a subdiscipline that has been changing rapidly in recent years, presents fewer (putative) results and concentrates instead on broad underlying concepts of syntax. Semantics (chapter 11), which enjoys even less consensus than syntax, is taken up in three distinct but related parts. The first delineates the domain of the subject, the second explores traditional definitions of meaning, and the third presents the outlines of an informal semantic theory. Finally, in chapter 12, we present a two-part discussion of the very new subfield of pragmatics (the study of language use), which is not even old enough to have developed opposing schools. Here again we delineate the domain of the field, independently of any particular theory, and follow up with a sketch of an informal theory, which stresses the interesting complexity of actual linguistic communication without obscuring and mystifying it. In short, structural uniformity in part II would be artificial at best; therefore, the different states of the art in different subdisciplines have guided our conceptions of the individual chapters. In addition, the different chapter formats in parts I and II reflect even greater differences in the states of the two arts: the study of animal communication and the study of human language.

Finally, in part III, we present two special topics. Our discussion of the first, language and the brain, presents the student with information that forms the basis of the nascent field of neurolinguistics. The second topic, teaching language to chimpanzees, allows the student to integrate material from parts I and II. With a background in both natural animal communication systems and human language, the student can undertake a critical evaluation of the recent work on teaching chimps to communicate with a language artificial to them.

Turning from the organization of the book to its contents, we cannot overemphasize our concern with imparting basic conceptual foundations of linguistics, and the methods of argumentation, justification, and hypothesis testing within the field. In no way is this book intended to be a complete survey of the facts or putative results that have occupied linguists in recent years. On the contrary we have chosen a small set of linguistic concepts that we understand to be among the most fundamental within the field at this time, and in presenting these concepts we have attempted to show how one argues for linguistic hypotheses. By dealing with a relatively small number of topics in detail, students can get a feeling for how work in different areas of linguistics is done. If an introductory course can impart this sort of feeling for the field, it will have largely succeeded.

With a few minor exceptions, all of the illustrative examples in part II are drawn from the English language. We recognize the great importance of studying language universals and the increasingly significant role that comparative studies will play in linguistic research. In presenting conceptual foundations of linguistics to students who have never been exposed to the subject before, however, we feel it is absolutely crucial that students should be able to draw upon their linguistic intuitions in making occasionally subtle judgments about language, in both following the text and doing exercises. This is not merely for convenience, to set up as few obstacles as possible in an introductory course; we feel, rather, that it is essential that students be able to evaluate critically our factual claims at each step, for this encourages a healthy skepticism and an active approach toward the subject matter. Given that the majority of our readers will be native speakers of English, our restriction to English examples provides benefits that we feel far outweigh the lack of data from other languages. Obviously, the general principles we discuss must be applicable to all languages, and some teachers may wish to emphasize universals and cross-language data in their lectures.

Finally, a few words about the use of the text. We have used the text quite comfortably for a one-semester course, with the following timetable: two weeks on part I, eleven weeks on part II, and two weeks on part III. Teachers working under different time constraints may wish to modify this schedule or to drop certain chapters from their courses; we have tried to facilitate modification by making the chapters as independent of each other as possible, short of harming the presentation of the subject matter. Furthermore, some chapters contain subsections labeled as optional. Teachers who need, or wish, to teach a fairly broad survey of linguistics can skip over these (and possibly other) sections without harm to the rest of the subject matter. Those who wish to teach a course that has more depth will probably want to include more sections as required reading. In short, by varying the selection of chapters and subsections, teachers from diverse backgrounds and in diverse academic departments will be able to design an introduction to linguistics that is custom-made for their own purposes.

A Note on the Exercises   The exercises at the end of each chapter are of two sorts: some are prefixed with an asterisk, others are not. The latter are mainly for review of the material in the chapters; starred exercises involve more creative thinking, extensions beyond particular chapters, and integration of material from more than one chapter.

NOTE TO
THE STUDENT

Phenomena can be so familiar that we really do not see them at all, a matter that has been much discussed by literary theorists and philosophers. For example, Viktor Shklovskij in the early 1920's developed the idea that the function of poetic art is that of "making strange" the object depicted. "People living at the seashore grow so accustomed to the murmur of the waves that they never hear it. By the same token, we scarcely ever hear the words which we utter. . . . We look at each other, but we do not see each other any more. Our perception of the world has withered away; what has remained is mere recognition." Thus, the goal of the artist is to transfer what is depicted to the "sphere of new perception"; as an example, Shklovskij cites a story by Tolstoy in which social customs and institutions are "made strange" by the device of presenting them from the viewpoint of a narrator who happens to be a horse.

Noam Chomsky, *Language and Mind* (1972, 24–25)

Beginning students of linguistics are often surprised to find that linguists spend considerable time trying to formulate theories to explain the workings of human language. After all, for most people, speaking their native language is the most natural and effortless task imaginable—it is carried out with great speed, with great ease, and even four-year-old children can do it with little conscious effort. It is a common belief that aside from a few rules of grammar and pronunciation there is nothing else to explain about human language.

But it turns out that there is a great deal to explain—if we "step outside" language and look at it as an object to be consciously studied and described, not merely used. Once we manage to "make strange" something as familiar as human language, we discover a new and exciting sphere of human knowledge previously hidden to us.

Imagine that you are an extraterrestrial linguist from a nearby galaxy, sent to Earth in order to report on the nature of human language. To you as an alien creature, nothing about human language (or customs or culture) is obvious or plain. Every detail of human language is new to you, and all of language appears strange. After careful study of this marvelous mechanism of humans, you might see the structure of human language in the way it is depicted in the chart.

How an extraterrestrial linguist might see universal properties of human language structure

Theory 1 (Order)	□	□	□	□	□	□
Theory 2 (Category)	△	★	⊕	◇	×	⊙
Theory 3 (Grouping)	△	★	⊕	◇	×	⊙
Theory 4 (Function)	△	★	⊕	◇	×	⊙
		F_1		F_2		F_3
Theory 5 (Dependency)	△	★	⊕	◇	×	⊙
		F_1		F_2		F_3

How might you arrive at this "strange" view of language? By the time you have finished this book the answer will be clear. But it might be useful to see how you, as the alien linguist, might arrive at the picture we have drawn. When you first arrive on Earth, you would notice humans emitting continuous streams of sound, which apparently have some sort of effect on other humans. As surprising as it may seem, it would not be at all obvious to an extraterrestrial creature that these streams of sound are actually made up of discrete units, for example, words. In reality, the sentences we utter in real speech are physically continuous and not broken down into convenient separate chunks. It is therefore a major breakthrough for you as an alien linguist to propose theory 1, based on your discovery that human language is made up of *discrete units* in some sequential *order* (see theory 1 on chart). The discrete units all seem to be alike to you—they all appear to have the same status at first, as though they were identical boxes in a row. This is very much the way human linguists describe the abstract properties of most bird songs (see chapter 3).

After more study, however, you quickly discover that the discrete units of human language are not all identical but, rather, come in different categories. This leads you to theory 2: human language is made up of discrete units of *different categories* (for example, the traditional parts of speech), strung out in a sequential order. Now the units no longer resemble the identical boxes of theory 1 but take on distinctive shapes, just as the words in the following English sentence are all of distinct categories:

the	old	man	left	didn't	he
↕	↕	↕	↕	↕	↕
△	★	⊕	◇	✕	⊙

Every human language has this property, and, in fact, some researchers have claimed that certain artificial languages taught to chimpanzees have discrete units of different categories (see chapter 14).

Your continuing exploration of human language begins to reveal an even more interesting property, formulated as theory 3: human language is made up of a sequential order of discrete (and distinctly categorized) units that are *grouped together* in various ways to form larger units, or phrases. In our particular English example, we have the following grouping:

the old man   left   didn't he
△ ★ ⊕   ◇   ✕   ⊙

This is a significant discovery: to an alien linguist it is not obvious that words should go together to form phrases. Yet every human language has the property of grouping, and we know of no animal language with this property; from here on we seem to be in an exclusively human domain.

Another important property of all human languages is revealed when you discover facts that lead to theory 4: the structural groupings of the discrete units have specific and distinct *functions*. Thus, the first grouping might have F_1, or function 1; the second grouping F_2, or function 2; and so on. In our English example, the first grouping has traditionally been called the subject, the second grouping the predicate, and the third grouping the tag question:

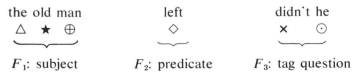

F_1: subject F_2: predicate F_3: tag question

Even though you as an alien linguist have already discovered that human language is a very sophisticated communication system, the story is not yet finished. Your further investigations show you that theory 5 must be postulated: in all human languages there are dependencies between words in completely different locations in a sentence. In our concrete example from English the dependency is this: the pronoun in the tag question (*he*) must agree in person, number, and gender with the subject of the sentence:

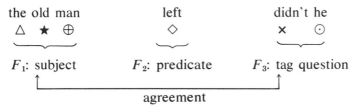

Thus, the symbols $\oplus$ and $\odot$ (*man, he*) are distinct but related units, bound together by a dependency relation traditionally called agreement.

By the time you finish this book, it will be clear why the alien linguist might arrive at the picture of all human languages shown as theory 5. The properties represented by theory 5 do not exhaust the known abstract properties of human language, but they are certainly among the most important. As you read, refer back to the picture chart often: it can help to organize the material and can take you "outside" language to get a clearer picture of its abstract properties.

LINGUISTICS:
AN INTRODUCTION
TO LANGUAGE AND
COMMUNICATION

Chapter One

WHAT IS LINGUISTICS?

People have been fascinated with language and communication for thousands of years, yet in many ways we are only beginning to understand the complex nature of this aspect of human life. If we ask, What is the nature of language? or How does communication work? we quickly realize that these questions have no simple answers and are much too broad to be answered in any direct way. Similarly, questions such as What is energy? or What is matter? cannot be answered in a direct fashion, and indeed the entire field of physics is an attempt to answer them. The field of linguistics is no different: the field as a whole represents an attempt to break down the broad questions about the nature of language and communication into smaller, more manageable questions that we can hope to answer and in so doing to establish reasonable results that we can build on in moving closer to answers to the larger questions. Unless we limit our sights in this way and restrict ourselves to particular frameworks for examining different aspects of language and communication, we cannot hope to make much progress in answering the broad questions that have fascinated people for so long.

What is linguistics, then? As the reader will see, the field covers a surprisingly broad range of topics related to language and communication.

Part I of this text deals with animal communication systems, a topic not traditionally considered part of linguistics. Its inclusion reflects our interest in communication in general as well as a growing interest, in many disciplines, in comparing animal systems with human language. For example, consider this statement by Premack:

It is often said that language is unique to the human species. Yet it is now well known that many other animals have elaborate communication systems of their own. It seems clear that language is a general system of which human language is a particular, albeit remarkably refined, form. Indeed, it is possible that certain features of human language that are considered to be uniquely human belong to the more general system, and that these features can be distinguished from those that are unique to the human information-processing regime. (1972, 92)

Can we test the truth of these claims? Our purpose in exploring animal systems will be to set up a contrast and comparison with human language so that we are in a better position to evaluate claims about the relatedness of animal systems and human language. Chapters 2 through 4 are written as fairly independent chapters presenting basic facts about bee, bird, and primate communication. Readers, however, should begin to tie together for themselves the information in these chapters, so that our own summary and integration of this material in chapter 5 will be that much more meaningful.

Part II deals with human language and communication. This section covers major areas of the field of linguistics; in our discussion we present a number of universal properties of human language. Each chapter in part II is an attempt to impart to the reader a feeling for how work in a particular subfield of linguistics is actually *done;* the differences in scope and approach in these chapters reflect differences in developmental progress in each of the subfields. We hope that by the end of part II the reader will be in a good position to determine whether human language is a refined version of animal communication systems or not.

Although not all linguists would agree with *all* the details of our approach in part II, linguists do agree that the fundamental ideas we present represent important basic concepts of the field. These concepts, furthermore, are of importance to students and teachers interested in fields related to linguistics: philosophy, cognitive psychology, artificial intelligence and computer science, speech and hearing sciences, neuroscience, anthropology, sociology, language teaching, and education, among others.

In part III we present two perspectives on the capacity for language. Chapter 13 deals with an exciting area known as *neurolinguistics,* a field concerned with the way the human brain stores and processes language. Chapter 14 deals with some of the recent attempts to teach various forms of language to chimpanzees. One increasingly finds chimps compared with humans in the popular literature on this subject, and some people have gone so far as to claim that the chimps' mastery of language is comparable to human linguistic ability. In evaluating claims about the linguistic abilities of chimpanzees, the student will have an opportunity to integrate various topics covered throughout the text.

To turn now from the particular to the general: What are some of the background assumptions that linguists make when they study language? Perhaps the most important fundamental assumption is that human language at all levels is rule-governed. Every language that we know of has systematic rules governing pronunciation, word formaation, and grammatical construction. Further, the way in which meanings are associated with expressions of a language is characterized by regular rules. And, finally, the *use* of language to communicate is governed by important generalizations that we can express in rules. As the reader will see, the ultimate aim of each chapter of part II is to formulate linguistic rules to describe and explain the phenomena under consideration. (Indeed, chapter 9 shows that even so-called casual speech is governed by systematic regularities expressible in rules.)

At this point we must add an important qualification to what we have just said. That is, we are using the terms *rule* and *rule-governed* in the special way that linguists use them. This usage is very different from the layman's understanding of the terms. In school, most of us have been taught so-called rules of grammar, which we were told to follow in order to speak and write "correctly"—rules such as "Do not end a sentence with a preposition," or "Don't say "*ain't*"," or "Never split an infinitive." Rules of this sort are called *prescriptive rules*; that is to say, they all prescribe, or dictate to the speaker, the way the language supposedly should be written or spoken in order for the speaker to appear correct and educated. Prescriptive rules are really rules of style rather than rules of grammar.

In sharp contrast, when linguists speak of rules, they are not referring to prescriptive rules from school grammar books. Rather, linguists try to formulate *descriptive rules* when they analyze language, rules that describe the actual language of some group of speakers (and not some hypothetical language that speakers "should" use). Descriptive rules, as we will see in part II, actually express generalizations and regularities about various aspects of a language. Thus when we say that language is rule-governed, we are really saying that the study of human language has revealed numerous generalizations about and regularities in the structure and function of language.

Another important background assumption that linguists make is that the various human languages constitute a *unified phenomenon:* linguists assume that it is possible to study human language in general, and that the study of particular languages will reveal features of language that are universal. What do we mean by universal features of language?

So far in our discussion we have used the terms *language* and *human language* without referring to any specific language, such as English or Chinese. Students are sometimes puzzled by this general use of the term *language;* it would seem that this use is rarely found outside of linguistics-related courses. Foreign language courses, after all, deal with specific languages such as French or Russian. Further, specific human languages appear on the surface to be so different from each other that it is often difficult to understand how linguists can speak of language as though it were a single thing.

Although it is obvious that specific languages indeed differ from each other on the surface, if we look closer we find that human languages are surprisingly similar. For instance, all languages that we know of are at a similar level of complexity and detail—there is no such thing as a primitive human language. All languages provide a means for asking questions, making requests, giving orders, making assertions, and so on. And there is nothing that can be expressed in one language that cannot be expressed in any other. Obviously, one language may have terms not found in another language, but it is always possible to invent new terms to express what we mean: anything we can imagine or think, we can express in any human language.

Turning to more abstract properties, even the formal structures of languages are similar: all languages have sentences made up of smaller phrasal units, these units in turn being made up of words, which are themselves made up of sequences of sounds. We find, too, that sentences and phrases are structured in similar hierarchial ways across languages. All of these features of human language may seem obvious, and that perhaps is the problem: these features are *so* obvious to us that we may fail to see how surprising it is that languages share them. When linguists use the term *language* (or *human language*), they are revealing their belief that at an abstract level, beneath the surface variation, languages are remarkably similar in form and function and conform to certain universal principles

In relation to what we have just said about universal principles, we should observe that virtually all the illustrative examples in part II of this book are drawn from the English language. This should not mislead the reader into supposing that what we say is relevant only to English. We will be introducing fundamental concepts of linguistics, and we believe that these have to be applicable to all languages. We have chosen English examples so that the reader can continually check our factual claims and decide whether our claims are empirically well founded. We encourage readers to use their knowledge of English as actively as possible in evaluating our discussions.

Finally, a brief observation about the general nature of linguistics. To many linguists the ultimate aim of linguistics is not simply to understand how language itself is structured and how it functions. We hope that as we come to understand more about human language, we will correspondingly understand more about the processes of human thought. In this view the study of language is ultimately the study of the human mind. This goal is perhaps expressed best by Noam Chomsky in his book *Reflections on Language* (1975, 3–4):

Why study language? There are many possible answers, and by focusing on some I do not, of course, mean to disparage others or question their legitimacy. One may, for example, simply be fascinated by the elements of language in themselves and want to discover their order and arrangement, their origin in history or in the individual, or the ways in which they are used in thought, in science or in art, or in normal social interchange. One reason for studying language—and for me personally the most compelling reason—is that it is tempting to regard language, in the traditional phrase, as "a mirror of mind." I do not mean by this simply that the concepts expressed and distinctions developed in normal language use give us insight into the patterns of thought and the world of "common sense" constructed by the human mind. More intriguing, to me at least, is the possibility that by studying language we may discover abstract principles that govern its structure and use, principles that are universal by biological necessity and not mere historical accident, that derive from mental characteristics of the species. A human language is a system of remarkable complexity. To come to know a human language would be an extraordinary intellectual achievement for a creature not specifically designed to accomplish this task. A normal child acquires this knowledge on relatively slight exposure and without specific training. He can then quite effortlessly make use of an intricate structure of specific rules and guiding principles to convey his thoughts and feelings to others, arousing in them novel ideas and subtle perceptions and judgments. For the conscious mind, not specially designed for the purpose, it remains a distant goal to reconstruct and comprehend what the child has done intuitively and with minimal effort. Thus language is a mirror of mind in a deep and significant sense. It is a product of human intelligence, created anew in each individual by operations that lie far beyond the reach of will or consciousness.

References

Chomsky, N. (1975) *Reflections on Language,* Pantheon Books, New York.

Premack, A., and D. Premack (1972) "Teaching language to an ape," *Scientific American* 227, no. 4, 92–99.

Part One

ANIMAL
COMMUNICATION
SYSTEMS

Chapter Two

BEE COMMUNICATION

One of the most remarkable communication systems found in the nonhuman world is that of the European honeybee. Imagine the evolutionary advantage for a honeybee if it is able to communicate the location of an especially rich food source to its hivemates when it returns to the hive. The honeybee is, in fact, able to do this.

Beekeepers had long suspected that bees communicated with each other before the properties of this communication system were scientifically established. For example, beekeepers noticed that if a single bee happens upon a particularly rich source of nectar or pollen, other bees from the hive will soon be found at the food source in significant numbers. It was also noted that large numbers of bees from a certain hive may all be gathering at the same type of food source, while large numbers of bees from an adjacent hive may be gathering food from an entirely different type of flower. This selective food gathering suggested a coordination of efforts on the part of the bees which could be the result of some method of communication.

These facts about bee behavior are now much better understood. We now know that honeybees do communicate, and the most important properties of their communication system have been identified through the research of Karl von Frisch and his colleagues (von Frisch 1967). They have established that when a foraging bee has discovered a rich food supply and returns to the hive, it is able to communicate a surprisingly complex message to its hivemates. The transmitted message is actually a recruitment device, indicating to the hivemates how far to fly, what direction to fly, and what type of food to seek. How is this accomplished?

The scout bee's message is communicated through patterns of movement, called dancing, on the vertical walls of the hive. There are two major types of dance depending on the location of the food source with respect to the hive: the round dance, and the tail-wagging dance. If the source is within 10 meters of the hive, the bee performs the round dance. For distances greater than 100 meters the bee performs the tail-wagging dance.

The Round Dance

Structure

In performing the round dance, the bee traces a circular path in one direction, turns around and retraces the same path in the opposite direction, a pattern that is repeated several times within a small area (see figure 2.1). The dancing bee will frequently stop and pass out samples of food to its hivemates who have been alerted by the dancing activity. The round dance has the following major features:

1. It is used to signal that the food source is within 10 meters of the hive.
2. The intensity of the dance (speed and duration) signals the richness of the food source.

Figure 2.1
Pattern of the round dance. Adapted from von Frisch 1967.

3. The scent on the dancing bee signals to the new recruits the type of food source to seek.

Interestingly, a scout bee will not perform the round dance in an empty hive (nor in one that has been emptied for experimental purposes), which indicates that the dance is not merely an automatic response conditioned by the return to the hive with a rich supply of food. Other bees must be present to trigger the dance, thus underscoring its communicative nature.

Function

The primary function of the round dance is to recruit hivemates. In order to test the honeybees' ability to alert their hivemates to a good food source, von Frisch and his colleagues conducted a wide variety of experiments. In one experiment, bees were first trained to collect food at a feeding station near the hive. They were fed a relatively weak sugar solution, and during the feeding the bees were marked with small dots of paint so that they could be identified. When the supply was interrupted, most of the bees of the original group stopped coming, although a few scout bees would occasionally recheck the feeding station. When an extra-rich supply of a scented sugar solution was later introduced at the feeding station, the scout bees flew back to the hive and performed a vigorous round dance. Out of 174 bees of the original collecting group that came in contact with the dancing scout bee, no less than 155 returned to the feeding station within five minutes.

Dancing bees are also able to recruit new bees to gather at a recently discovered food source. The newly recruited bees do not waste time searching the wrong type of flower, since the scent of the food source on the dancing scout bee is noticed by the bees attracted to the dance. Once the recruited bees have been alerted by the round dance, they fly randomly around the hive seeking the scent they had noticed on the dancing bee. To aid recruited bees in finding their goal, a scout will often secrete a special scent over an especially rich food source.

The Tail-Wagging Dance

Structure

By far the most impressive aspect of the honeybees' communication system is the ability to indicate the location of sources of food beyond 100 meters. As was the case in the round dance, a returning scout bee performs a dance indicating that it has found a profitable gathering site. However, when the distance from the hive is great, it would not be efficient for the recruited bees to begin searching randomly for the source, as they do in response to the round dance. For example, for a source one kilometer away, the recruited bees would have to search an area of 3 million square meters. The European honeybee has therefore evolved a dance that not only indicates the direction the recruited bees must travel but enables the recruited bees to fly the proper distance. Both aspects of the dance have a remarkable degree of accuracy. The dance is known as the tail-wagging dance, and it consists of two roughly semicircular paths of movement with a straight-line portion in between, during which the bee waggles, as illustrated in figure 2.2.

Function: Communicating Direction of Source

Since the working surfaces inside the hive are vertical, the dancing bee is not able to point directly toward the location of the food source. Given this, how can it indicate the proper direction? For the purpose of

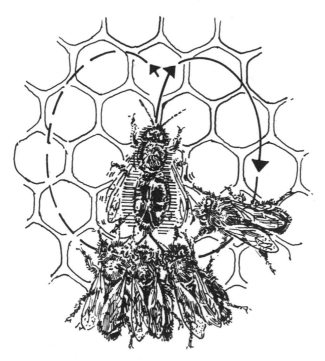

Figure 2.2
Pattern of the tail-wagging dance. Adapted from von Frisch 1967.

indicating the direction of the food source, the bee uses the direction of the force of gravity. For example, there are three typical situations that the bee faces, as shown in figure 2.3. First, if the recruited bees are to fly along the ground in the direction of the sun, the straight-line portion of the tail-wagging dance points directly upward (dance A, figure 2.3). Second, when the recruited bees are to fly along the ground away from the sun, the dancing bee will orient the straight-line portion of the dance directly downward (dance C). Third, if the recruited bees are to fly with the sun, say, 80° to their right, the dance will be oriented 80° to the left of vertical (Dance B). In other words the solar-oriented flight of the recruited bees is systematically related to the gravity-oriented dance of the scout bee.

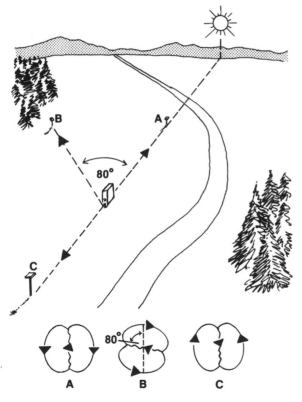

Figure 2.3
Relation of solar-oriented flight to force of gravity. Box at center of landscape is the hive; three test feeding stations, A, B, and C, surround it. At bottom: dances corresponding to the paths to the three feeding stations. Adapted from von Frisch 1967.

The accuracy of the bees' ability to communicate direction is best illustrated by another experiment performed by von Frisch. Several bees were first trained to feed on a meager food source at a station located 250 meters from the hive. The source was kept meager so that the bees would not become excited enough to start recruiting their hivemates. After a few bees had been induced to feed regularly at the station, a rich sugar solution scented with an essential oil was fed to them. The feeding station was then removed as soon as a few scout bees left it to return to the hive. At 200 meters from the hive, seven cards scented with the same essential oil used in the feeding solution were placed on an arc. The middle card was in a straight line from the hive to the feeding station and the other cards were 15° apart along the arc, as shown in figure 2.4a.

The recruited bees, flying from the hive looking for the food source, alighted upon the cards. The number of bees landing on the card in line with the original feeding station was substantially greater than the number alighting on cards further out along the arc, illustrating the accuracy of the message communicated by the dancing bees (see figure 2.4b).

One of the more remarkable aspects of the bee communication system is that the successful forager who returns to dance is able to indicate the direction to the source without having flown that exact same direction itself. Once a scout bee has located a profitable food

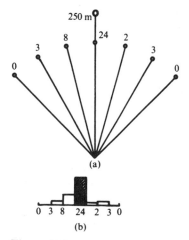

Figure 2.4
Number of bees alighting on scent cards placed 200 meters from hive. After von Frisch 1967.

source, it returns directly to the hive and there it must communicate the *reverse* of its own return trip.

Function: Communicating Distance of Source
There is increasing evidence that the length of time the dancing bee spends in the straight-line portion of the tail-wagging dance is the critical feature representing the distance to the food source. During this portion of the dance the bee also makes a special buzzing sound, and it has been proposed that it is the length of the buzzing which actually communicates the distance. The length of time that the bee spends in the straight-line portion of the tail-wagging dance is also related to the number of complete circuits the bee makes per unit of time. The fewer circuits per unit time (or equivalently the longer the bee spends in the tail-wagging portion of the dance), the farther the source is from the hive. For example, if nine or ten circuits are made within a 15-second period, the distance to the food source is 100 meters; for six circuits per 15 seconds, the distance indicated is 500 meters; and if the number of circuits is four per 15 seconds, the distance is 1500 meters (almost a mile). Experiments have shown that bees can communicate distances up to 11 kilometers—almost 7 miles.

The accuracy of the dancing bees' communication of distance is revealed by the results of a typical experiment in which a small number of bees were induced to fly out to a feeding station located 2000 meters from the hive, where they were fed a meager sugar solution. On the following morning the same meager feeding was continued, but for a period of two and a half hours an extremely rich sugar solution scented with an essential oil was substituted for the meager feeding. The feeding station was then removed, and scent cards were placed at intervals in a straight line from the hive out to and beyond the feeding station. Most of the recruited bees landed on the cards that were closest to the original feeding station (see figure 2.5). What is remarkable is that bees flew over and ignored scent cards *closer* to the hive than those near the feeding station—even at 1200 meters only one bee alighted on a closer card. Had the bees been seeking scent alone, more of them would have landed on the cards closest to the hive.

The clustering of the bees at the cards closest to the original feeding station offers an excellent indication of the quality of information that the bee has when flying to a target food source. There is even evidence that the recruited bee anticipates the distance before flying to a food

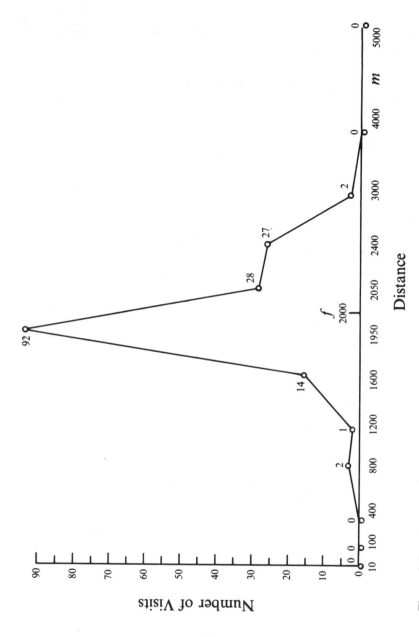

Figure 2.5
Number of bees visiting scent cards when feeding was at 2000 meters. Adapted from von Frisch 1967.

source, inasmuch as the bee takes on fuel (honey) in proportion to the distance it must fly to the source (see table 2.1).

In summary, the tail-wagging dance conveys the following information: the *orientation* of the straight-line portion of the dance communicates the *direction* that the bees must fly with respect to the position of the sun; the length of *time* spent during the tail-wagging portion of the dance communicates the *distance* that must be flown; and, finally, the general level of *excitation* during the dance communicates the *richness* of the source.

Dialects in the Communication System

Not all honeybees of the same or related species communicate in the same way; the bee system, like human language, may have dialectal variation. The dancing patterns discussed in the previous sections belong to the black Austrian honeybee. In contrast, the Italian honeybee, a member of the same species as the black Austrian honeybee, has a slightly different mode of dancing. For distances up to 10 meters the Italian bee, like the black Austrian honeybee, does the round dance. But for distances between 10 and 100 meters the Italian honeybee performs a dance called the sickle dance, which is not used by the black Austrian honeybee. The sickle dance is a flattened figure-eight pattern bent into a semicircle; the center of the semicircle points toward the food source (see figure 2.6).

For distances beyond 100 meters the Italian honeybee does the same type of tail-wagging dance as the black Austrian honeybee. The only difference is that the tempo of the Italian honeybee dance is somewhat slower than that of the Austrian honeybee. When these two types of honeybee are placed together in the same hive and the black Austrian honeybee is aroused by the dance of the Italian bee, it will search for

Table 2.1
Distance Bee Must Travel Related to Amount of Honey Taken in Before the Trip (Based on data from von Frisch, 1967)

Distance	Weight of Honey Taken In
5 meters	.782 mg.
500	1.6
1000	2.2
1500	4.13

Food source

Figure 2.6
Sickle dance of Italian honeybee. Adapted from von Frisch 1967.

food at a point *beyond* the location actually indicated in the framework of the Italian bee.

Acquisition of the Communication System

The bees' ability to dance and navigate is innate, but experience can play a role in increasing the accuracy of these activities. Von Frisch reports: "During their first outward flights, young bees have to acquire individual experience with the sun's course in order that their compass orientation shall function properly. But in this process, becoming acquainted with the sun's course over a few hours suffices for them to find the proper direction later, at another time of day" (1967, 525).

Outside of increasing the precision of its activities through experience, there is no evidence that the bee has to learn any of its behavior. Individual bees raised in isolation from the hive function normally when they are introduced to the hive for the first time. Thus it appears that the general communication system is innate but that the finer details of the system can be modified by learning. The same characteristic seems to hold for some species of birds and primates (see chapters 3 and 4).

Additional support for the innateness of the bee communication system has come from studies of the dances of hybrid offspring of black Austrian and Italian honeybee parents. "Offspring that bear the Italian bee's yellow body markings often do the Sickle Dance. In one experiment sixteen hybrids strongly resembling their Italian parent used the Sickle Dance to represent intermediate distances 65 out of 66 times, whereas fifteen hybrids that resembled their Austrian parent used the Round Dance 47 out of 49 times" (von Frisch 1962, 80). In other words, the offspring inherit the dance patterns of the parents they resemble physically, just as they would inherit any other genetic trait.

In sum, the honeybee has a remarkably complex communication system, especially for an organism with a brain the size of a grass seed. Indeed, the system shows a degree of internal complexity that is unrivaled in the more advanced species we will take up in chapters 3 and 4.

Exercises

1. What is the structure of the European honeybee's communication system?

2. What is the function of the communication system? How do aspects of the message correlate with aspects of the structure?

3. Why does the black Austrian honeybee search *beyond* the food source when aroused by the dance of the Italian honeybee?

4. What is the role of learning in the honeybee's communication system?

*5. In discussing communication systems, the terms *icon* and *symbol* are sometimes used. An icon is a sign that bears some type of physical resemblance to its referent. For example, statues, road maps, and photographs are all examples of icons. A symbol is an arbitrary sign: it bears no necessary physical relation to its referent. For example, the word *dog* does not resemble a dog. Discuss whether the communication system of the honeybee is iconic or symbolic.

*6. Does bee language share any features with human language?

References

Esch, H. (1967) "The evolution of bee language," *Scientific American* 216, no. 4, 96–104.

Lindauer, M. (1961) *Communication Among Social Bees,* Harvard University Press, Cambridge, Mass.

von Frisch, K. (1962) "Dialects in the language of bees," *Scientific American,* 207, no. 2, 78–87.

———— (1967) *The Dance Language and Orientation of Bees,* translated by C. E. Chadwick, Harvard University Press, Cambridge, Mass.

Wenner, A. (1964) "Sound communication in honeybees," *Scientific American,* 210, no. 4, 116–124.

Chapter Three

BIRD
COMMUNICATION

Human beings have long responded poetically to the songs of birds. As simple as these songs may sound to us at first, it is no easy task to discover the structure and function of bird vocalizations, which range from a single note to intricate melodies. An important task in ornithology at the present time is to determine what communicative functions these vocalizations might be serving. It is clear that birds also use many visual devices to communicate. The mating dance of grebes, the bobbing dance before mating of the mockingbird, the brilliant display of the peacock, and even the bright colors of the males of most bird species are all prime examples of visual displays related to communication. But though these visual features belong in a complete account of bird communication, they have not been studied extensively. In contrast, bird vocalizations have long been studied in great detail, and with the advent of the sound spectrograph (a device that displays sounds visually), more careful qualitative and quantitative studies have been undertaken. In this chapter we will limit ourselves to the vocal aspects of bird communication.

Ornithologists distinguish two major classes of vocalizations—calls and songs. Although there is some overlap in structure and function between these two categories, the distinction is useful for purposes of discussion.

Bird Calls

Structurally, calls are sound patterns consisting of single notes or short note sequences associated with the following functional events and activities: flight, specialized alarm (for example, mobbing call, aerial predator call), pleasure, distress, territorial defense, feeding, nesting, flocking, aggression, and general alarm (Thorpe, 1961). We will discuss here the first two types of calls.

Flight Calls

The tree sparrow lives in colonies that may consist of as many as a hundred birds; they have at their disposal three different calls relating to flight. One call is used just before takeoff; another is used during flight; and the third is used while looking for food and just before landing at nesting sites. The function of these calls seems to be to coordinate the activities of the numerous members of the colony. For instance, the in-flight call seems to be used to keep the flock together in flight, and the landing call seems to be used to announce an imminent landing.

Specialized Alarm: Mobbing Call

There is an interesting convergence among distinct bird species with respect to the mobbing call. The call itself is a sharp note, which often sounds like the word "chink." When a predator is discovered nearby, such as an owl in a tree, the birds will fly up to the predator and announce its presence with their mobbing calls. These calls attract other birds, who in turn also make the mobbing call. One of the effects of this activity is that the predator may be driven off. The primary effect, however, is that the chance of a predator's capturing a bird with the element of surprise is greatly reduced. It is easy for a small bird to evade a predator if the bird can keep the predator in sight. The function, then, is to alert the birds in the area to the presence and location of a potential predator.

The mobbing call shows an interesting structure–function adaptation. Because the call has an abrupt onset and offset, it is easy for birds to establish the direction from which the sound comes. The sound arrives at slightly different times at the left and right ears of each bird, allowing the direction of the sound to be localized. Thus, because of the structure of the sound, a bird giving the call attracts attention to itself and so helps other birds locate the predator.

The structure of this alarm is shared by many birds, and an alarm sounded by one bird will cause a mobbing reaction among different species. The similarities in the structure of this call can be seen in figure 3.1, a collection of spectrograms of mobbing calls. Spectrograms are made by a device called a spectrograph, which analyzes acoustic signals (sounds) and displays them visually. Frequency is shown on the

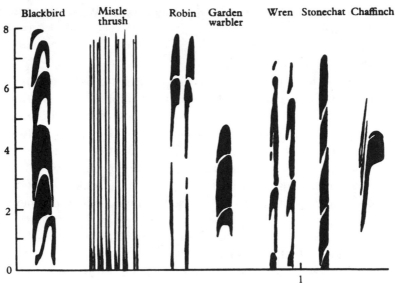

Figure 3.1
Mobbing calls of different bird species. Frequency (vertical axis) is in kilocycles per second. From Thorpe 1961.

vertical axis and time is shown on the horizontal axis. The relative darkness of the figure on the spectrogram represents the intensity of the sound. The call of the blackbird, for example, is shown with six concentrations of sound energy (called resonances), all of which rise and fall abruptly. The first (lower) resonance begins at 300 cycles per second (or 300 Hertz), and rises to almost 2000 Hertz before it falls again. To the human ear the call represented by the blackbird spectrogram sounds like a metallic "chink", whereas the call represented by the mistlethrush spectrogram sounds like a short hiss (a "psh" rather than the more common "chink"). Just as these differences are represented graphically by spectrograms, so also is an important similarity, namely, the abruptness of the beginning and the end of each call. (Contrast the sharp beginnings and ends of the calls in figure 3.1 with the tapered beginnings and ends of the calls in figure 3.2.)

Specialized Alarm: Aerial Predator Call
If a predatory bird is spotted flying overhead, many ground birds will emit a call whose structure is decidedly different from that of the mobbing call. Instead of beginning abruptly, the aerial predator call begins gradually and is at a much higher frequency. It is referred to as

the "seet" call. When birds feeding near the ground hear it, they may either become motionless or move rapidly for cover. These reactions are clear evidence that the function of the call is to minimize the birds' chances of being caught by surprise from above.

Again, there is an interesting type of structure–function adaptation involved with the aerial predator call. In contrast to the mobbing call, the aerial predator call has an imperceptible onset combined with a high-frequency "seet"; thus locating the source of this call is very difficult. Using this call, a bird can announce the presence of an overhead predator while minimizing its own danger of being located and captured. The "seet" call too is shared by birds of many different species and when given by one bird, members of other species will take evasive action. Figure 3.2 shows a striking similarity in the structure of the "seet" calls of different species, given when a hawk flies overhead. Each of the spectrograms in figure 3.2 begins with a slow taper on the left, remains fairly uniform, and then tapers off to a point on the right.

In sum, these representative bird calls demonstrate that this aspect of the bird communication system consists mainly of a small collection of *discrete* sounds, each with a fixed range of functions. This system is surprisingly similar to that of a totally unrelated species, the primates, as will be seen in chapter 4.

Bird Songs

It is instructive to compare these typical bird calls with some bird songs. The songs of birds are more complex than their calls and are used chiefly by male birds to establish territories and attract mates during the breeding season.

Territorial Song

In experiments carried out by Falls (1969), recordings of several white-throated sparrow songs were played in areas where particular male white-throated sparrows had established their territory. Songs of both neighboring birds and of strangers that had never before been heard in the established male's territory were played. The established male, when confronted with a song of another male in his territory, flew up to the source (in this case a loudspeaker) and performed his song. When the songs of strangers were played, the established males responded much more aggressively and sang more frequently than they

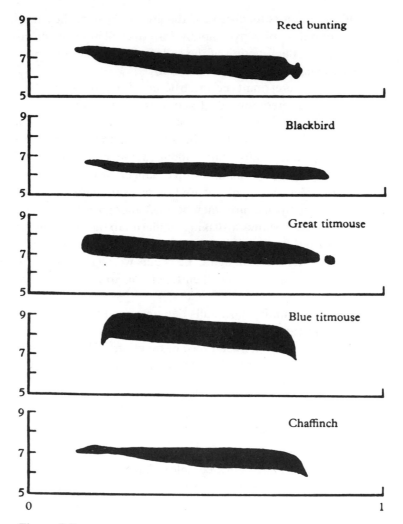

Figure 3.2
Aerial predator calls of five species, given when a hawk flies overhead. Frequency (vertical axis) is in kilocycles per second. From Thorpe 1961.

did when the songs of neighbors were played. Moreover, when the song of a neighbor was played from a direction that did not correspond to the location of the neighbor's territory, the established male responded to the song as if it were the song of a stranger. Thus, the white-throated sparrow is able to recognize the individual songs of its neighbors.

One function of the song is to allow males to delimit their territory and to minimize overlap with other males. Singing, then, is a highly efficient device for maintaining territory, since less energy is expended than would be the case if the bird had to patrol and actually battle to defend its territory. Once the male bird has established his territory, the song then functions to attract females, which is shown by the fact that unpaired chaffinch males sing more than those who have found a mate (Thorpe 1961). Since the song serves two major functions (establishing territory and attracting mates), it is not surprising that some species have two distinct songs, one for each of these separate functions. The Pekin robin, for example, has one song for establishing and holding territory and another that is uses to keep in contact with its mate. Since these birds mate permanently, the separate song functions to allow the birds to keep in contact with each other throughout the year.

Antiphonal Singing (Duetting)
For most bird species only the male sings, but some species of birds have evolved a system of countersinging among couples (Hooker and Hooker 1969). This kind of singing has reached its most remarkable form in the Bou-Bou shrike of East Africa. Each couple shares its own distinctive song and a typical song may consist of as many as fourteen notes. For example, the male may take the first four notes of the song, the female the next three notes, the male the next four, and the female the final three. Alternatively, the male or female may sing the whole song alone, or they may even switch parts. These elaborate possibilities are represented in figure 3.3, which further illustrates the differences between songs and calls in terms of structure. (Compare figure 3.3, in terms of general complexity, with figures 3.1 and 3.2.) Readers familiar with musical notation will see that the songs (2–8) are elaborate in structure and strikingly different from each other in their melodies, rhythms, and overall time spans. Scientists hypothesize that the bird couples use these songs to keep in touch in the brushy areas where they live.

Dialects in Calls and Songs

One of the best-known examples of dialect variation in bird calls is found in the chaffinch rain call (so named because many believe that the bird uses it before it rains), which will vary depending on the geographic location of the birds. Figure 3.4 displays the wide variety of

Figure 3.3
Antiphonal songs of the Bou-Bou shrike of East Africa; *x* and *y* indicate the parts taken by the two members of the bird pair. Duration of the song is given in seconds. From Thorpe 1974.

acoustic signals corresponding to the rain call. The functions of these different rain calls have not been established.

Dialects are much more common in bird songs than in bird calls. Two questions immediately present themselves: Are the different dialects learned or part of the genetic inheritance? And what functions do dialects serve? In the case of the chaffinch, the answer to the first question is known, but the answer to the second has not been established.

It has been shown that the young male chaffinch learns the dialect of the area in which it sings during its first breeding season. The basic structure of the song is learned during the first four months after hatching, but the dialects appear to be the result of more careful learning during the following spring when the one-year-old bird is acquiring its final song. Banding experiments have shown that birds will return to the general area where they were raised. Suppose we have a number of adjacent dialect areas, such as shown in figure 3.5. If a brood is raised at the intersection of dialect areas a, b, and c, it is equally probable that the offspring will settle in any of the three adjacent areas. Thus brothers from the same original nest will acquire different dialects, each learning the dialect of the area where he ends up

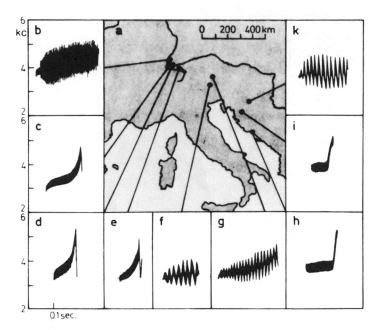

Figure 3.4
Spectrograms of rain calls of the chaffinch. From Thielcke 1976.

breeding: a, b, or c. This is excellent evidence that the dialects of the chaffinch are learned.

Acquisition of Calls and Songs

Bird calls are largely innate; nevertheless, there are species in which learning of calls has survival value. In one of these species the function of a certain call is to allow prompt reuniting of parent and offspring whenever they become separated. For instance, common murre families brood on rock ledges in very close proximity to each other. Disturbances will cause the parents to abandon their ledges and fly into the air, while the chicks scurry for cover under the nearby rocks. When the danger is past, the parents return, each giving a distinctive call. Parents and chicks are thus immediately reunited, and the chicks' exposure to cold and hunger is minimized, increasing their chances for survival.

How do the chicks learn to recognize the distinctive calls of their parents? There is good evidence that the chick of the common murre learns to recognize the distinctive call in the two and a half to four and a

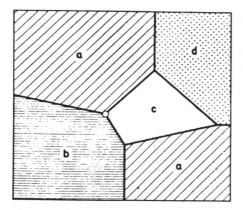

Figure 3.5
Mosaiclike spread of dialects. From Thielcke 1976.

half days *before* hatching (Thielcke 1976). They respond to the call of their own parents immediately after hatching, and calls from neighboring murres do not attract them.

During the first part of the brooding, the two parents alternate incubating the eggs in sixteen- to twenty-four-hour shifts; they are usually quiet during this period. Shortly before the eggs begin to hatch, the chicks inside begin to make a peeping sound, which activates a new set of behavior patterns in the parents. They begin to bring food to the nest, and they also begin to emit their distinctive training call which will eventually be used to summon the chicks. The actual hatching takes three days and fourteen hours, during which the chick saws its way out of the egg with its egg tooth. It is during this cutting period that it hears and learns the training call of its parents.

In controlled experiments, a particular training call was played by means of a tape recorder to hatching chicks. Immediately after hatching, the chicks would run only to the loudspeaker that played the training call they had been exposed to when hatching, ignoring other loudspeakers playing calls that they had not heard before.

Whereas most calls in birds are innate, songs may be either entirely or partially learned. The European cuckoo's song is completely innate. Birds reared in isolation, deafened, or exposed to all songs but their own, still sing the typical song of their species. In contrast, the song of the male bullfinch is almost completely learned. Investigators reared a young bullfinch in a cage with a canary (Nicolai 1959). In the spring during the breeding season, the bullfinch sang the song of the canary.

Moreover, when the offspring of this particular bullfinch matured, they sang the canary song they learned from their father. One of these offspring raised yet another brood in a different cage and passed the canary song on to one of its offspring, who became a third generation canary singer. An interesting feature of the acquisition of the canary song is that the second generation offspring were also raised with normal bullfinches and heard the normal bullfinch song. In spite of this, they nevertheless acquired the canary song of their father.

One of the most interesting features of bird song acquisition has been revealed by the work of Thorpe (1961) on the chaffinch song, which clearly exhibits a complex interplay of innate and learned characteristics. The song of a hand-reared, totally isolated chaffinch is a song of normal length (two and one-half seconds) but without any typical chaffinch structure. This rudimentary song prototype is apparently the biologically innate chaffinch song. In contrast, under normal conditions a chaffinch at around four months of age *learns* the structure of the chaffinch song (three phases and flourish), although it does not *produce* this sequence until the following spring. At that time the young chaffinch produces this imprinted pattern and refines the song by countersinging with other chaffinches in its community. The usual development of the chaffinch song takes place in several critical stages.

Table 3.1 shows the normal developmental stages, matched with the seasons of the year. It also indicates points (A–F) at which experiments were performed. We will discuss the experiments and their significance in succession. At point A, hand-reared birds that are isolated from other chaffinches do not sing the normal chaffinch song; instead they develop a song that is the proper length but is not divided into phrases. If a chaffinch is deafened at three months (point B), the following spring its song will be similar to the food-begging call it performed as a three-month-old chick. Birds captured in September (point C) and kept in isolation during the following spring develop a song with the typical three initial phrases and flourish, but otherwise the song is not like that of normal chaffinches. September-captured birds that are allowed to countersing with each other develop more complex songs than isolated birds. During the breeding season (point D) females injected with the male hormone testosterone performed the song of the male. This experiment shows that though females do not normally perform the song, they nevertheless learn it, which they need to do in order to be attracted to males. During the early spring of the second year (point E), the young chaffinches develop an ever closer

Table 3.1
Stages in the development of the song of the chaffinch

	Spring, First Year	Summer
Developmental stages of typical song	(hatching) First subsong 2–3 seconds	Chirps and rattles
Point at which experiments were performed	↑ A	↑ B

Source: Based on data from Thorpe 1961

approximation to the final song of their species. Countersinging apparently accelerates, and is crucial to, final song development. Isolation of a chaffinch at any of the various stages between D and F will result in an imperfect approximation to the final song. At thirteen months (point F), the ability to acquire the song ends. A chaffinch kept in isolation from others of its species up to this point will never acquire the chaffinch song, regardless of the learning conditions.

Having examined various properties of bird calls and songs in this chapter, we will end on a speculative note. In spite of the vast differences between birds and humans, there are nevertheless some interesting similarities. For instance, we have seen that many birds develop dialects in their songs (and the chaffinch has dialectal variation in one of its calls). Dialect variation is also a characteristic of human language (see chapter 9). Furthermore, as we will see in chapter 13, the human language faculty is dominated by one hemisphere of the brain. Surprisingly, there is evidence that hemispheric dominance in the brain plays a role in the control of bird song (Nottebohm 1970, 952). For instance, the chaffinch song is controlled by the left hypoglossus nerve; cutting that nerve causes the song to be destroyed or impaired. In contrast, if the right hypoglossus is cut, either the song is not altered or only a few of the simpler elements of the song are missing. Interestingly, if either of the nerves (but not both) is cut when the bird is young enough (before maturation), the song develops normally, under control of the other hemisphere. As we will see in chapter 13, in humans, too, one hemisphere can take over the language faculty if the other is impaired.

Finally, we have noted the complex interplay between innate and learned aspects in the chaffinch song: the general characteristics appear to be fixed biologically, whereas the details of the system seem to be learned. One of the more exciting proposals for human language

Fall	Winter	Early Spring	Spring Second Year
Sustained series of chirped notes of varying pitch	Relatively quiet	Subsong	Full song development
↑		↑ ↑	↑
C		D E	F

acquisition, advanced by Noam Chomsky (1965), is that the general structure of human language is fixed biologically and the human language learner learns those aspects of a language that differentiate it from other languages. Interesting though these similarities are, however, the reader should not be misled into thinking that bird communication and human language are even remotely analogous systems. The similarities are overshadowed by vast differences between human language and bird vocalizations, a contrast we will pursue further in chapter 5.

Exercises

1. What are the structural and functional differences between the mobbing call and the aerial predator call?

*2. Compare and contrast the bee communication system with some particular bird song in terms of structure and function.

3. The European cuckoo lays its eggs in the nests of over 120 different bird species, who raise the young cuckoos as their own. Would you expect the cuckoo song to be learned or innate, and why? Compare and contrast the song acquisition of the cuckoo with that of the chaffinch.

*4. Bird calls are usually much shorter than songs. In terms of the functions calls and songs serve, conjecture why this difference in relative length and complexity may exist.

References

Armstrong, E. A. (1963) *A Study of Bird Song,* Dover Press, New York.

Chomsky, N. (1965) *Aspects of the Theory of Syntax,* MIT Press, Cambridge, Mass.

Falls, J. (1969) "Functions of the territorial song in the White-Throated Sparrow," in Hinde, *Bird Vocalizations*.

Hinde, R. (1969) *Bird Vocalizations,* Cambridge University Press, Cambridge, England.

Hooker, T., and B. Hooker (Lade) (1969) "Duetting," in Hinde, *Bird Vocalizations.*

Nicolai, J. (1959) "Familientradition in der Gesangentwicklung des Gimpels (Pyrrhula pyrrhula L.)," *Journal of Ornithology* 100, 39–46.

Nottebohm, F. (1970) "Ontogeny of bird song," *Science* 169, 950–956.

Thielcke, G. (1976) *Bird Sounds,* University of Michigan Press, Ann Arbor, Mich.

Thorpe, W. (1956) "The language of birds," *Scientific American,* 195, no. 4, 129–138.

——— (1961) *Bird-Song,* Cambridge University Press, Cambridge, England.

——— (1974) *Animal Nature and Human Nature*, Anchor Press, Doubleday, Garden City, New York.

Chapter Four

PRIMATE COMMUNICATION

People have been fascinated with the question of primate communication for centuries. The fascination sometimes takes the form of wondering why, if primates are so smart, they don't talk. Probably the most ingenious answer to this question is the one reported by the seventeenth-century Cartesian, Antoine Le Grand (Chomsky 1972, 102), about some peoples of the East Indies who hold that apes and baboons do not talk because they know that if they did, humans would put them to work.

Although it is virtually certain that primates in the wild do not talk in anything like the way a normal human being does, it is an open question how close the various primate communication systems are to human language. Our interest in cracking the communicative code of another species is in this case augmented by our being related to these creatures by evolution, and so there is the suspicion that since we are primates too, here might be some clue to the origin of human language. At present the results on this count must go down as disappointing. There seems to be nothing in the way of a *linguistic* system in use among primates, and the gap between primate communication systems and human linguistic communication is huge. As the noted primatologist Thelma Rowell (1972, 84) remarks, "Communication by monkeys is not qualitatively different from that of other animals, and the same principles apply to them. There is a complete break between people and other primates in this area, with the development of a verbal language capable of communicating . . . ideas, rather than objects or events in the immediate surroundings." In fact, one anthropologist (Lancaster 1975, 56) goes so far as to contend that "the interest in human evolution and in the origin of human language has distorted the study of the communication systems of the nonhuman primate. These systems are not steps toward language."

If it is not the disparity between primate intelligence and linguistic accomplishments nor a search for insight into the origins of human language that motivates us to consider primate communication systems, what is it? In brief, it is for contrast. By looking at primates we complete a spectrum of different animal systems, all of which have striking similarities. We will then be in a better position to contrast natural animal systems both with human natural language and with some recent attempts to teach primates systems of communication that are artificial to them (see chapter 14). In this way normal human linguistic achievements will be thrown into dramatic relief.

General Background

There are a number of different competing classifications of primates, many of which were set up, at least in part, on the basis of rather superficial physical and behavioral characteristics. As more biologically oriented scientists become involved in primate communication research, we hope that a more unified and coherently motivated scheme will emerge; "until that day arrives, the student new to primate biology carries the unfair burden of learning his teacher's mistakes" (Rosen 1974, 24). For convenience we will adopt a taxonomy used fairly extensively in the study of primate communication (see Altmann 1968b), given in figure 4.1.

Primatologists customarily divide studies of forms of behavior into laboratory and nonlaboratory conditions, each setting having its own methodological strengths and weaknesses for studying communication.

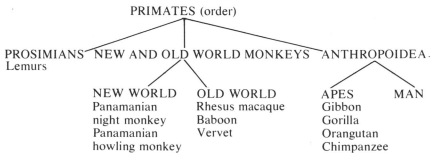

Figure 4.1
Classification of primates

The laboratory allows investigators to control many variables they can not normally control in the wild, such as what the animal is attending to; on the other hand, limiting the study to the laboratory introduces the problem of how much can be inferred, from laboratory results, about behavior in the wild.

Nonlaboratory environments for primates are of three general sorts: colonies living in compounds, free-ranging but artificially fed groups, and free-ranging groups in their natural habitats. We saw in chapters 2 and 3 that it is possible to experiment with both bee systems and various bird calls and songs by manipulating the natural environment in various ways and observing how the organisms react to the changes: food sources were moved to test the accuracy of the bee dance, and tapes of bird calls and songs were played to test their effects. Such manipulative studies (in the natural habitat) are much more difficult to carry out with primates; as a consequence, theories of communication among members of groups living in any of the three nonlaboratory environments are built almost exclusively on the basis of naturalistic observation and theoretical inference.

Some authors (see Altmann 1962, 1965, 1968a) have attempted to reduce the role of theory by applying sophisticated statistical techniques to naturalistic data, but as one primatalogist (Jolly 1972, 149) concludes, "quantitative analysis of communication has the seeds of detailed explanation in the future but so far tells us less than does intelligent empathy."

Technological advances (and nonadvances) also have had their effects on this field. With the development of the sound spectrograph, precise analyses of sound waves have become possible and economically feasible. Nothing analogous has emerged for visual systems. Cameras are expensive and clumsy, and the analysis of pictures is still impressionistic and anecdotal; to compensate for these problems, most authors resort to cartoons and the like to represent visual aspects of primate communication. These difficulties have biased serious work in favor of auditory communication even though it seems that the visual mode is the central form of primate communication.

Another problem in studying primates is accessibility. Ground dwellers are more likely to be studied than arboreal species just because of the comparative ease of observation. All in all, then, the sample of primates and their communication systems is not, at present, very representative.

Communication Context

According to Lancaster (1975, 56–57), communication between complete strangers is very rare among primates. For the most part, communication takes place within a social group composed of members of both sexes and of disparate ages, who have spent most, if not all, of their lives together. "The context, then, of any communicative act includes a network of social relations that have a considerable history behind them, all of which is relevant to the message and how it is received and responded to." For example, primates form a variety of social relationships, one of which is dominance, wherein one primate has "priority of access to desirable goods" over another—the dominance usually being enforced by superior strength. Since dominance tends to organize groups hierarchically, a particular signal can be interpreted differently depending on the location of the sender and receiver in the hierarchy: "a juvenile would ignore, or even respond with teasing to a threat from a female of lower rank than his mother, but would flee screaming from the same gesture from a female of higher rank" (Rowell 1972, 96).

In short, (a) primate signals tend to be *context-bound* in that the message sent is heavily dependent on the salient features of the context, and (b) signals are *multimodal* in that a variety of sensory channels may be operating and contributing simultaneously: vision, audition (hearing), and olfaction (smell) being the commonest.

In primate studies, the operative conceptions of "meaning" and "communication" are often quite inflationary by (human) linguistic standards. Consider two typical examples: Jolly (1972, 143) says that we can determine the "*meaning* of a message . . . from the reactions of the other animal," and Rowell (1972, 84) comments that "communication occurs when any signal given out by one animal is used by another to predict the behavior either of the first animal, or of something else in their environment." If one applies Jolly's conception of meaning to expressions in a human language, one gets preposterous results. For instance, if there were no overt response to one's utterance by the hearer, then the expression uttered would have no meaning. But surely one can simply sit and listen to what someone has to say—we do it all the time. Or suppose someone sneezed and startled someone else; by Jolly's definition the sneeze would have meaning.

Similarly, if one applies Rowell's conception of communication to humans, one again obtains bizarre results; since virtually any form of

behavior can be used to signal, the definition applies without constraints. Suppose a detective observes a gangster planting a bomb in a
senator's car and thereby predicts that the car (and driver) will blow up
when it is started. According to Rowell's conception, the gangster communicated to the detective the fact that the senator was going to be
blown up. Surely this is a loose conception of communication, not our
normal notion. Thus one should be cautious when reading about communication between primates, since no more may be meant than that
one primate acts on the basis of something another primate did.

Visual Communication

Primates in general have excellent vision, and at close range, where
foliage is not a problem, they tend to rely mainly on the visual mode of
communication. At longer ranges where obstacles can interfere with
vision, they tend to rely more on auditory signals. We have noted that
the closer, visual mode is the more important in primate social interaction, and it is also fairly well understood. Some of the main forms of
visual communications are summarized in figure 4.2.

A typical example of communicating by *postural* signals is communicating confidence versus timidity. In general, the posture of a
confident (usually dominant) primate is loose and relaxed; it sits comfortably (sprawls, actually) and walks with a sort of swagger. The timid
primate, by contrast, is tense. It sits rigidly, usually hunched over, and
walks with its back arched as if to spring away at any moment (see
figure 4.3).

Although these postural signals are quite general characteristics
among primates, there are also some interesting variations between
species: "The confident rhesus monkey carries its tail hanging rather
loosely, one lacking confidence carries it stiffly out behind, while most
high-ranking adult males carry their tails curled over the back. In

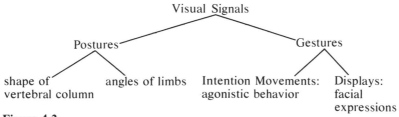

Figure 4.2
Types of primate visual signals

a.

b.

c.

d.

e.

f.

g.

h.

Figure 4.3
Typical primate postures. From Rowell 1972, 88–89.

baboons, by contrast, a vertical tail indicates fear, an unsure animal carries its tail rather stiffly and held slightly up, while the tail of a confident baboon hangs loosely after the first few stiffly fused verte-brae" (Rowell 1972, 86).

As an example of communication by means of *intention movements*, primates often exhibit forms of agonistic behavior, that is, behavior that spans the scale from agression to submission. For instance, an aggressive monkey might sequentially bob its head, slap the ground, lunge, or attack with an open mouth, as the expression of agression increases. Finally, the communicative behavior of most primates seems to include some common *displays*, including facial expressions. It has been claimed by McNeill (1970, 42), for instance, that all pri-mates have some variant of an open-mouth threat, a grimace for pac-ification, and lip-smacking for showing neutrality. It is difficult to illustrate these facial expressions without motion pictures, but the drawings in figure 4.4 may help convey the differences in these ex-pressions. Although the notion of a display is not altogether precise, the term generally refers to forms of behavior that have become some-what ritualized. Such behavior is characteristically exaggerated, ste-reotyped, and often repeated, which suggests that the communicative function of these forms of behavior has affected their evolutionary selection from less-ritualized but highly emotive forms of behavior (see Andrew 1972).

Vocal Communication

Although most primate signals are multimodal and the visual element is generally the more important, we will concentrate on the vocal mode. This is necessary, given our interest in comparing natural primate communication with human spoken language. We will look at two types of Old World monkeys: the vervet (*Cercopithecus aethiops*) and the rhesus (*Mucaca mulata*). The main reason for this selection is that from the point of view of vocal communication these are two of the most intensively studied primates.

Vervet
The vervet is a rather elegant looking semiterrestrial Old World monkey found and studied mainly in the grassy forests of southeast Africa—especially at the Amboseli Reserve in Kenya.

One preliminary estimate of the vervet's vocal repertoire puts the

Figure 4.4
Equivalent expressions of the grimace (*left*) and the open-mouthed threat (*right*) in rhesus monkeys (*top*), bonnet macaques (*middle*), and langurs (*bottom*). From Marler 1965, by permission of I. De Vore.

number of physically distinct sounds at about 36, evoked by 21 different situations, and carrying roughly 22 different messages (Struhsaker
1967, 313). Some of these possibilities are given in table 4.1.

Three of the more interesting vocalizations of the vervet are the
alarm calls listed in figure 4.5. These are of particular interest because
they are apparently used to convey information about the vervet's
environment and so "are rare and represent important specializations
of the few species that use them" (Lancaster 1975, 64).

Snake chutter This alarm call (table 4.1, no. 15) is emitted almost
exclusively by juveniles and adult females. It is of low amplitude and is
produced with teeth exposed in a sort of grimace. Of five species of
snake observed in the vicinity of vervets, only two species evoked this
call—the Egyptian cobra (*Naja haje*), and the puff adder (*Bitis
arietans*). The monkeys cluster together about five feet from the snake;
while emitting the call they stare at the snake and follow it through the
brush. The survival value of isolating a dangerous predator in this
manner is obvious.

Airborne predator call This call (table 4.1, no. 18) is also emitted
almost exclusively by adult females and juveniles; it is used to signal
the presence of such airborne predators as the (monkey-eating) martial
and the crowned hawk eagle. It is a call of low frequency and high
amplitude, making it a sort of "chirp," and is audible to ¼ mile. Upon
hearing this call, vervets tend to drop out of the trees into the high grass
or bushes for cover.

Terrestrial predator calls Sometimes these calls (table 4.1, nos. 16 and
19) resemble the airborne predator call, but their function is just the
opposite—to get the hearers to climb nearby trees and go out to the
ends of the branches.

Having examined the vervet call system, let us now turn to the vocal
repertoire of the rhesus monkey to see in what ways these systems can
be compared (see exercises).

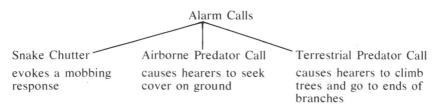

Alarm Calls

Snake Chutter — Airborne Predator Call — Terrestrial Predator Call

evokes a mobbing
response

causes hearers to seek
cover on ground

causes hearers to climb
trees and go to ends of
branches

Figure 4.5
Vervet alarm calls

Table 4.1
Stimulus situations evoking sounds, in vervet monkeys (A = adult, SA =

Stimulus Situation	Name of Sound
1. Intragroup agonism	Chutter
	Squeal
	Chutter-squeal
	Squeal-scream
	Scream
	Bark
2. Attempted copulation by SA or A male with anestrous female	Anti-copulatory squeal-scream and squeal
3. Red, white, and blue display	*Woof, Woof*
	Waa
	Woof-waa
	Lip smacking
	Teeth chattering
4. Close proximity of subordinate and dominant individuals	*Wa-waa*
	Long *raugh*
	Short *raugh*
	Lip smacking
	Teeth chattering
5. Initial phase of group progression	Progression grunt
6. Play	Purr
7. Approach of strange A male to infant	Scream
8. Weaning of infant	Scream
	Squeal
	rrr
9. Separation of infant and mother	Lost *rrr*
	Lost *eee*
	Lost squeal
	Lost scream
	Lost *rrah*
10. Reunion of infant and mother	*Eh, eh*
11. Ambivalent situation (proximity of foreign group and close proximity of subordinate and dominant)	Long *aarr-rraugh*
	Short *aarr-rraugh*

subadult, J = juvenile, yJ = young juvenile, inf = infant)

Message Probably Communicated	Apparent or Probable Response Evoked in Other Animals
Solicitation for aid and aggressive threat	Solicits aid and evokes flight
Solicitation for aid and defensive threat	Solicits aid and inhibits attack
Aggressive threat	Disrupts fighting
Indicates that female is anestrous	Inhibits copulatory attempts by male
Expresses subordination	Inhibits attack
Expresses subordination	Inhibits attack
Expresses subordination	Inhibits attack
Expresses nonaggression	Permits subordinate to approach dominant
Expresses nonaggression	Permits close proximity of subordinate and dominant animals
Indicates temporal proximity of group progression	Facilitates coordination of group progression and/or group coherency
Not apparent	May enhance play bond
Indicates approach of strange A male	Evokes rapid retrieval of infant by mother and rapid retreat of strange male
Not apparent	Not apparent
Not apparent	Attracts attention of mother and evokes eventual retrieval of infant by mother
Not apparent	May facilitate social bond between mother and infant
Indicates approach and/or proximity of foreign group and/or aggression	Others look toward foreign group; permits vocalizer to approach dominant individual

Table 4.1

Stimulus Situation	Name of Sound
12. Proximity of foreign group	Long *aarr*
	Short *aarr*
	Wawooo
	Intergroup grunt
13. Intergroup agonism	Intergroup chutter A
	Intergroup chutter B
	Bark
	Chirp
14. Near proximity of human observer	Chutter-toward-observer
15. Proximity of snake predator	Snake chutter
16. Proximity of minor mammalian predator	*Uh!*
17. Sudden movement of minor predator (mammalian and avian)	*Nyow!*
18. Initial perception of major avian predator	*Rraup*
19. Proximity of major predator (mammalian and avain)	Threat-alarm bark
	Chirp
20. Interference with respiration	Coughing
	Sneezing
21. Indigestion	Vomiting

Message Probably Communicated	Apparent or Probable Response Evoked by Other Animals
Indicates approach and/or proximity of foreign group	Others look toward foreign group
Not apparent	Evokes intergroup grunt
Indicates intergroup chase and/or fight; possibly solicitation for aid; aggressive threat	Others look toward foreign group and may solicit aid
Indicates intergroup chase and/or fight; possibly solicitation for aid; aggressive threat	Others look toward foreign group and may solicit aid and evoke fight
Moderate- to low-intensity threat toward observer	Not apparent
High-intensity warning of snake predator	Others look toward snake
Low-intensity warning of proximity of minor mammalian predator	Others look toward predator
Moderate-intensity warning of sudden movement of minor predator (mammalian and avian)	Others look toward predator and sometimes run toward trees
High-intensity warning of proximity and/or approach of major avian predator	Others run into thickets and away from open areas and treetops
High intensity warning and aggressive threat toward major predator (mammalian and avian)	Others look toward predator and run to appropriate cover; predator ignores threat or gives aggressive threat in return
High intensity warning of major mammalian predator and possibly aggressive threat toward major predator (mammalian and avian)	Others run into trees; predator's response not apparent
Indicates the obvious	None
Indicates the obvious	Others sometimes approach and investigate vomiter's mouth and the vomit

Rhesus

One of the best available and most widely used descriptions of the rhesus vocal repertoire comes from Rowell and Hinde (1962) and Rowell (1962), who divide the vocalizations into two classes, Harsh Noises and Clear Calls. Although this system was based on captive groups, it has been applied successfully in field studies by Lindburg (1971). Acoustically, one of the main differences between these vocalizations is that the harsh noises contain a mixture of many frequencies at a given level of intensity whereas the clear calls contain a few distinct frequencies and sound tonal. Although Rowell's classification correlates sounds with eliciting conditions, harsh noises are categorized in terms of the sounds, clear calls in terms of the conditions. Figure 4.6 shows Rowell's classification of the various vocalizations.

The connection between the agonistic vocalizations and their eliciting conditions is given in table 4.2. Acoustically, these agonistic vocalizations have spectrograms like the ones in figure 4.7. (See chapter 3 for a discussion of spectrograms.) We have not reported the friendly harsh noises, since they are similar in relevant respects to agonistic harsh noises.

Having examined two primate communication systems that have been studied in some detail, the reader can now see interesting similarities and differences between these systems (see exercises). Unlike the bee

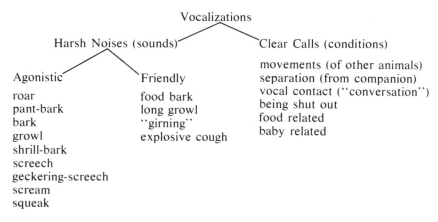

Figure 4.6
Classification of rhesus vocalizations. Based on Rowell 1962 and Rowell and Hinde 1962.

Table 4.2
Rhesus agonistic harsh noises and their eliciting conditions

Call	Situational Context
Roar	Made by a very confident animal when threatening another of inferior rank
Pant-threat	Made by a less confident animal who wants support in making an attack
Bark	Made by a threatening animal who is not aggressive enough to move forward
Growl	Made by a mildly alarmed animal
Shrill-bark	Alarm call
Screech	Made when threatening a higher-ranked animal
Geckering screech	Made when threatened by another animal
Scream	Made when losing a fight and being bitten
Squeak	Made by a defeated and exhausted animal at the end of a fight

Source: After McNeill 1970.

dance, but like bird calls, the vocal repertoires of the vervet and the rhesus seem to consist of simply a small vocabulary of distinct calls, which are not combined with each other in any systematic fashion. We will explore these issues in greater detail in chapter 5.

Processing and Acquisition

Not much is known about the neurological and psychological mechanisms underlying primate communication. Nor is much known about the details of its development and acquisition, especially in the wild. What seems to be emerging from preliminary work in the field of primate learning is that the general structure of the communication system is biologically fixed and learning fills in the more detailed structure of the system. A comparison of the communicative repertoires of laboratory rhesus monkeys with repertoires of free-ranging ones illustrates this point (Mason 1960, 1961). Although the two groups used the same basic repertoire of postures, gestures, and vocalizations, the communicative system of the free-ranging group showed more detail and subtlety.

There is also evidence that productive aspects of primate systems are differentially fixed (Altmann 1973). An infant monkey raised with monkeys of another species will apparently come to comprehend sig-

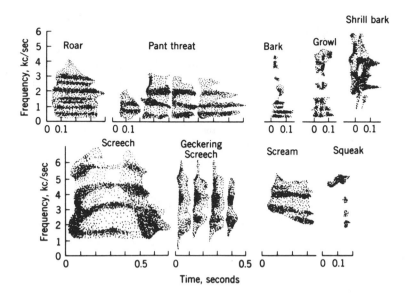

Figure 4.7
Spectrograms of rhesus harsh noises. From Marler and Hamilton 1966, after Rowell 1962.

nals of the other species but will produce only those signals characteristic of its own species. These features are reminiscent, not of human language, but of human emotional displays such as laughing, crying, smiling, frowning, screaming, gasping, and so on, in that these human expressions are also fairly fixed biologically in general form and function (expressing happiness, sorrow, fear, and so on) even though the details may be modified or filled out by imitation and innovation. Like many if not most forms of behavior, communication systems in primates are probably complicated mixtures of genetic disposition, circumstances, and learning.

In conclusion, it is interesting to compare the acquisition of communicative behavior with a particularly striking example of the contributions of circumstances and learning to the acquisition of noncommunicative behavior patterns in primates. Primatologists studying the Koshima Island (Japan) macaques placed sweet potatoes on the beach as rations for the macaque troop. A two-year-old female initiated the procedure of washing the sand off of the potatoes before eating them, first in a stream, later on in the sea. Other young macaques copied her, then older female monkeys also began copying her, until finally the tradition spread to all but the adult males. Previously water-shy adults waded into the sea and the tradition was passed on to newborn monkeys. The practice is now a normal part of an infant macaque's process of growing up on the island. The primatologists decided to try the experiment again with wheat. Surprisingly the same female placed the wheat in the water, allowing the sand to sink and leaving the edible portions clean. Thus, still another tradition was born (see Rosen 1974).

Exercises

1. What are the features of visual communication in primates?

2. Suppose *synonymy* is sameness of meaning and *ambiguity* is multiplicity of meaning. How would these terms be applied to human language given the primatologists characterization of *meaning*?

*3. Comment on the following description of one experimental approach to communication in primates: Is this really an example of communication? "Two restrained monkeys, equipped with a battery of physiological recorders, are linked by closed-circuit television that shows one a picture of the other's face. One monkey sees a stimulus indicating either shock or a food reward. The second monkey, watching the first one's facial expression, presses appropriate levers so that both avoid shock or both receive the reward. This would be ridiculous gadgetry if it merely made the trivial point that one monkey can tell whether another is frightened. It becomes interesting when the monkeys cannot tell. Isolated monkeys, reared for the first year of life without companions, neither respond to facial expressions nor 'send' them so that normal monkeys can respond effectively" (Jolly 1972, 148).

4. Compare and contrast the vocal repertoires of the vervet and the rhesus monkeys.

*5. Compare and contrast the mobbing calls of birds with the alarm calls of the vervet and rhesus monkeys.

*6. Recall that adult male vervets do not make alarm calls, although females and juveniles do; and recall that the adult males on Koshima Island have not developed the potato and wheat washing tradition of the females. What might account for this differentiation of behavior between adult males and the other members of the primate group?

References

Altmann, S. (1962) "A field study of the sociobiology of Rhesus monkeys, *Macaca Mulatta,*" *Annals of the New York Academy of Science*, 102, 338–435.

————(1965) "Sociobiology of Rhesus monkeys II: stochastics of communication," *Journal of Theoretical Biology* 8, 490–522.

————(1967) "The structure of primate social communication," in S. Altmann, ed., *Social Communication among Pirmates,* University of Chicago Press, Chicago.

————(1968a) "Sociobiology of Rhesus monkeys III: the basic communication network," *Behavior* 32, 17–32.

————(1968b) "Primates," in T. Sebeok, ed., *Animal Communication,* University of Illinois Press, Urbana, Ill.

————(1973) "Primate communication," in G. Miller, ed., *Communication, Language, and Meaning,* Basic Books, New York.

Andrew, R. (1972) "The information potentially available in mammal displays," in R. Hinde, ed., *Non-Verbal Communication,* Cambridge University Press, Cambridge, England.

Chomsky, N. (1972) *Language and Mind* (enlarged ed.), Harcourt Brace Jovanovich, New York.

Hinde, R., and T. Rowell (1962) "Communication by postures and facial expressions in the Rhesus monkey," *Proceedings of the Zoological Society of London* 138, 1–21.

Jolly, A. (1972) *The Evolution of Primate Behavior,* Macmillan, New York.

Lancaster, J. (1975) *Primate Behavior and the Emergence of Human Culture,* Macmillan, New York.

Lindburg, D. (1971) "The Rhesus monkey in North India: an ecological and behavioral study," in L. Rosenblum, ed., *Primate Behavior,* vol. II, Academic Press, New York.

Marler, P. (1965) "Communication in monkeys and apes," in I. DeVore, ed., *Primate Behavior,* Holt, Rinehart & Winston, New York.

Marler, P., and W. J. Hamilton (1966) *Mechanisms of Animal Behavior,* Wiley, New York.

Mason, W. (1960) "The effects of social restriction on the behavior of Rhesus monkeys, I. Free serial behavior," *Journal of Comparative and Physiological Psychology* 53, 582–589.

————(1961a) "II. Tests of gregariousness," *Journal of Comparative and Physiological Psychology* 54, 287–290.

————(1961b) "III. Dominance tests," *Journal of Comparative and Physiological Psychology* 54, 694–699.

McNeill, D. (1970) *The Acquisition of Language,* Harper & Row, New York.

Rosen, S. (1974) *Introduction to the Primates,* Prentice-Hall, Englewood Cliffs, N.J.

Rowell, T. (1962) "Agonistic noises of the Rhesus monkey," *Symposia of the Zoological Society of London* 8, 91–96.

Rowell, T., and R. Hinde (1962) "Vocal communication by the Rhesus monkey," *Symposia of the Zoological Society of London* 8, 279–294.

Rowell, T. (1972) *Social Behavior of Monkeys,* Penguin Books, Baltimore, Maryland.

Struhsaker, T. (1967) "Auditory communication among Vervet monkeys," in S. Altmann, ed., *Social Communication among Primates*.

Chapter Five

COMPARING ANIMAL
COMMUNICATION
SYSTEMS

Classifying Communication Systems

It is a common experience of travelers in another land not to be able to discern the various words within sentences of the foreign tongue—the sentences all sound like one continuous noise. In contrast, with a language we speak and understand, we are able to perceive sentences as sequences of independently meaningful elements: words. This indicates quite clearly that the detection of significant units can depend on knowing a language.

With respect to (natural) animal communication systems, we are all nonspeakers: we are faced with the task of recognizing the significant units of these systems, given the movements, postures, and sounds that we can observe. For example, often the same superficial behavior can have a different role in different species. This is evident from Jolly's observation that "in Old World monkeys 'smiles' or grimaces frequently grade into fearful screaming; in the chimpanzee they are related to bared-teeth screaming but also have a greeting and reassuring function, whereas in ourselves smiles more often grade into laughter or play faces. Thus, the same continuum would be grouped differently for man and monkey" (1972, 148).

Because our purpose is to describe and compare animal communication systems, we must find a framework for classifying animal behavior. The choice of such a framework is both important and hard to justify. What constitutes a good framework? We will assume that a good one must have one central feature: it must provide descriptive categories that allow one to state the fundamental principles governing animal communication. A variety of systems have been proposed, but most of them fail in some respect to have this central feature.

Hockett's Framework

One influential system for classifying animal communication has been developed by the linguist Charles Hockett. Hockett's strategy is to determine what he calls the *design features* of human language and next to determine which of the features are found in various other animal communication systems. The design features are given in table 5.1. The basic idea behind this way of comparing communication systems is to find a list of features, or characteristics, such that each communication system has at least one of the features, and no two systems share all the same features. Each system of communication is therefore distinguished from every other system in possessing at least one feature the other lacks.

Adapting from Hockett (1960), we define the features in table 5.1 as follows:

1. *Vocal-auditory.* The sender of the signal employs a vocal tract to produce the message, and the receiver employs an auditory mechanism to receive the signal.
2. *Broadcast transmission and directional reception.* A signal travels out in all directions from the sender because of the physical properties of the medium. The receiver, however, is usually able to locate the direction from which the signal has been sent.
3. *Rapid fading (transitoriness).* Because of the physical properties of the transmitting medium, the signal quickly dissipates.
4. *Interchangeability.* Individuals can be both senders and receivers of messages.
5. *Total feedback.* Senders are able to monitor their own signals.
6. *Specialization.* The communication system is specialized to the extent that its use does not serve any additional physiological function. For example, human speech is not necessary for respiration.
7. *Semanticity.* Expressions in the communication system have a fixed meaning.
8. *Arbitrariness.* There is no necessary connection between the sign and its referent. Note, for example, some of the different words (signs) for the referent "dog" in various of the world's languages: *perro* (Spanish); *chien* (French); *łééchąą'í* (Navajo).
9. *Discreteness.* The signaling system can be subdivided into repeatable units: for example, the sounds, words, and sentences of a human language.

Table 5.1
The Hockett framework

	A Bee Dancing	B Western Meadowlark Song
1. Vocal-Auditory Channel	No	Yes
2. Broadcast Transmission and Directional Reception	Yes	Yes
3. Rapid Fading (Transitoriness)	?	Yes
4. Interchangeability	Limited	?
5. Total Feedback	?	Yes
6. Specialization	?	Yes?
7. Semanticity	Yes	In part?
8. Arbitrariness	No	If semantic, yes
9. Discreteness	No	?
10. Displacement	Yes, always	?
11. Productivity	Yes	?
12. Traditional Transmission	Probably No	?
13. Duality of Patterning	No	?

Source: Adapted from Hockett 1960
Note: Five systems of communication possess in varying degrees the 13 design features of language; a question mark means that it is doubtful or not known whether the system has the particular feature.

10. *Displacement.* The referent of the signal does not have to be immediately present in time or space. For example, humans can talk about things that they have never encountered, such as Julius Caesar.
11. *Productivity.* The system allows novel messages to be sent.
12. *Traditional transmission.* The communication system is learned from those who have already used it.
13. *Duality of patterning.* The communication system can be described as consisting of two levels, one a physical system and the other a system of interpretation or meaning. Different combinations of physical signals may have different interpretations. For example, the mean-

C	D	E
Gibbon Calls	Paralinguistic Phenomena	Language
Yes	Yes	Yes
Yes	Yes	Yes
Yes repeated	Yes	Yes
Yes	Largely Yes	Yes
Yes	Yes	Yes
Yes	Yes?	Yes
Yes	Yes?	Yes
Yes	In part	Yes
Yes	Largely No	Yes
No	In part	Yes, often
No	Yes	Yes
?	Yes	Yes
No	No	Yes

ingless sounds represented by *a, p,* and *t* can be arranged as *apt, tap,* and *pat,* which have different and idiosyncratic meanings.

These features, which are claimed to be the salient features of human language (speech), are sought in other animal communication systems for purposes of comparison. When we consider Hockett's method critically, however, we encounter two fundamental problems, one regarding the selection of the features, the other regarding the superimposition of these features onto animal communication systems.

The first problem is that Hockett defines human communication in terms of speech and thus biases it towards its acoustic features. However, the more interesting and important features of human communication are contained in the more abstract properties of the system. This more abstract side is usually identified as *language* and is the system that underlies speech. For example, the term *vocal-auditory*, although valid for speech, is not critical for human communication: a widespread communication system of the deaf, American Sign Language (ASL), has all of the important features of human language.

The second basic problem with Hockett's framework is that the features that characterize human speech do not apply naturally and insightfully, for purposes of comparison and contrast, to other animal communication systems. His framework assumes that human language is a more complicated variant of, and ultimately derives from, features of other systems. However, it is more fruitful to consider each system on its own and then on that basis to make a careful comparison.

As an illustration of the weakness of Hockett's framework, let us examine his description of the bee dance, to which he assigns two of the most important properties of human language: productivity and semanticity (see table 5.1).

Consider, first, productivity. Although there is an enormous difference between the type of productivity found in human language and the type found in the bee dance, Hockett's framework does not reveal this difference. Recall from chapter 2 that the bee dance (tail-wagging form) is productive only with respect to variations of a single type of message (a food source of a certain richness is located a certain distance and direction from the hive). Since there are an infinite number of possible food points on a plane, the bee system is able to transmit an unlimited number of messages corresponding to these food sources. Human communication, however, is not limited to food sources on a plane. In fact, there is no meaningful way to define the limit on what may be talked about. Thus, the use of the same term, *productive*, in describing the domain of reference of the bee dance and in describing the creative aspect of human language use fails to highlight the fundamental difference between those two systems of communication.

Hockett also applies the term *semantic* to the bee communication system, but a bee semantics must be first worked out before it can be compared to the complex and abstract theories that have been developed to account for meaning and reference in human language (see chapter 11). The difference between the two systems will certainly turn out to be more than a difference in degree. We leave it as an exercise for the reader to analyze critically the remaining design features of the bee dance (see the exercises).

Problems similar to those found in the bee dance description are also found in each of the other animal communication systems Hockett describes. To see this, let us consider Hockett's discussion of the gibbon in contrast with Thorpe's adaption of Hockett's scheme applied to primates in general, shown in table 5.2. Note the points of contention at design features 9–13. We will leave it to readers to decide on the basis of the data in chapters 2 through 4 which version of the design feature framework is best. As an example of how complicated the resolution of such conflicts can be, consider the conflict surrounding feature 12, traditional transmission. Hockett places a question mark and Thorpe a *no?* for this feature of the gibbon system. Our remarks in chapter 4 concerning the differential acquisition of production and comprehension may help explain why there should be this uncertainty. Since comprehension can be learned to a greater extent than production can, in order to reflect the facts adequately, a design feature scheme should split *traditional transmission* into production and comprehension aspects. In short, no straightforward answer to the question is possible and it is clear why these different marks of uncertainty should have been registered. These problems are typical of the difficulties that one encounters in evaluating the design feature framework in detail.

McNeill's Framework

McNeill's classification (1970, chapter 4) is based on two kinds of principles, structural and functional. If one focuses on *structural* aspects of the communication system, two extreme types can be isolated. First, there are *graded* systems. In these a new message is produced by changing the signal along some physical dimension; certain changes in the physical signal are correlated with concomitant changes in the message. For example, the angle of the tail-wagging dance is correlated with the angle of the food source from the sun, and the intensity of a monkey's roar can be correlated with the aggressiveness it communicates. On the other end of the scale of structural characteristics are *combining* systems. In these systems new messages are created not by varying the signal along some physical dimension but by combining the elements of the system in different ways. For example, natural human languages are combining systems.

Turning to *functional* aspects of these systems, three main functions can be distinguished: nominal, expressive, and predicative. Signals fulfill their *nominal* function when they serve to pick out an object,

Table 5.2
Comparison of communicative systems, animal and human

Design Features (all found in verbal human language)	Human Paralinguistics
	1
1. Vocal-Auditory Channel	Yes (in part)
2. Broadcast Transmission and Directional Reception	Yes
3. Rapid Fading	Yes
4. Interchangeability (adults can be both transmitters and receivers)	Largely Yes
5. Complete Feedback ("speaker" is able to perceive everything relevant to his signal production)	Partial
6. Specialization (energy unimportant, trigger effect important)	Yes?
7. Semanticity (association ties between signals and features in the world)	Yes?
8. Arbitrariness (symbols abstract)	In part
9. Discreteness (repertoire discrete not continuous)	Largely No
10. Displacement (can refer to things remote in time and space)	In part
11. Openness (new messages easily coined)	Yes
12. Tradition (conventions passed on by teaching and learning)	Yes
13. Duality of Patterning (signal elements meaningless, pattern combinations meaningful)	No
14. Prevarication (ability to lie or talk nonsense)	Yes
15. Reflectiveness (ability to communicate about the system itself)	No
16. Learnability (speaker of one language learns another)	Yes

Source: Adapted from W. H. Thorpe 1974

| 2 | 3 | 4 | 5 |
Honeybee dancing	Buntings, finches, thrushes, crows, etc.	Mynah	Primates (vocal)
No	Yes	Yes	Yes
Yes	Yes	Yes	Yes
?	Yes	Yes	Yes
Partial	Partial Yes, if same sex	Yes	Yes
No?	Yes	Yes	Yes
?	Yes	Yes	Yes
Yes	Yes	Yes	Yes
No	Yes	Yes	Yes
No	Yes	Yes	Partial
Yes	Time No Space Yes	Time No Space Yes	Yes
Yes	Yes	Yes	Partial
No?	Yes	Yes	No?
No	Yes	Yes	Yes
No	No	No(?)	No
No	No	No	No
No(?)	Yes (in part)	Yes	No?

Table 5.3
McNeill's classification of animal communication systems

	Grading	Combining
Nominal	bees	finches
	ants	cicadas
Expressive	wolves	
	gulls	
	monkeys	
	human paralanguage	
Predicative		grammatical speech

Source: McNeill 1970.

event, or situation outside the sender. For instance, an alarm call might bring attention to a particular predator in the animal's environment. A signal fulfills its *expressive* function when it serves to express or give vent to an internal emotional state of the sender. Thus various forms of aggressive behavior can serve this expressive function. Finally, a signal fulfills a *predicative* function when it serves to comment on either internal states or outside events. McNeill's summary of his scheme appears in table 5.3. McNeill goes on to comment, though, that this table does not adequately reflect his views. Although there is a strong tendency for systems to be of one type or another, "all communication systems include messages of both expressive and nominal types, and some systems use both grading and combining" (McNeill 1970, 38).

It is instructive to see in some detail why this last remark might be true. Consider the categorization of monkey vocalizations as grading-expressive. Recall the vervet alarm-call repertoire as well as the rhesus harsh noises, and remember that in an expressive system, signals "stand for internal states" (McNeill 1970, 38). However, when we turn back to table 4.2, we find very little in the way of specification of internal states; rather we find (somewhat loaded) descriptions of various external situations.

Similar problems arise with McNeill's characterization of grading: "new messages are produced by moving the signal along a physical dimension in correlation with a shift in content" (McNeill 1970, 38). McNeill, following Rowell (1962), suggests that rhesus sounds are graded as the arrows in figure 5.1 indicate. But we do not find the necessary correlation between this sequence of calls and the messages suggested by table 4.2. Remember that in a grading system the messages must correlate with a physical dimension of the signal. Although there may be portions of the rhesus system that are grading, it looks as

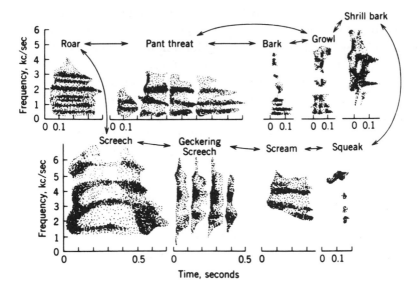

Figure 5.1
Grading of rhesus harsh noises. From Marler and Hamilton 1966, after Rowell 1962.

if the system as a whole is discrete: the physical dimensions of the calls are either not continuously connected or blur off into one another acoustically. The same thing can happen in human speech, particularly in rapid speech—the (discrete) words can blurr off into one another acoustically. When the blurring is extreme, we describe such speech as slurred.

Other systems of communication we have considered reinforce the suspicion that table 5.3 does not really partition animal languages into distinct classes. Bird songs and calls do not appear to have the structural property of combining. In fact, we disagree with McNeill's contention regarding some birds that "in many cases novel songs are produced by combining categories; combinations enter into combinations to form hierarchical structures" (McNeill 1970, 43). In the literature on bird songs we have found no examples that can be analyzed as consisting of hierarchically arranged elements. Rather, it appears that the songs and calls of birds consist of discrete units with some degree of internal complexity (but the complexity is not of the combining type). Structurally, the bird communication systems are very much like primate systems, both being systems of discrete signals with graded possibilities for each signal.

Finally, there also seems to be a general problem with McNeill's category of combining: "messages are produced by combining elements, each new combination standing for a new message" (1970, 38). This definition rules out the possibility of synonymy in combining systems, since synonyms are different combinations that mean the same thing. The definition also suggests that combinations have only one meaning, thereby ruling out ambiguous expressions. In either case such a definition of *combining* would exclude from table 5.3 human natural languages (grammatical speech), which contain both synonyms and ambiguous expressions.

Chomsky's Framework

According to Chomsky (1966), there is a series of differences between animal communication systems and human linguistic systems. Animal systems make use of two sorts of principles of correlation: "Each known animal communication system either consists of a fixed number of signals, each associated with a specific range of eliciting conditions or internal states, or a fixed number of 'linguistic dimensions' each associated with a nonlinguistic dimension in the sense that selection of a point along one indicates a corresponding point along the other" (Chomsky 1966, 77–78). We will call the first sort of system *bounded and discrete,* the second sort of system *unbounded and nondiscrete.* These can be diagrammed as in figure 5.2.

How would one classify animal systems within Chomsky's framework? Chomsky is not very specific about the nature of the association between the discrete signals and their eliciting conditions

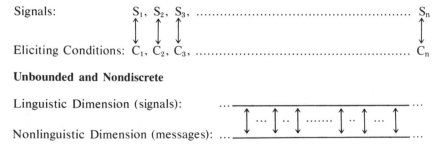

Bounded and Discrete

Signals: $S_1, S_2, S_3,$ .... S_n

Eliciting Conditions: $C_1, C_2, C_3,$ .... C_n

Unbounded and Nondiscrete

Linguistic Dimension (signals):

Nonlinguistic Dimension (messages):

Figure 5.2
Chomsky's framework

(external or internal), nor is he very specific about the nonlinguistic dimension involved in nondiscrete systems. However, a natural categorization of these animal systems can be represented as in table 5.4.

We consider the bee system to be unbounded and nondiscrete and consider both bird calls and bird songs to be bounded and discrete. Apparently, primate calls, postures, and gestures should also be considered as bounded and discrete.

In the course of describing animal communication systems, Chomsky contrasts such systems with human language and human language use. According to Chomsky (1966, 4–5), "human language is available for the free expression of thought or for appropriate responses in any new context and is undetermined by any fixed association of utterances to external stimuli or physiological states."

This creative aspect of language use, so central to human language and linguistic communication, includes three important characteristics:

Unbounded scope. Human language is available for the free expression of novel thoughts and for communicating novel messages by means of novel signals.

Stimulus freedom. Human language is not under the control of either external stimuli or internal emotional states.

Contextual appropriateness. Human language can be used appropriately in novel situations.

It is interesting to note that these characteristics are all independent and that although each can be possessed by systems other than human language, not *all* of them are. For instance, a computer program with two responses, but with a randomizer controlling its production, will be stimulus-free but bounded in scope. On the other hand, the bee system seems to be unbounded in scope (in the sense of having an unlimited number of potential messages) but stimulus-bound. In contrast to animal systems, human language and language use seem unbounded in

Table 5.4
Categorization of systems in Chomsky's framework

	Bounded	Unbounded
Discrete	Bird calls and song Primate calls, postures, gestures	Human language
Nondiscrete	?	Bee dance: direction, distance, quality

scope, stimulus-free, and contextually appropriate. Notice that the last two features are characteristics not of human languages themselves but of normal language *use*. One can imagine a bounded system (such as bird or monkey calls) coming to be used by humans in a way that is stimulus-free and contextually appropriate.

Chomsky seems to be on the right track in his comparison of animal and human communication. *Structurally,* human languages are primarily discrete at the minimal meaning-bearing level (for example, at the word level); they are compositional in that the meaning of complex expressions is determined by the meaning of their constituent parts and their grammatical relations; and human languages are unbounded in scope and subject matter in that they can be used to talk about anything imaginable. *Functionally,* human language use is almost completely stimulus-free and contextually appropriate. Finally, in normal communication situations virtually anyone who knows the language is able to separate various central functions that an expression can have:

(1) a. There is a black limousine in the driveway. (report)
    b. Oh! A spider! (expression of fear)
    c. Leave! Quick! (warning)

Animal signals, on the other hand, are not functionally separable in this sense; we are again in the position of a foreign traveler in not being able to distinguish the functions of a signal. For example, the mobbing calls of various birds (see chapter 3) could be described as reporting the presence of a predator, expressing fear (at the presence of the predator), or warning others to look out. There is no way at present to decide which of these functional characterizations is *not* correct. The same point holds for most primate vocalizations and visual gestures.

In summary, human natural language and communication is discrete, compositional, unbounded in scope and subject matter, stimulus-free, contextually appropriate, and functionally separable. Part II of this book expands on some of these topics: Chapters 6–11 investigate *structural* characteristics of human language at the level of sound, syntax, and meaning; chapter 12 elaborates on the *functions,* or *uses,* of language and explores issues related to the concept of contextual appropriateness.

Exercises

*1. Give three examples of some human gestures or postures that can be interpreted in different ways in different contexts.

*2. Are there any cases of nonarbitrariness in human language; that is, are there cases where words resemble certain aspects of what they refer to?

3. Critically assess Hockett's feature analysis of the tail-wagging dance of the honeybee. How would this analysis extend to the round dance and the sickle dance? Could Hockett's framework distinguish these dances?

*4. Discuss the disagreement between Hockett and Thorpe concerning features 9–13 of primate communication. Given the data from chapter 4, which framework seems more adequate?

5. Compare the design features assigned to the mynah bird and to human language in table 5.2. Do you agree with the designations for the mynah? Use specific examples in your answer.

*6. How might one define a *combining* system in such a way as to allow for synonymous and ambiguous signals?

7. Does any animal system in our survey contain two signals that mean the same thing? Defend your answer.

8. Does any animal system in our survey contain an ambiguous signal (a signal that means two things)? Defend your answer.

9. What does it mean to categorize the rhesus system as expressive?

10. Why does McNeill think that the rhesus system is graded? What is the correlation that is required for a grading system?

11. Compare (as best you can) what Hockett and McNeill say about (natural) primate communication systems. Where do they agree? Where do they disagree? Given the data in chapter 4, who do you think is right?

*12. Think up an example of a bounded but nondiscrete system (see figure 5.2). Is there a comparable animal system? (See table 5.4)

*13. How is contextual appropriateness and inappropriateness related to stimulus freedom?

*14. Human language use can be inappropriate as well as appropriate. Give some examples of contextual inappropriateness in human language use. Are there any examples of inappropriateness in animal communication?

*15. Give an example of a situation where human language use is not stimulus-free.

*16. Suppose someone utters the sentence *The bull is about to charge!* How might this be a report, an expression (of fear), and a warning all at once? Does this show that human language use is not functionally separable? Defend your answer.

*17. Recall the chart picturing the structure of human language given in The Note to the Student at the beginning of this book. Which theories from the chart are reflected in bird and primate communication? Which are not? Defend your answer.

References

Chomsky, N. (1966) *Cartesian Linguistics,* Harper & Row, New York.

Hockett, C. (1960) "The origin of speech," *Scientific American* 203, 88–96.

Jolly, A. (1972) *The Evolution of Primate Behavior,* Macmillan, New York.

Marler, P., and W. J. Hamilton (1966) *Mechanisms of Animal Behavior,* Wiley, New York.

McNeill, D. (1970) *The Acquisition of Language,* Harper & Row, New York.

Rowell, T. (1962) "Agonistic noises of the rhesus monkey (Macaca mulata)," *Symposia of the Zoological Society of London* 8, 91–96.

Thorpe, W. (1974) *Animal Nature and Human Nature,* Doubleday, Garden City, New York.

Part Two

HUMAN LANGUAGE
AND COMMUNICATION

INTRODUCTION

Turning from the study of animal communication systems to the study of human language, we take up in seven individual chapters various subfields in linguistics. This division reflects the need to break down the broad questions about language into smaller ones that we can hope to answer. Although this is a good strategy, the reader should nevertheless be aware at the very beginning that the various subfields can in fact be integrated and unified at a more abstract level and should look for the following themes that run through each chapter:

Linguistic phenomena can be described in terms of small collections of *discrete units.*

These discrete units are governed by *rules: rules of combination* and *rules of use.*

Throughout part II readers should attempt to integrate, as far as possible, the material from the different chapters. Especially relevant in this regard are chapter 9 (the subsection entitled "Where phonology, morphology, syntax, and pragmatic context meet"), chapter 11 (section 11.3), and chapter 12 (section 12.2). Finally, a periodic review of The Note to the Student at the beginning of this book may provide a useful way to organize the material in part II, especially for chapters 7 and 8.

Chapter Six

PHONOLOGY: THE STRUCTURE OF SOUNDS

6.1 SOME BACKGROUND CONCEPTS

A grammar of a language can be viewed as a system of rules relating sound and meaning; that portion of a grammar that describes the sounds, and the rules governing the distribution of the sounds, is the *phonological component* (or simply, the *phonology*). Among the basic phonological units of all human language sound systems are discrete elements called *phonemes* (the contrasting speech sounds of a language). The pronunciation of the phonemes is highly structured; even our so-called casual pronunciation of words is governed by regular, but abstract, principles.

For an illustration of the structural conditions that govern pronunciation, we begin by considering the following pairs of words, each consisting of a verb and its corresponding agentive noun.

(1) Verb   Agentive Noun
   (to) write   writer
   (to) shout   shouter
   (to) bat   batter
   (to) hit   hitter

The words in the left column end in a "t" sound. In the related words in the agentive column, the *t* (or *tt*) is regularly pronounced as a "d" sound by most speakers of American (but not British) English. Because of the rapidity of the articulation of the "d" sound, it is referred to as a *flap*. Thus, the "t" sounds in the words on the left in (1) correspond to the flapped "d" sounds in the words on the right.

Rules Governing the Pronunciation of the Sounds of Language

Two important questions immediately arise: What is the nature of the relation between the "t" and flapped "d" sounds? And if there is a relation, how is it to be expressed? Perhaps the simplest account would be that there is *no* relation between the two sounds. Speakers of American English may have simply memorized the different pronunciations of the words in the separate columns and any relation between the members of the pairs is in terms of meaning only. If this were true, however, how could we account for the fact that words we have never encountered before will exhibit the same pattern of distribution of sounds as the examples in (1)? Consider the nonsense words in (2):

(2) Verb   Agentive Noun
    (to) grite   griter
    (to) bloyt   bloyter
    (to) plat   platter

If you pronounced a flapped *d* in the agentive forms in (1), then you will automatically and unconsciously pronounce a flapped *d* in the agentive forms of the nonsense words of (2). This rule of pronunciation in American English is only one of many rules governing the pronunciation of our words. Given that pronunciation is rule-governed, we must now ask how these rules are stated. Before we can understand the nature of phonological rules, however, we must know something about the physiological mechanisms that underlie our ability to pronounce the utterances of our language.

Physiology of Speech Production

The articulation of human speech is an enormously intricate process involving over one hundred muscles and a complex nervous system that must control and synchronize these muscles. Lenneberg (1967) discusses several instances of special adaptations of human physiology to speech. We will discuss three of these adaptations here:

the adaptation of respiration to speech,

the rate of speech production,

the ordering of events in speech production.

Adaptation of Respiration to Speech

The rhythm of respiration during speech is radically different from the rhythm of respiration during normal breathing. Lenneberg states that "we are endowed with special physiological adaptations which enable us to sustain speech driven by expired air" (1967, 81). His point is made clear by the observation that only certain types of disruptions of the normal breathing pattern can be tolerated. For example, if one intentionally breathes too rapidly or too slowly, hyper- or hypo-ventilation results. As another example, if one were to attempt to speak during inhalation (it will sound whispered) and then breathe out rapidly in order to carry on a normal conversation, one would soon experience severe respiratory difficulties. Thus, not all distortions of normal breathing can be tolerated and compensated for by the respiratory mechanisms.

One of the greatest distortions of the breathing rate occurs during speech: breath is drawn in rapidly and let out over a much longer period than during normal breathing. Even this radical distortion of the normal breathing pattern causes none of the effects of discomfort that accompany the previously mentioned distortions of normal breathing. It is apparent that the human body has special physiological adaptations to compensate for the distorted breathing patterns that occur during speech.

Rate of Speech Production

The sounds of speech are articulated (as well as processed and understood) at a very rapid rate. Goldman-Eisler (1954) calculated an average rate of production of 200 to 210 syllables per minutes during normal conversational speech. (Rates as high as 500 syllables per minute are also possible.) Using the figure of 2.4 phonemes per syllable as an average for English, we arrive at an average rate of articulation of about 8 phonemes per second. The matter is complicated by the fact that during speech, signals are constantly being sent to every muscle used in producing speech. Basically, three types of instructions are sent to these muscles: maintain tension, contract, or relax. Thus, 8 times a second an order must be given to all one hundred muscles involved in speech. The number of events taking place every second is therefore extremely large.

Ordering of Events in Speech Production

The brain's signaling to the articulatory muscles is complicated further by the fact that innervation (activation) times vary considerably for the various muscles that must act in unison to produce a given speech sound. Consider, for example, the pronunciation of the sequence *pa* (pronounced "pah"). Oversimplified somewhat: in order to coordinate the pronunciation of "p" and "ah," part of the signal to articulate the "ah" must be sent from the brain to the vocal tract *earlier* than part of the signal to articulate the "p," since part of the signal for the "ah" has a longer distance to travel. This can be seen in figure 6.1.

Notice that the nerves that connect the brain to the jaw and lips, (a) and (b), which must be activated to make a "p" sound, are short and thick and therefore able to transmit nerve impulses quickly. On the other hand, one of the nerves controlling the laryngeal muscles in the throat (c), which is necessary for the articulation of the "ah" sound, is longer and thinner than nerves (a) and (b). Thus, in articulating a sequence such as "pah," the signals from the brain to the vocal tract do not follow the neat, linear sequence of our spelling p-a.

It is not always the case in actual speech that the different parts of the articulation of a phoneme all occur at the same time. The reader can

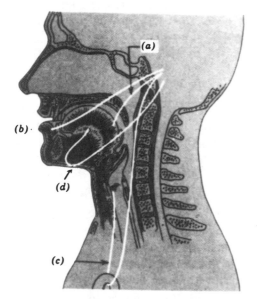

Figure 6.1
Schematic cross section of vocal tract showing nerves connected to muscles. From Lenneberg 1967.

directly observe the phenomenon of the different sequencing of the vocal tract gestures for a particular phoneme in the word *construe*. The rounding of the lips which must accompany the final vowel of the word (the part spelled *-ue*) begins three phonemes earlier (on the "s" sound). In contrast, pronouncing the *-str-* sequence in *constrict* does not require the lip rounding found in *construe*. Roughly speaking, the lip rounding for the last vowel sound in *construe* arrives three phonemes early.

Thus we see that, first, respiration is adapted to speech; second, the sounds of speech are articulated at a very rapid rate and involve over a hundred muscles; and, third, a very complex sequencing of brain signals must be sent to the vocal tract. These features of speech are complex and automatic physiological gestures which cannot be learned, but are among the biologically innate features that facilitate the acquisition of speech by the human species.

Babbling and the Acquisition of Language

Before children begin to acquire the language they are exposed to, they go through a phase that is referred to as babbling. The first babbled sequences are physiologically complex combinations: "bah," "pah," "mah," "dah," "gah," and so forth. These babbled sounds are produced by all normal children (and even deaf children). Moreover, a baby who will eventually learn Swahili as its native language will begin to babble with the same or similar sounds as the baby who will acquire English. In fact, the ability to babble is a necessary prerequisite for the later acquisition of the language to which the child is exposed. Young children who will learn English are physiologically able to make a wider range of complex sounds than are actually found in English, and thus they must learn to restrict their potential repertoire of sounds to conform to the rules of English pronunciation (such as the rule governing the flapped "d"). For children acquiring a sound system of a particular language, the task is not so much to learn how to utter sequences of speech sounds (the ability to do so being biologically innate) but rather to refine their ability to speak in accordance with the sound system to which they are exposed. We turn next to a discussion of the human vocal tract, which children must learn to manipulate in order to speak their language correctly.

The Vocal Tract and the Production of Speech

In all human languages speech sounds are for the most part formed in the vocal tract, the area between the vocal cords and the lips (see figure 6.2). The number of vocal tract configurations (and therefore phonemes) found in the world's languages is enormous, but we limit ourselves here to a discussion of the major articulatory features most commonly found across languages (see Smalley 1968 for a description of the richness of articulatory possibilities). For purposes of discussion we divide speech sounds into two major categories: *syllabics* (vowels) and *nonsyllabics* (consonants). This binary division obscures a number of subtleties, but the division is a useful one for beginning our discussion.

Articulation of Syllabics

During the production of vowel sounds the vocal tract is an open chamber within which air molecules vibrate, causing sound to be produced. The energy for the production of vowels is supplied by the vibration of the vocal cords (see no. 7 in figure 6.2). The vocal cords are elastic bands of tissue located in the larynx, and they can be brought

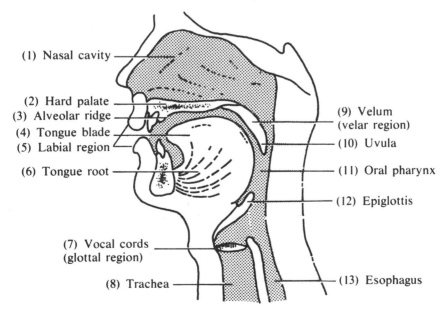

Figure 6.2
Cross section of human vocal tract

into mechanical vibration if (a) they are brought close enough together and (b) the air passing between the cords is moving fast enough. This mechanical vibration of the vocal cords is called *voicing,* and the *rate* of vibration is the *frequency* (or *pitch*) of the vowel.

The different vowels are formed by different shapes of the open, *resonating* vocal tract, the shape of which is determined by several factors. The primary factors are the position of the tongue (blade and root: nos. 4 and 6 in figure 6.2); the relative openness of the lips (no. 5, figure 6.2); the constriction of the oral pharynx (no. 11, figure 6.2); and the position of the jaw. Each of these features of articulation plays an important role in the production of vowels. For instance, an "ah" vowel (as in the English word *father*) is formed when the upper part of the vocal tract is relatively open (the tongue is lowered), the lower part of the vocal tract is relatively narrow (the tongue is moved back and the pharynx is constricted), and the lips are relatively open (see figure 6.3).

Other vowels are formed by different configurations of the same features of articulation used to form the "ah" vowel, written as /a/ in figure 6.3. For example, to form the vowel sound "ee," written as /i/ in figure 6.3, the tongue is moved forward and upward creating a rather narrow cavity along the roof of the mouth. In contrast, the lower vocal tract is relatively open, caused by the forward position of the tongue yielding a widening in the pharyngeal region. Also, the lips are brought closer together than is the case in the formation of "ah."

Articulations such as tongue position, pharyngeal constriction, lip position, and so forth, are for the most part independently controllable. These articulations combine in various ways in the world's languages

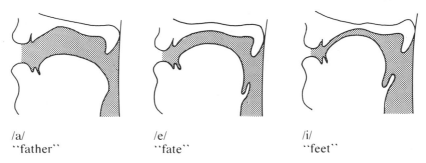

/a/   /e/   /i/
"father"   "fate"   "feet"

Figure 6.3
Vocal tract shapes for some English vowels

to form the different vowels; we will discuss them in more detail when we discuss the vowel system of American English in section 6.2.

Articulation of Nonsyllabics (Consonants)

Whereas the different *vowels* are formed by various degrees of *openness* at points in the vocal tract, *consonants* in all human languages are formed with various degrees of *constriction* at points along the vocal tract. Linguists generally cross-classify the consonants in terms of *manner* and *place* of articulation, both of which can be independently controlled by the speaker. The primary *manners of articulation* that are common to all languages are the following:

Stops are formed when the airflow in the vocal tract is completely blocked at points between the vocal cords and the lips (see figure 6.2). Examples from English are the initial consonants in p*in* and b*in*.

Constrictives (also called *fricatives*) are formed when the stream of air must flow through a very narrow opening in the vocal tract, so that turbulence (friction) is created. Examples from English are the initial consonants in s*ing* and f*oot*.

Affricates are single phonemes, each beginning with a *stop* but being secondarily released into a *constrictive*. Examples from English are the initial consonants in the words ch*ip* and j*oy*.

Nasals are formed with *open* nasal cavity (no. 1 in figure 6.2) so that resonances of the nasal cavity are present. The nasal cavity can be blocked to form nonnasals by raising the velum (no. 9, figure 6.2). The first consonants in the words m*ile* and N*ancy* are nasals.

Liquids occupy an intermediate position between the more extreme consonants (such as stops and constrictives) and vowels. The liquid consonants in English are "r" and "l," found in the initial position of the words r*ed* and l*ike*, respectively.

Glides, similar to liquids, are intermediate between consonants and vowels. In initial position in the words w*ind* and y*es* are the glides "w" and "y," respectively. Because of the similarity of articulation of the glides to the vowels in *boot* and *beet*, respectively, these glides are frequently referred to as *semivowels*.

Voicing is one of the more important features found in the articulation of consonants. Recall that voicing is the result of the vibration of the vocal cords. All of the manners of articulation discussed so far can be further cross-classified with the feature of voicing. For example, in English the stops have two different forms, depending on the presence or absence of voicing. The first and last consonants of b*i*g and d*i*g are voiced, whereas the first and last consonants of p*i*ck and t*i*ck are voiceless.

The *points of articulation* are located along the vocal tract between the lips and the vocal cords. Among the more common points are the bilabial, labiodental, dental (and interdental), alveolar, palatal, velar, uvular, and glottal regions (see figure 6.2). For the most part, the terms for these positions refer to points along the roof of the mouth, and there is an implicit assumption that some articulator from below (usually the lower lip or some part of the tongue) approaches or touches the designated point along the roof of the mouth.

Bilabials are consonants formed when the upper and lower lips approach each other (or touch). The English words **M**ike and **b**i*g* begin with bilabial consonants (see no. 5, figure 6.2).

Labiodental consonants are formed when the upper teeth and lower lip approach (or touch) each other. The English words **f**ish and **v**oice begin with labiodental consonants (see no. 5, figure 6.2).

Dental consonants are formed when the tip of the tongue approaches (or touches) the upper teeth. The English words **th**in and **th**en begin with *interdental* constrictives (the tongue is between the teeth).

Alveolar consonants are those formed when the tip of the tongue approaches (or touches) the alveolar ridge (no. 3, figure 6.2). The English words **s**ing and **d**og begin with alveolar consonants.

Palatal consonants are formed when the tongue (tip or blade) approaches (or touches) the roof of the mouth behind the alveolar ridge along the hard palate (no. 2, figure 6.2). The final consonants in ri**ch** and ri**dge** are palatal consonants. (These are sometimes referred to as pre-palatal consonants because of their relative closeness to the alveolar area.

Velar consonants are formed when the blade of the tongue approaches (or touches) the roof of the mouth in the velar region (no. 9, figure 6.2). The English words **g**ood and **k**id begin with velar consonants.

Uvular consonants are formed when the back of the tongue approaches (or touches) the roof of the mouth near the uvula (no. 10, figure 6.2). There are no uvular consonants in English, but Parisian French *r* is uvular.

Glottal consonants are formed by the vocal cords (the opening between the vocal cords is called the glottis). The sound of the *tt* in the English word *bu***tt***on* is not an alveolar stop, but a glottal stop for many speakers of American English.

6.2 THE PHONEMES OF AMERICAN ENGLISH

In our discussion we will present a special set of symbols to represent the sounds of American English, since they are not adequately represented by the contemporary orthography (spelling system). The letter *t*, for example, can represent a "t" sound (*tin*), a "sh" sound (*nation*), and, as we saw in section 6.1, a flapped "d" sound (*batter*). On the other hand, various letters other than *j* can represent the first sound in *jug: dge* in *bridge* and *g* in *logic*. Many features of the current orthography are based on the way English was pronounced hundreds of years ago; because English has changed, a different alphabet is required to represent the contemporary pronunciation. We will use a set of symbols that is in general use by American linguists.

American English Vowels

There are two major classes of American English vowels; they have been characterized as *short* versus *long,* or *lax* versus *tense,* respectively.

Short (Lax) Vowels of English

If we imagine that figure 6.4 is superimposed on a cross section of the vocal tract, such as that in figure 6.2, then the relative positions of the vowels represent the relative positions that the tongue assumes in forming these vowels (with the mouth on the left). The oral cross section is divided into subsections; in describing the English vowels, linguists frequently cross-classify the vowels in terms of their position in one of the six sections in figure 6.4. Thus, /ɪ/ is a high, front vowel, and /ɛ/ is a mid (nonhigh and nonlow) front vowel. The set of symbols we now present is often referred to as a phonemic alphabet. These

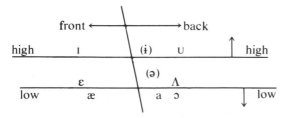

Figure 6.4
Short (lax) vowels of American English

symbols accurately represent the *major* features of articulation of American English, but do not represent finer phonetic details.

/ɪ/ A high front lax vowel. Typical words exhibiting this vowel are *sin* /sɪn/ and *big* /bɪg/. (Note that orthographic forms are in italics, phonemic forms are enclosed in slashes.)

/ɛ/ A mid front lax vowel. It is found in words such as *get* /gɛt/ and *mend* /mɛnd/.

/æ/ A low front lax vowel. This vowel is called *ash* by many linguists, and in fact it is the vowel sound in the word *ash* /æš/.

/ʌ/ A mid central unrounded lax vowel. It occurs in words such as *putt* /pʌt/ and *luck* /lʌk/.

/ʊ/ A high back slightly rounded lax vowel. It is found in words such as *put* /pʊt/ and *book* /bʊk/.

/a/, /ɔ/ Low back lax vowels. These two vowels show considerable variation of occurrence in American English; it will be up to your instructor to let you know which variant(s) you have in your speech. Some diagnostic words can enable you to determine whether you have both of these vowels in your speech: If you make a phonetic distinction between *cot* and *caught,* you probably will have the vowels represented by /kat/ and /kɔt/, respectively. (If you're from New York City, all bets are off.) You may have more than these two low lax vowels in your speech, especially if you have three different vowels in *father, cot* and *caught.* Many, if not most, Americans in the western United States have a single low back vowel; linguists use either /a/ or /ɔ/ to represent this sound.

Reduced Vowels
There are two vowels in English called reduced vowels; they are shown in parentheses in figure 6.4. The most common reduced vowel is called schwa and is written as an upside down *e* /ə/. It is the first vowel sound in *about* /əbawt/ and sounds very much like /ʌ/ (some linguists, in fact, use the same symbol for both sounds). The two are slightly different, however, in that ʌ is at least somewhat longer than ə. Say the word *abut* /əbʌt/ a few times to try to hear the difference. The /ə/ is called a reduced vowel because it is frequently a reduction of a regular vowel. Note the different vowels in the word *democrat* /déməkræt/ and in the word *democracy* /dəmákrəsiy/. The /ɛ/ in /déməkræt/ corresponds to the first unstressed /ə/ in /dəmákrəsiy/.

The other reduced vowel is /ɨ/ and is referred to as *barred i* by linguists. It is the vowel sound in the second syllable of *children* /čɪldrɨn/. The reduced vowels of English occur only in unstressed positions (in unemphasized syllables in a word).

Long (Tense) Vowels and Diphthongs
The long vowels of English differ from their short vowel counterparts not only in terms of length but in the place of articulation. If one compares the two vowel sounds in *beat* and *bit*, one will notice that the vowel in *beat* is not only longer, it even sounds higher in pitch. In addition, all of the long vowels of Modern English are diphthongal, which means that these vowel sounds can be divided into two parts: a vowel part that carries the main stress (emphasis), and an offglide, /y/ or /w/. For example, in pronouncing the word *tie*, note that at first the tongue is low (as in the vowel /a/) and gradually rises into a front *ee* /iy/ sound. (Even the vowel in English *beat* /biyt/, which is already a high vowel, rises slightly toward the end). Hence, a common practice is to represent all the long vowels and diphthongs as clusters of vowels and offglides as follows:

(3) iy   uw
     ey   ow
     ay   aw
     oy

/iy/   A high front vowel, with a slightly rising offglide represented by /y/. It occurs in words such as *beat* /biyt/ and *three* /θriy/.

/ey/   A mid front vowel with an accompanying high front offglide. Words such as *clay* /kley/ and *weigh* /wey/ exhibit this sound.

/ay/   Begins as a low back vowel, followed by a rising front offglide. It is found in *my* /may/ and *thigh* /θay/.

/oy/   A sequence of a back rounded vowel followed by a rising front offglide. It is found in words such as *boy* /boy/ and *Floyd* /floyd/.

/uw/   A sequence of a high back rounded vowel followed by a slightly rising back offglide, represented by *w*. It occurs in words such as *boot* /buwt/ and *screw* /skruw/.

/ow/   A mid back rounded vowel followed by a rising back offglide. It occurs in *boat* /bowt/ and *toe* /tow/.

/aw/   A low back unrounded vowel followed by a back offglide. It occurs in *cow* /kaw/ and *plough* /plaw/.

Table 6.1
The consonants of English

	Voicing	Bilabial	Labiodental
Stops	voiceless	p	
	voiced	b	
Constrictives	voiceless		f
	voiced		v
Affricates	voiceless		
	voiced		
Nasals		m	
Liquids			
Glides		w	

Consonants and Glides

Table 6.1 displays the consonants of English according to the two major categories of description, manner and place of articulation. The reader may wish to refer again to figure 6.2 for an illustration of where the points of articulation are located in the vocal tract. The consonant sounds represented by the symbols in table 6.1 can be described in terms of the articulatory features discussed in section 6.1.

Stops

/p/ A voiceless bilabial stop. It is the initial sound in the word *pin* /pɪn/.

/b/ A voiced bilabial stop. It occurs twice in *Bob* /bab/.

/t/ A voiceless alveolar stop. it is the initial sound in *tin* /tɪn/.

/d/ A voiced alveolar stop. It occurs twice in the word *dad* /dæd/.

/k/ A voiceless velar stop. The position of *k* will vary along the roof of the mouth, depending on what vowels precede or follow it. Thus, the /k/ in *keep* /kiyp/ is articulated in a more forward position than the /k/ in *cool* /kuwl/.

/g/ A voiced velar stop. It occurs twice in the word *gig* /gɪg/.

/ʔ/ A glottal stop. It is formed by blocking the passage of air through the vocal tract by means of closing the vocal cords. The American English pronunciation of *button* /bʌʔən/ frequently contains a glottal stop in place of /t/. Also, every word that appears to begin with a vowel actually begins with a glottal stop (/ʔæpəl/ *apple*).

Interdental	Alveolar	Palatal	Velar	Glottal
	t		k	ʔ
	d		g	
θ	s	š		h
ð	z	ž		
		č		
		ǰ		
	n		ŋ	
	r, l			
		y		

Constrictives (Fricatives)

/f/   A voiceless labiodental constrictive. An /f/ is found in initial position in the word fish /fɪš/.

/v/   A voiced labiodental constrictive. It is the initial sound in *vine* /vayn/.

/θ/   A voiceless interdental constrictive. It is usually spelled in English as *th*. It is the initial sound in *theta* /θeytə/, and its symbol is called *theta*.

/ð/   A voiced interdental constrictive. This symbol is also represented by *th* in English spelling. The difference between /ð/ and /θ/ can be easily heard if one says *then* and *thin* slowly. You will hear (or feel) the voicing that accompanies *then* /ðɛn/ and the lack of voicing at the beginning of *thin* /θɪn/.

/s/   A voiceless alveolar constrictive. It is the initial sound in the word *sit* /sɪt/.

/z/   A voiced alveolar constrictive. It is the initial sound in the name *Zeke* /ziyk/.

/š/   A voiceless palatal constrictive. It is pronounced further back in the mouth and with a greater tongue area than the sound /s/. It is the initial sound in the word *ship* /šɪp/.

/ž/   A voiced palatal constrictive. It is the second sound in the word *azure* /æžər/.

/h/   Has many variants. In front of high front vowels it is actually a palatal constrictive as in the word *he*. Before other vowels it is a whispered (voiceless) variant of that vowel with an accompanying constriction in the glottal region. It is the initial sound in *hop* /hap/.

Affricates

/č/   A voiceless palatal affricate. The term affricate indicates that friction (constriction) is part of the articulation of this sound. As already noted, an affricate is analyzed as a stop with a secondary release into a constrictive. A /č/ is the last sound in the word *crutch* /krʌč/.

/ǰ/   A voiced palatal affricate. It is found twice in the word *judge* /ǰʌǰ/.

Nasals

/m/   A bilabial nasal stop. The nasal stops are analogous to the voiced stops discussed earlier. When the nasal passages are opened by lowering the velum (see figure 6.2) as a /b/ is being articulated, an /m/ will be produced. An /m/ is the initial sound in *mice* /mays/.

/n/   An alveolar nasal stop. An /n/ is the initial sound in *nice* /nays/.

/ŋ/   A velar nasal stop. As /b/ is to /m/ and as /d/ is to /n/, so /g/ is to /ŋ/. The /ŋ/ is called an *engwa* by many linguists. The normal English spelling for this sound is *ng,* although not all /ŋ/s are represented by *ng,* and not all *ng*'s represent an engwa. For example, there is a difference between *singer* /sɪŋər/ and *finger* /fɪŋgər/. The *ng* in *congress* is the velar nasal, but the *n* in *congressional* is an alveolar /n/ for many speakers of English.

Liquids

/r/   An alveolar liquid in which the tongue tip approaches the alveolar ridge. American English /r/ has concomitant lip rounding (labialization) and some degree of pharyngeal constriction.

/l/   A lateral alveolar liquid. The term *lateral* indicates that the air flows past both sides of the tongue during the articulation of this sound. It is the first sound in *luck* /lʌk/.

Glides

/y/   A high front glide. It occurs only before and after vowels. It is the initial sound in *yes* /yɛs/.

/w/   A high back glide. As in the case with y, w only occurs before and after vowels. It is the initial sound in *wet* /wɛt/.

Phonetic Feature Analysis of Phonemes

Refer again to figure 6.4 and list (3), showing the English vowels, and to the table of consonants (table 6.1). Notice that there is a regularity in the distribution of phonemes. The phonemes in these displays are not random lists but are grouped into systematic classes. In talking about the sound structures of different languages, linguists frequently refer to groupings of phonemes as *series* of sounds. Thus, in table 6.1 the reader can identify the series of voiced /b, d, g/ and voiceless /p, t, k/ stops. Similarly, one can talk about the series of high vowels /ɪ, ɨ, ʊ/ or the front vowels /ɪ, ɛ, æ/. These groupings are not accidental; they are a reflection of a deeper organizational principle governing the sound system of human language. That is, it is not the phonemes themselves but a more basic set of phonetic features that are the fundamental units of phonological systems. Not only are the phonemes of a language grouped into systematic classes according to phonetic features; but as we will see in section 6.3, these systematic classes of sounds play a crucial role in the description of the phonological regularities found in human languages.

The next question to be asked, then, is what are *phonetic features*? One view of phonetic features is that for the most part they represent the individually controllable aspects of the pronunciation of the phonemes of a language. Just as we break the continuous stream of sound down into words and words into discrete phonemes, we analyze each phoneme into smaller discrete units called phonetic features. Phonemes can be viewed, then, as simultaneous bundles of phonetic features. We now turn to a discussion of the phonetic features of English, but the reader should keep in mind that the principles we discuss are applicable to the phonological systems of all human languages.

Phonetic Feature Characterization of English Vowels

The phonetic features used in this text are, for the most part, based on a proposal made by Chomsky and Halle in their book, *The Sound Pattern of English* (1968). In table 6.2 we present a list of syllabic phonemes (vowels) of English with their respective phonetic feature specifications. The features in the chart represent a breakdown of the vowel sounds in terms of the various vocal tract shapes that produce these sounds.

Table 6.2
Phonetic feature composition of English vowels

	i (iy)	ɪ	e (ey)	ɛ	æ	u (uw)	ʊ	ʌ	o (ow)	ɔ	a	ə	ɨ
syllabic	+	+	+	+	+	+	+	+	+	+	+	+	+
high	+	+	−	−	−	+	+	−	−	−	−	−	+
back	−	−	−	−	−	+	+	+	+	+	+	+	+
low	−	−	−	−	+	−	−	−	−	+	+	−	−
round	−	−	−	−	−	+	+	−	+	+	−	−	−
long (tense)	+	−	+	−	−	+	−	−	+	−	−	−	−
reduced	−	−	−	−	−	−	−	−	−	−	−	+	+

At the top of the table we have listed the English vowels and on the left the phonetic features that characterize them. Every plus mark indicates that a vowel has a certain feature, and every minus indicates the lack of this feature. For example, /i/ has the feature *high* but lacks the feature *round,* whereas /u/, which also has the feature *high*, possesses the feature *round.* In other words, the features allow us to distinguish all the vowels, while at the same time allowing us to cross-categorize them into classes. The vowels /i, ɪ, u, ʊ, ɨ/ are members of the class of high vowels.

Let us examine each of the phonetic features of table 6.2. The terms *high, low,* and *back* refer to the relative positions the tongue may have in the mouth. These terms have already been used in the description of the vowels in figure 6.4. The term *round* refers to the rounding of the lips (also called labialization), which is a feature of English back vowels such as /uw, ʊ, ow and ɔ/. The term *long* is used to distinguish /ɛ/ and /ey/, although we have already noted that there is more than a length difference between these vowels: the /ey/ phoneme begins in a higher position in the mouth than the /ɛ/ phoneme, and the /ey/ also has a high offglide. We have therefore listed the long vowels /iy, ey, uw, ow/ in terms of the features of their first segment. The remaining diphthongs /ay, aw, oy/ are not listed in table 6.2; they are to be analyzed as clusters of two phonemes: for example, /ay/=/a/+/y/. Finally, *reduced* is a tentative term used to indicate that relatively less effort is used in the articulation of the vowels /ə/ and /ɨ/. Table 6.2 should be used to find the feature specification for vowels needed to do the exercises.

Phonetic Feature Description of English Consonants
The phonetic feature compositions of English consonants are listed in table 6.3. Some of the phonetic features used to describe vowels are

Table 6.3
Phonetic feature composition of English consonants

	p	b	m	t	d	n	k	g	ŋ	f	v	s	z	θ	ð	š	ž	č	ǰ	l	r	w	y	h	ʔ
consonant	+	+	+	+	+	+	+	+	+	+	+	+	+	+	+	+	+	+	+	+	+	−	−	−	−
voiced	−	+	+	−	+	+	−	+	+	−	+	−	+	−	+	−	+	−	+	+	+	+	+	−	−
nasal	−	−	+	−	−	+	−	−	+	−	−	−	−	−	−	−	−	−	−	−	−	−	−	−	−
stop	+	+	+	+	+	+	+	+	+	−	−	−	−	−	−	−	−	+	+	−	−	−	−	−	+
affricate	−	−	−	−	−	−	−	−	−	−	−	−	−	−	−	−	−	+	+	−	−	−	−	−	−
sibilant	−	−	−	−	−	−	−	−	−	−	−	+	+	−	−	+	+	+	+	−	−	−	−	−	−
labial	+	+	+	−	−	−	−	−	−	+	+	−	−	−	−	−	−	−	−	−	−	+	−	−	−
interdental	−	−	−	−	−	−	−	−	−	−	−	−	−	+	+	−	−	−	−	−	−	−	−	−	−
glottal	−	−	−	−	−	−	−	−	−	−	−	−	−	−	−	−	−	−	−	−	−	−	−	+	+
sonorant	−	−	+	−	−	+	−	−	+	−	−	−	−	−	−	−	−	−	−	+	+	+	+	+	+
high	−	−	−	−	−	−	+	+	+	−	−	−	−	−	−	+	+	+	+	−	−	+	+	−	−
back	−	−	−	−	−	−	+	+	+	−	−	−	−	−	−	−	−	−	−	−	−	+	−	−	−
low	−	−	−	−	−	−	−	−	−	−	−	−	−	−	−	−	−	−	−	−	−	−	−	+	+
coronal	−	−	−	+	+	+	−	−	−	−	−	+	+	+	+	+	+	+	+	+	+	−	−	−	−
lateral	−	−	−	−	−	−	−	−	−	−	−	−	−	−	−	−	−	−	−	+	−	−	−	−	−
distributed	−	−	−	−	−	−	−	−	−	−	−	−	−	−	−	+	+	+	+	−	−	−	−	−	−

also used for consonants. The consonant /k/, for example, requires that the back of the tongue be raised toward the roof of the mouth; /k/ thus has the feature description [+high] and [+back]. Because some of the terms have not been used up to now, we will describe each of the features in table 6.3. As you will see, most of them are described in articulatory terms already encountered in section 6.1.

Voiced. Recall that vibration in the vocal cords can accompany the articulation of various sounds. Examples: /b, g, ǰ/.

Nasal. In nasal sounds the velum is lowered to activate resonances in the nasal cavity. Examples: /m, n, ŋ/.

Stop. The air stream through the vocal tract is completely stopped. Examples: /b, m, t/.

Affricate. The air stream is stopped temporarily, but the stop releases into a constrictive. The release into the constrictive is secondary, and the sequence of stop plus constrictive is actually a single sound. Examples: /č, ǰ/.

Sibilant. The class of sibilants in English contain sounds with a high degree of friction noise (''hissing''). Examples: /s, š, ǰ/.

Labial. Articulation involves the lips. Examples: /p, m, b/.

Interdental. The tongue is pushed forward between the teeth, forming a constrictive sound as the air passes between the upper teeth and the tongue. Examples: /ð, θ/.

Glottal. The vocal cords constrict or stop the flow of the air. Examples: /h, ʔ/.

Sonorant. Sonorant sounds are those produced when the vocal tract is open to the extent that spontaneous vibration of the vocal cords occurs (see Chomsky and Halle 1968, 300). Sonorants are consonants and vowels produced in such a way that the degree of constriction in the upper vocal tract is not sufficient to prohibit spontaneous voicing. Examples: /r, l, m/. Sounds made with greater degrees of constriction, such that spontaneous voicing is impossible, are called nonsonorants, or, more commonly, *obstruents*.

High. The body of the tongue is raised toward the roof of the mouth. Examples: /č, g/.

Back. The body of the tongue remains in its normal back position. Examples: /w, g/. The tongue root can also move forward to a nonback or front position. Examples: /č, ǰ/.

Low. The tongue is lowered to the bottom of the mouth. Examples: /ʔ, h/.

Coronal. The blade of the tongue moves up toward the teeth and teeth ridge. Dental, alveolar, and palatal stops are coronal. Examples: /θ, d, ǰ/.

Lateral. If the tip of the tongue is partially blocking the air stream but the air is allowed to pass along both sides of the tongue, the sound is called lateral. Example: /l/.

Distributed. This term refers to the relative amount of contact that the tongue makes along the roof of the mouth. The tongue has a relatively longer point of contact in /š/ than in /s/; thus /š/ is distributed and /s/ is nondistributed.

As one can see, individual phonetic features are, in general, related to specific shapes of the vocal tract which produce the consonants and vowels found in human language. Each feature is also related to a specific group of controllable muscles in the vocal tract. Figure 6.5 illustrates this in an oversimplified schematic manner, ignoring certain subtleties.

Suppose we have listed on the left of figure 6.5 all the hundred or so

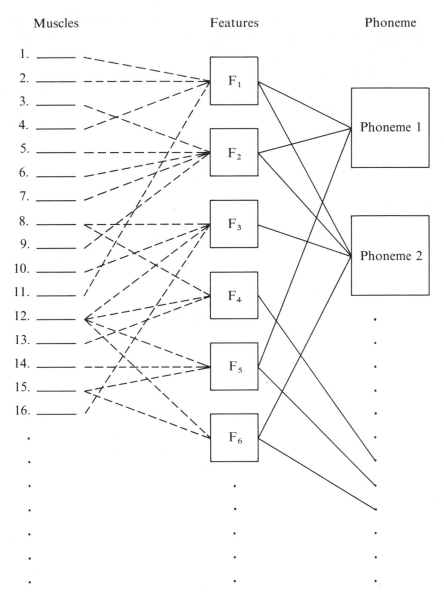

Figure 6.5
Phonetic features in an intermediate position between muscles and phonemes.

that we have just discussed, and on the right all of the phonemes of English. The important relationship is this: each feature is an abstract cover term for a grouping of muscle gestures, and each phoneme, in turn, is made up of a group of features. In this way the features are abstract units of muscle organization, which act in an intermediate position between the muscles involved in speech and the phonemes. For example, let us suppose that feature 1 is the feature *labial,* and feature 2 is the feature *nasal.* In our diagram we have connected feature 1 to a set of muscles that we have arbitrarily labeled 1, 2, 4, and 11. These could stand for muscles in the jaw, lips, and so forth. We have connected feature 2 to another group of arbitrarily labeled muscles, which could represent the muscles involved in lowering and raising the velum. The chart thus shows both the similarities and the differences in the articulation of /p/ versus /m/. To say that the two phonemes share the feature *labial* is to say that the same muscle groups are involved as part of the articulation of these two consonants. On the other hand, since feature 2 (*nasal*) is associated only with phoneme 2 (/m/), and not with phoneme 1 (/p/), only phoneme 2 will be articulated with the muscles involved in lowering the velum. In sum, the phonetic features link the muscle groupings and the phonemes.

Phonetic Features, Phonemes, and the Notion of Contrast

The phonemes of the world's languages are constructed from differing subsets of the universally available set of phonetic features. Although all languages draw from the same universal set of phonetic features, individual languages can differ in the sets of features that make up their phonemes. The features *coronal, lateral, affricated,* and *distributed* are all found in English, but they never occur together in a single phoneme. By contrast, in Navajo (as well as in many other North American Indian languages), these features do occur together in a single consonant, called a lateral affricate; the Navajo word *tɬah* ("ointment") begins with this phoneme, which is represented by two letters (tɬ) in the Navajo alphabet. Different feature combinations also occur in vowels. English, for example, does not have the feature of rounding in front vowels, but many European languages do (French, German, and Finnish among others). Thus, the widely differing sounds occurring in the world's languages are actually based in large part on various combinations drawn from a relatively small, restricted set of phonetic features.

A crucial property of phonetic features is that they are not all of equal value with respect to each other in particular languages. It is necessary, at this time, to introduce the distinction between phoneme and phone, since this is an important one in phonological theory. Up to this point we have been using a phonemic alphabet for writing words of English. Linguists have at their disposal a more precise alphabet, however, frequently referred to as a phonetic alphabet.

The nature of the relation between a phonemic and a phonetic alphabet can be made clear with some examples. Just as phonemes are analyzed as simultaneous bundles of phonetic features, phones are likewise bundles of phonetic features, but phones represent much finer phonetic detail than do phonemes. In English the *phones* [tʰ], [t˺], and [t] are varying pronunciations (or simply, variations of) the phoneme /t/. We follow here the traditional practice of writing phonemes in slash lines and phones in square brackets. The phones of /t/ all share the features listed in table 6.2 for /t/; that is, all are voiceless, coronal stops.

The differences in the phones, however, are as follows: the phone [tʰ], found in initial position in words such as *tin* [tʰɪn], is a stop whose release is accompanied by an extra puff of air, referred to as aspiration (indicated by a raised *h* with the *t*). The presence of aspiration can be observed if one dangles a piece of paper close in front of one's mouth when saying the word *tin*. The paper will move immediately after the /t/ is pronounced. In contrast, no such movement will be noticed when the /t/ follows an /s/ in a word such as *sting:* voiceless stops following /s/ in word-initial position are never aspirated in English.

The phone [t˺] is an unreleased *t*. For example, many speakers of American English do not release the final /t/ of *write*—the tongue remains touching the alveolar ridge. In contrast, the phone [t] is released, but not aspirated. For many speakers, then, a physical difference exists between the final /t/ of *print* and the final /t/ of *write*. Phonetically, the word *print* ends in [t], and the word *write* may end in [t˺]. There are thus several phonetic variations of the phoneme /t/ in English; these variants are referred to as different *phones*.

The phones of a phoneme bear certain relations to each other. For instance, since each of the three phones of the phoneme /t/ [tʰ, t˺, t] (also called *allophones* of the phoneme /t/) can occur in final position in a word, more or less freely, they are said to occur in *free variation* in that position. By contrast, the aspirated and unreleased phones [tʰ, tˀ] can never appear after word-initial /s/, though the released, unaspirated phone [t] can. The two phones [tʰ, tˀ] are therefore said to be in *complementary distribution* with [t] after word-initial /s/: [tʰ, tˀ] never appear in that position; [t] does. Thus the phones of a phoneme are generally describable as being in either complementary distribution or in free variation with each other.

The phones [tʰ] and [tˀ] can now be compared to the phone [d], the latter being a phone of the phoneme /d/. These three phones are phonetically (physically) distinguishable, yet the difference between [tʰ] and [d] and between [tˀ] and [d] is not of the same nature as the difference between [tʰ] and [tˀ]. The pair [d] and [tʰ] functions as a contrasting pair in English words and so do [d] and [tˀ], whereas [tʰ] and [tˀ] do not. That is to say, words will differ in meaning by the mere substitution of [tʰ] for [d]: in English, *tin* [tʰɪn] is a different word from *din* [dɪn]. Moreover, even in nonsense words—for example, *plit*— replacing a [tʰ] with a [d] creates a different word, in this case *plid*. Similar facts do not hold for [tʰ] and [tˀ]. Replacing one of these sounds by the other does not yield a new English word. Whether one pronounces a final voiceless coronal stop /t/ with aspiration or without aspiration, a native speaker of English will perceive the word as ending with the same consonant. Thus, *write* pronounced as [raytʰ] or as [raytˀ] is still the same word. Hence one can say that the phonetic difference between [tʰ] and [tˀ], aspiration, is nondistinctive. In general, the feature of voicing (which distinguishes /d/ from /tʰ/ functions *distinctively* (or *phonemically*) in English, whereas, aspiration functions nondistinctively (or nonphonemically).

Languages differ as to what features function distinctively. In Hindi, a language of India, the feature of aspiration functions distinctively in voiceless stops. For speakers of Hindi, the consonants [kʰ] (aspirated) and [k] (nonaspirated) are perceived as two different consonants. For example, *khiil* means "parched grain" whereas *kiil* means "nail".

In sum, if a phonetic feature functions distinctively—that is, if it can be used to distinguish one word from another—then it may be called a *distinctive feature*. All of the phonetic features discussed in this chapter are often called distinctive features because of the phonemic (or distinctive) role that these features play in the sound systems of human languages.

6.3 PHONOLOGICAL RULES, NATURAL CLASSES, AND THE SPEAKER'S KNOWLEDGE OF PHONOLOGY

The Role of Phonetic Features in the Expression of Phonological Rules

As we have seen, speech sounds can be described in terms of small units that represent very fine and detailed aspects of the articulation of each sound. It is these phonetic features—and not the phonemes themselves—that underlie the phonological regularities (rules) of natural language. We illustrate some phonological regularities with three examples, of increasing complexity.

Example 1: English

In section 6.1 we discussed some cases of verb and agentive noun pairs:

(4) Verb　　　　　　　　　　　　Agentive Noun
   (to) write　　　　　　　　　　writer
   (to) shout　　　　　　　　　　shouter
   (to) bat　　　　　　　　　　　batter
   (to) hit　　　　　　　　　　　hitter

As we noted, for most Americans the final dental stop in the verb *write* is voiceless but appears as a voiced flap (which we now write as [D]) in the agentive noun. We can now describe this phenomenon of the appearance of the [t] and the [D] more precisely, in terms of phonetic features.

Recall that the occurrence of the [D] is not random but rather results from a principle of pronunciation of contemporary American English. Words we have never encountered before will exhibit the same variation between [t] and [D]. Linguists refer to the differing corresponding phonological segments in related words as phonological alternations. The final [t] in *write* [rayt] is said to alternate with the medial [D] in *writer* [rayDər].

Note that the alternation might have a direction and could go either of two ways. Either the [D] must be pronounced as a [t] when it occurs in final position; or, conversely, a [t] must be pronounced as a [D] when it occurs before the /-ər/ agentive suffix. We might formulate the first possibility as follows: Whenever an agentive noun with a [D] is used as a verb, the [D] becomes a [t]. This cannot be correct, however, since the medial [D] of *rider* [rayDər] does not become a final [t] in *ride* [rayd]. Thus the rule seems to be that alveolar stops [t, d] must be pronounced as [D] if preceded by the stressed vowels /áy, í, and so on, and if followed by /-ər/. This rule is expressed schematically in (5).

(5) $\begin{bmatrix} t \\ d \end{bmatrix}$ → D / áy——ər (writer)

í——ər (kidder)

ǽ——ər (batter)

áw——ər (powder)

éy——ər (later)

In rule (5) the arrow indicates the direction of the change ([t] and [d] become [D]), the slash means "in the environment of," and the dash indicates where the change occurs. Thus the rule in (5) expresses that a [t] or a [d] becomes a [D] between /áy/ and /ər/, between /í/ and /ər/, between /ǽ/ and /ər/, and so on.

At this point we can hypothesize that our theory of phonology must consist of a description of the phonemes and a set of conditions describing aspects of the occurrence of these phonemes.

Theory 1
The phonological system of a natural language consists of (i) a set of phonemes and (ii) a set of conditions (rules) that define aspects of the pronunciation of those phonemes. The rules that account for phonological alternations are stated by listing the phonemes that condition the phonological change.

Rule (5) will, in fact, cover all the examples mentioned so far. However, it does not account for additional cases of the [t] → [D] alternation. Consider the examples in (6):

(6) Verb   Agentive noun

(to) butt   butter   (ʌ́——ər)

(to) bait   baiter   (éy——ər)

(to) beat   beater   (íy——ər)

(to) exploit   exploiter   (óy——ər)

. . .   . . .

Rule (5) fails to generalize to these cases, since the stressed vowels listed in (5) are not found in the words in (6). Indeed, the ellipsis points in (6) indicate that *any* preceding stressed English vowel can condition the change of [t] to [D]; a list completely fails to express this generalization. The correct statement for the alternation between [t] and [D] is that an alveolar stop will be pronounced as a flap when it occurs between *any* vowels if the left (preceding) vowel bears primary stress. This leads us to our next theory.

Theory 2
The phonological system of a natural language consists of (i) a set of phonemes, and (ii) a set of conditions (rules) that define aspects of the pronunciation of those segments. The rules account for phonological alternations by referring to phonetic features, not by listing phonemes.

Following Theory 2 we will write the rule that expresses the alternation between [t, d] and [D] in English in terms of the phonetic features introduced earlier.

(7) Flap Rule

$$
\begin{bmatrix} +\text{coronal} \\ +\text{stop} \\ -\text{affricate} \\ -\text{sonorant} \end{bmatrix} \rightarrow \begin{bmatrix} +\text{voice} \\ +\text{flap} \end{bmatrix} / \begin{bmatrix} +\text{syllabic} \\ +\text{stress} \end{bmatrix} \text{——} [+\text{syllabic}]
$$

$$
(d, t) \quad \rightarrow \quad D \quad / \quad V \quad \text{——} \quad V
$$

The Flap rule (7) states that a nonaffricate coronal stop ([d, t]) must be pronounced as a voiced flap ([D]) whenever it occurs between vowels, if the first vowel is stressed. The feature [+stress] is necessary because a coronal stop remains voiceless if the preceding syllable does not bear the main stress of the word (as witness the final [t] in *rapidity* [rəpíDɨtiy]).

Example 1 illustrated that phonological systems are not organized according to whole phonemes. Rather, each phoneme is made up of phonetic features, and phonological rules sensitive to these *features* govern our pronunciation. If the Flap rule were to be expressed in terms of phonemes, all of the English vowels would have to be listed in the rule. However, the feature notation allows us to capture the generalization that any syllabic segment will provide the conditioning environment for rule (7). This is a good illustration of how classes of sounds (here the class of all vowels) play a role in phonological descriptions.

Rule (7) is typical of the rules one finds in the phonological systems of natural language. Languages may differ in the types of rule they have, or even in the number they have, but phonological regularities are describable by rules formulated in phonetic features such as (7). Rule (7), moreover, is not limited to the dental stops in agentive nouns.

Forms such as *nutty* [nʌDiy], *beating* [bíyDɨŋ], and *butter* [bʌDər], all satisfy the conditions expressed in rule (7). Any English speaker who has the flap [D] in the agentives in (1) will also have a flap in any word in which the conditions specified in rule (7) are satisfied.

Example 2: Mongolian
Mongolian has two sets of stops in the velar region, a front set /g,k/, which are pronounced in a more forward position in the vocal tract, and a back set /ɣ,q/, which are pronounced further back in the vocal tract. The exact additional phonetic qualities of these stops are not important for this example and will not be discussed. (Interested readers may find more details in Grønbech and Krueger 1955.) Some examples are listed in (8).

(8) aɣula   "mountain"
    degü   "younger brother"
    bari-ɣ-ad   "taking"
    üje-g-ed   "seeing"

The consonants /g,k/ occur before the vowels /e, ö, ü/ and the consonants /ɣ,q/ occur before /a, o, u/. The vowels /ö/ and /ü/ are the front vowels /e/ and /i/ pronounced with lip rounding (vowels found in, for example, French and German). The distribution of the /g,k/ set versus the /ɣ,q/ set is predictable, in that the former occurs before front vowels, the latter before back vowels:

(9) The consonants /g,k/ occur before $\begin{bmatrix} +\text{syllabic} \\ -\text{back} \end{bmatrix}$

The consonants /ɣ,q/ occur before $\begin{bmatrix} +\text{syllabic} \\ +\text{back} \end{bmatrix}$

Once again, if we stated the facts in terms of two lists of phonemes, /e, ö, ü/ versus /a, o, u/, we would fail to express the relevant generalizations that are captured by the phonetic feature notation in (9). This notation reveals that the groups of phonemes /e, ö, ü/ and /a, o, u/ pattern as two natural classes.

Example 3: Navajo
Most speakers of Navajo have a phonological alternation in the prefix meaning "my." This alternation is demonstrated in (10).

(10) shi-forms   si-forms

    shi-má "my mother"   si-k'is "my friend"
    shi-béézh "my knife"   si-tse' "my rock"
    shi-taa' "my father"   si-dziid "my strength"

The accent marks on some of the vowels are tone markers, where the presence of an accent indicates a high tone, its absence a low tone. (The tone, however, does not play a role in the alternation between *si-* and *shi-*.) The sequences of letters *ts* and *dz* actually represent a single sound; one is the voiceless and the other the voiced nondistributed alveolar affricate (similar to the English sounds in *ċats* and *la*ds).

Navajo speakers automatically alternate between the prefixes /šɪ/ (represented in the Navajo alphabet by *shi*) and /sɪ/ (represented in the Navajo alphabet by *si*), depending on the phonemes in the word that follows. Whenever a following noun has an *s, z, ts,* or *dz* in it, the *shi-* prefix is pronounced as *si-*. What *s, z, ts,* and *dz* share in common is that they are all nondistributed, strident consonants. The rule changing *shi-* to *si-* will have the following shape:

$$(11) \quad \begin{bmatrix} +\text{consonant} \\ +\text{strident} \\ +\text{coronal} \end{bmatrix} \text{i} \rightarrow \begin{bmatrix} -\text{distributed} \\ +\text{anterior} \\ -\text{high} \end{bmatrix} \text{i/} \underline{\quad} \ldots \begin{bmatrix} +\text{coronal} \\ +\text{strident} \\ -\text{distributed} \\ +\text{anterior} \\ -\text{high} \end{bmatrix}$$
$$\quad\quad\quad (/\text{š}/) \quad\quad\quad\quad (/\text{s}/)$$

Rule (11) expresses the fact that whenever a noun has a segment that is strident, coronal, nondistributed, anterior, and nonhigh, the *shi-* prefix becomes *si-* to match these features. A change of this type is called *regressive assimilation*. The *shi-* assimilates to (becomes more like) a later consonant: *s, z, ts,* or *dz*. The term *regressive* expresses the fact that some of the features of *s, z, ts,* and *dz* are being transferred backwards in the word, thereby influencing the pronunciation of basic *shi-*. Regressive assimilation changes are among the most common phonological regularities found in phonological systems. The production of speech is not a linear phoneme-by-phoneme process. Certain features of the pronunciation of subsequent segments are anticipated and may even be transferred to preceding phonemes in a word. For example, recall the pronunciation of *construe:* the rounding of the /u/ is already present on the /s/, which is three phonemes ahead of the /u/.

Phonetic Features and Natural Classes

An important justification for the system of phonetic features presented in this chapter comes from the study of the phonological systems of the world's languages. It is the patterning of phonological regularities which reveals the role of phonetic features, in that the phonemes that participate in the formulation of the rules can usually be described in terms of a relatively small number of phonetic features. Each of these small lists of phonetic features defines what is referred to as a *natural class* of phonological segments (see Halle 1962).

Natural Class (approximate description)
A set of phonemes sharing a small set of phonetic features, where that set of features plays a significant role in expressing phonological regularities found in natural language.

In the examples discussed, each of the classes of phonemes appearing in the environmental statements of the rules was a natural class. In English (example 1) the class of all stressed vowels is a natural class; in Mongolian (example 2) the set of front vowels and the set of back vowels are two natural classes; and in Navajo (example 3) the set of s, z, ts, and dz also form a natural class.

Additional examples of natural classes can be displayed directly by a chart such as figure 6.6. The groups of enclosed vowels form natural classes in that each group can be exclusively described in terms of a small set of phonetic features; further, each set of features reappears in the phonological systems of many of the world's languages. The vowels /i, e, æ/ constitute a natural class in that they are uniquely describable with the features [+syllabic, −back]. Likewise, the vowels /i/ and /u/ form a natural class since they are uniquely describable with the features [+syllabic, +high]. In contrast, an unnatural class would consist of the segments /u, æ/ or /i, a/: no phonetic feature specification uniquely groups /u/ and /æ/ together while still excluding the other vowels. This is also the case with /i/ and /a/. It seems that phonological rules rarely, if ever, make reference to groups such as the unnatural classes /u, æ/ or /i, a/.

The major point of this section is simply this: *The phonological regularities found in natural languages are generally describable in terms of rules in which feature specifications define natural classes of phonological segments.* Thus the ultimate patterning of phonological

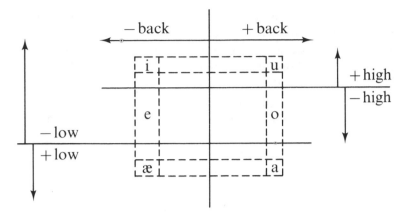

Figure 6.6
Typical natural classes found in languages

segments is not actually in terms of phonemes; rather it is in terms of the phonetic features that make up these segments.

Interaction of Phonological Rules in English

The theory of phonology outlined so far consists of two major parts: a set of segments (phonemes or phones) and a set of rules. The phonological segments are specified in terms of sets of phonetic features. The rules express regularities of pronunciation. For example, we discussed a rule in which an unvoiced alveolar stop must be pronounced as a voiced flap between vowels when the first vowel is stressed (rule (7)). Standard American English has a large number of rules of this type.

Another rule that affects medial /t/ (that is, /t/ inside a word) is the Glottal Stop rule, which has the following form:

(12) Glottal Stop Rule: t → ? / V́——n̩

This rule indicates that /t/ becomes a glottal stop /?/ when it occurs after a stressed vowel and before a syllabic /n/, which accounts for the typical American pronunciation of *button* [b ʌ́ ? n̩]. (Recall that a glottal stop is produced by blocking the airstream by closing the vocal cords, something English speakers consistently do in the middle of the phrase *oh oh* [ów?ow].) In other words the point of closure is shifted from the alveolar region where /t/ is produced to the glottal region resulting in /?/.

The /n/ following the glottal stop is referred to as a syllabic nasal, represented by [n̩]. The term *syllabic* is used to describe the [n̩] because in many ways this nasal element functions as an independent syllable. To see this, first note that the word *button* is bisyllabic (has two syllables) and carries the normal bisyllabic stress and tone contour of English nouns—that is, the major emphasis is on the first syllable. Second, the segment following the glottal stop is nasal throughout: it is not possible to isolate any nonnasal vowel between the glottal stop and the nasal. Hence the nasal itself functions as the second syllable.

So far we have discussed the phonological rules as isolated and indeed autonomous from other phonological rules. Now notice that the Glottal Stop rule (12) interacts in interesting ways with the Flap rule (7) in normal American English. Consider the two words *beating* and *beading*. In casual speech a final *-ing* ending can be reduced to a syllabic nasal /-n̩/, and rules (7) and (12) give us different results depending on whether the ending is /ɨŋ/ or /n̩/:

(13)	Formal Speech		Casual Speech	
	beating	beading	beatin'	beadin'
	biyt-ɨŋ	biyd-ɨŋ	biyt-n̩	biyd-n̩
Flap Rule (7)	biyD-ɨŋ	biyD-ɨŋ	——	——
Glottal Stop Rule (12)	——	——	biyʔ-n̩	——
Pronunciation	[biyDɨŋ]	[biyDɨŋ]	[biyʔn̩]	[biydn̩]

Given the rules represented in this section, we see that in more formal speech *beating* and *beading* are pronounced in the same way, but in casual speech the forms end up differently. For some speakers the sentence /ðə reyn ɨz biyDɨŋ an ðə wɪndow/ is ambiguous. It can mean either "The rain is beating on the window," or "The rain is beading on the window."

Ordered Rules? (optional section)
In chapter 10 (section 10.3) we will consider a pair of rules whose interaction raises a very important question: must the order in which certain rules apply be specified? As matters now stand, the Flap rule (7) would apply to the form /biyt-n̩/ because the /t/ occurs between syllabics, thus satisfying the conditions for the application of the rule. But that would derive an incorrect form. In order to derive the correct forms for casual speech with our current rules, we would have to specify that rule (12) must apply *before* rule (7) in order to prevent the

application of rule (7). However, the question of ordering does not arise if the feature [-nasal] is added to the feature specification [+syllabic] on the right side of the environment in which the Flap rule (7) applies. With this form, rule (7) and the Glottal Stop rule (12) would apply in mutually exclusive environments. An adjustment to one of the rules to avoid the question of ordering is not possible in the case of the rules discussed in chapter 10. We will pursue the question of ordering further in that chapter.

The Speaker's Knowledge of Phonology: "Possible Words"

When Madison Avenue advertisers want to create a brand name for a new product, they must follow the constraint that the name they invent must be a possible English word. *Possible word* here means a word that does not actually exist in English but that English speakers will readily claim sounds like an English word. Speakers have unconsciously extracted principles as to which sequences of sounds are possible English, and which are not. The soap product names *Fab* and *Biz* were excellent candidates for brand-name status, while hypothetical names such as *Vlk* or *Psulth* would not stand a good chance of being successful. Although all of the individual phonemes in *Vlk* occur in English, they cannot appear in this sequence.

The conditions on the possible sequences of phonemes in a given language is part of a study called *phonotactics*. For example, in English words beginning with three consonants, the first must be an /s/. If /p/ is the second consonant, then /r/, /l/, or /y/ can follow (*spread, spleen,* and *spew*). If the second consonant is /t/, then only /r/ can follow for most dialects of English (*stream*), though some dialects of English allow a /y/ after /st/ sequences if the phoneme /uw/ follows. (Thus, for *stew* one finds the pronunciation /styuw/ as well as the more common /stuw/.) If the second consonant is /k/, then /r/, /l/, /w/, or /y/ can follow (*scream, sclerosis, square,* and *skew*).

Native English speakers can easily recognize that made-up words like *Vlk* violate the sequential constraints on initial phonemes; the strangeness of such words is immediately apparent. It is unlikely that speakers check each new word they encounter against every other word in their vocabulary to judge whether or not it conforms to the patterns of the other words. The judgment is, instead, instantaneous and strongly suggests that speakers have internalized abstract principles that characterize the conditions on pronunciation of their language.

The Speaker's Knowledge of Phonology: Stress Patterns

One of the more remarkable features of the English speaker's knowledge has to do with the stress contours in words. It can be shown that the position of main stress (or emphasis) within a word is in part regular and predictable and is based on the phonological, morphological, and syntactic properties of the word. In this section we will discuss the rules for stress placement in nouns; we will test the validity of the rules by demonstrating how stress is assigned in words that have never been encountered before.

The position of main stress in bisyllabic (two-syllable) nouns is usually on the first syllable (the left one):

(14) móther   árgyle
      móuntain   cóntents
      tórrent   tórment

In words with three or more syllables the position of the main stress can vary. It is either on the second syllable from the right (the penultimate syllable) or on the third from the right (the antepenultimate), as shown in (15):

(15) Penultimate   Antepenultimate
      contrálto   América
      Arizóna   vánity
      eléctric   géneral

The difference in stress placement in these words is not random. Rather, stress will be on the penultimate syllable if that syllable consists of either a long vowel (as in *Arizona* /ærɨzównə/) or any vowel followed by at least two consonants (*electric* /əléktrɨk/). These two types of syllables are both designated as *strong* syllables. A *weak* syllable, on the other hand, consists of a short (or lax) vowel followed by at most one consonant; for example, all of the syllables in *America* /əmérɨkə/ are weak. One can state, then, that in words of at least three syllables the stress will be on the penultimate syllable unless that syllable is weak. If the penultimate syllable is weak, stress will be on the next syllable to the left, the antepenultimate syllable.

The English language is constantly acquiring new acronyms (words formed by combining the first letter (or letters) of the words in a descriptive phrase, like *Sunoco* from **Sun O**il **Co**mpany), and English speakers automatically stress these novel words according to principles based on syllable strength. Some typical examples follow:

(16) Penultimate Stress   Antepenultimate Stress

    Nabísco   Únicef

    Unésco   Cónoco

    Sunóco   Téxaco

In each of the words with penultimate stress the stressed syllable is strong. In all words with antepenultimate stress the penultimate syllable is weak. An interesting comparison can be made with the two acronyms *Sunóco* and *Cónoco* (**Con**tinental **O**il **Co**mpany). On the East coast, where Sunoco stations are found, stress is on the penultimate syllable [sənówkow]. The stress on *Conoco*, the name of a West coast company, is on the antepenultimate syllable /kánəkow/. These two different stress patterns are not counterexamples to the claim that stress placement is determined by regular rules, but rather this difference is consistent with the principles of English stress. In the word *Sunoco* the second syllable is strong because the /o/ is long (/ow/), and thus we have /sənówkow/. In *Conoco*, however, the penultimate syllable is weak /kánəkow/. Many readers may have "incorrectly" stressed the word *Conoco* in the penultimate syllable and pronounced the name as /kənówkow/. Note that in this case the second syllable is now pronounced with a long vowel, and thus stress is ultimately assigned based on whether or not the speaker decides that the penultimate syllable is weak or strong. If the penultimate vowel is interpreted as long, it will be stressed. It is important to note that it is not the stress itself that *causes* a syllable to be strong. In the noun *America*, for example, the stress is on the *e* (pronounced /ɛ/); nevertheless, that vowel is not long. There is, of course, an interaction between vowel length and stress placement, but once one decides the vowel length in the penultimate syllable of *Sunoco* or *Conoco*, the stress placement will follow automatically.

In sum, a theory of phonology can be viewed as a theory that represents native speakers' knowledge of the sounds and regularities of their language. The currently most promising theory of phonology is the following: for all human languages the knowledge of the native speaker is represented in the form of (a) a set of phonemes and (b) a set of phonological rules formulated in terms of phonetic features. The ability of a child to master a phonological system is part of the child's biologically inherited disposition to acquire a spoken language.

Exercises

Section 6.1

*1. What are some similarities between acquisition of song in the chaffinch (discussed in chapter 3) and the acquisition of a spoken language by children.

*2. In many of the world's languages there are so-called nursery names for parents. In English, for example, corresponding to the word *mother* is the nursery name *mama*, to the word *father* one finds *dada* and *papa*. There is a remarkable similarity across different languages in the form of these nursery names for parents. For example, in Chinese and Navajo *ma* corresponds to English *mama*. Why do you think that this is the case?

3. What type of physiological adaptations are present in humans to facilitate the speaking of language?

Section 6.2

*1. George Bernard Shaw, in ridiculing the English spelling system, claimed that a possible spelling for *fish* could be *ghoti*. Why did he claim this? (Hint: The *o* in *women* /wɪmɨn/ is pronounced as an /ɪ/.)

2. List the English phonemic symbol that corresponds to the following articulatory descriptions:

a. voiceless bilabial stop

b. voiced alveolar stop

c. high front short vowel

d. voiceless alveolar constrictive

e. lateral

f. voiced interdental constrictive

g. voiceless palatal affricate

h. high back long vowel

i. low front short vowel

j. voiceless velar stop

3. Describe each of the following phonemes with a small number of articulatory features:

a. /ŋ/

b. /u/

c. /š/

d. /z/

e. /m/

f. /ɑ/

g. /ɛ/

h. /h/

i. /g/

j. /ʌ/

4. Write the phonemic symbol for the first sound in each of the following words. Examples: *fish* /f/, *chagrin* /š/.

a. psychology

b. use

c. thought

d. though

e. pneumonia   h. knowledge
f. cybernetics   i. physics
g. cow   j. memory

5. Write the phonemic symbol for the last sound in each of the following words. Examples: bleach /č/, sigh /ay/.

a. cats   f. judge
b. dogs   g. rough
c. bushes   h. tongue
d. sighed   i. garage
e. bleached   j. climb

6. Write the phonemic symbol for the vowel sound in each of the following words. Examples: fish /ɪ/, table /ey/.

a. mood   f. five
b. caught   g. bait
c. cot   h. toy
d. and   i. said
e. tree   j. soot

7. Extra credit. Note the following pairs of phonemically written words:

a. /bæd/ bad   d. /bæg/ bag
b. /sɪn/ sin   e. /sɪŋ/ sing
c. /bɛd/ bed   f. /bɛg/ beg

You probably speak a dialect of American English in which the vowels in the words in the right-hand column differ from those in comparable words in the left-hand column. Describe the differences and make a guess as to why the vowels are different. (Hint: Consider tongue movement.)

8. Write the following words in the phonemic alphabet given in this chapter:

a. 1. through   6. though
    2. rough   7. blink
    3. gouge   8. hinge
    4. knox   9. hang
    5. draft   10. try

b. 1. miss   6. three
    2. his   7. paste
    3. shoe   8. trash
    4. edge   9. blunt
    5. foot   10. thigh

c. 1. bow (bend at waist)   6. lose
    2. bow (for shooting arrows) 7. which
    3. hand   8. witch
    4. hands   9. tasks
    5. loose   10. chat

d. 1. strengths   3. salve
    2. halve   4. cloths

5. clothes   8. mend
6. yeast   9. sixths
7. gym   10. boil

Section 6.3

The problem sets here are drawn from some of the world's languages, and serve to illustrate the role of natural classes of phonemes in describing the phonological regularities of these languages. In each of the problem sets a small number of phonetic features will serve to describe the class of segments that condition the change described in each problem. Assume that the data are representative of the phonological system of the particular language in question and that the phonemic symbols have the same phonetic feature specifications as the symbols in tables 6.2 and 6.3; refer to the tables in solving these problems. A sample problem and solution is given first, in order to acquaint the student with some strategies to follow in solving these problems.

Sample Problem: In English, the ɪ vowel becomes long (written /ɪ:/) under certain conditions. Consider the examples listed. (a) List the phonemes that condition the change of /ɪ/ to /ɪ:/. (b) What feature(s) uniquely specify this class of phonemes?

1. /hɪs/   8. /hɪ:d/
2. /tɪš/   9. /mɪθ/
3. /dɪ:d/   10. /rɪ:b/
4. /pɪt/   11. /lɪ:z/
5. /lɪ:m/   12. /snɪp/
6. /trɪk/   13. /rɪ:ǰ/
7. /bɪ:l/   14. /lɪ:ŋ/

Start with the fact the /ɪ/ is basic, that short /ɪ/ becomes long /ɪ:/. The change from short /ɪ/ to long /ɪ:/ is phonologically determined; that is, the lengthening takes place in the presence of certain phonemes. A good strategy is to first list the phonemes to the right of long /ɪ:/, then list those to the left. Since /h/ is on the left in both item 1 and item 8, it is not possible that the length is caused by a phoneme to the left. As an answer to part (a), then, one would propose that /ɪ/ becomes /ɪ:/ whenever the phonemes to the right (/d, m, l, b, z, ǰ, ŋ/) occur immediately after that vowel. This hypothesis looks promising because, in fact, the short variant /ɪ/ never occurs before these segments. The next question is, what is it about the phonemes on the right that unify them as a class? If one looks at their feature specifications in table 6.3, one will find that these phonemes are all voiced ([+voice]), and, in fact, the short /ɪ/ never lengthens before voiceless segments. Thus the answer to the (b) part of the problem is that the vowel /ɪ/ is lengthened before (the natural class of) voiced consonants.

*Problem A: English. In the following dialect of English there is a predictable variant /ʌy/ of the diphthong /ay/. (a) What phonetic segments condition this change? (b) What feature(s) characterize the class of conditioning segments?

a. /bʌyt/ bite   d. /fayl/ file
b. /tay/ tie   e. /lʌyf/ life
c. /rayd/ ride   f. /taym/ time

g. /rayz/ rise
h. /rʌyt/ write
i. /fʌyt/ fight
j. /bay/ buy
k. /rʌys/ rice

l. /tʌyp/ type
m. /naynθ/ ninth
n. /fayr/ fire
o. /bʌyk/ bike

*Problem B: Papago. In Papago, a Native American language of the southwest United States, the phone [č] is a variant of [t]. (a) List the set of segments that condition this change. (b) What feature(s) characterize this class? (c) How would a Papago speaker pronounce the word [tuksan] with a Papago accent? This pronunciation is found in Sells, Arizona. A colon after a vowel symbol indicates that the vowel is long; /ṣ/ is a voiceless fricative similar to English /š/. Unfamiliar phonemic symbols are not important for the solution to this problem.

a. ta:t
b. to:n
c. ton
d. čin
e. čɨm
f. čuk
g. čikpan
h. čɨ:kor

i. čuʔi
j. toha
k. čɨhok
l. toha
m tokit
n. tatk
o. ta:ñ
p. taṣ

*Problem C. Ganda. In the following words from Ganda, a language spoken in East Africa, the phone [ř] (a flapped "r" sound) is a predictable variant of [l]. (a) List the segments that condition the change of [l] to [ř]. (b) What feature(s) characterize the class of conditioning segments? A rising accent mark indicates high pitch, a falling accent mark indicates low pitch. Double vowels are long vowels. Data from Cole (1967).

a. mùkířà ("tail")
b. lùmóóndé ("sweet potato")
c. kùlímá ("to cultivate")
d. éfířímbí ("whistle")
e. kùwóólá ("to scoop or hollow out")
f. kùwólá ("to lend money")

g. kùtúúlá ("to sit down")
h. òkútábáálà ("to attach")
i. èříñá ("name")
j. òòlwééyó ("a broom")
k. kwàànířízá ("to welcome, invite")
l. kùùjjúkířá ("to remember")

*Problem D: English. For the following English words state the conditions under which the different forms of the past tense appear. What determines whether one uses /t/, /d/, or /ɨd/? Data: Write the past-tense marker phonemically to discover whether one has /t/, /d/, or /ɨd/. For example, *crushed* has final /t/, *pitted* has final /ɨd/. What phonetic features define each conditioning environment?

a. crushed
b. heaped
c. kicked
d. pitted
e. deeded

f. bagged
g. killed
h. nabbed
i. thrived
j. breathed

k.	turned	p.	hanged
l.	hissed	q.	cinched
m.	plowed	r.	played
n.	climbed	s.	hated
o.	singed	t.	branded

*Problem E: English. The occurrence of the plural marker is predictable in English (ignoring anomalies such as *geese* and *children*), and some children master a rule by the age of three. The three variants are /s/, /z/, and /ɨz/; the environment in which each occurs can be precisely and uniquely stated in terms of the phonetic features of English. To prove to yourself that you have mastered a rule and not simply memorized a plural form for each noun, you should use the following list of nonsense words as a source of data. (a) For each word determine the plural. (b) Next determine the class of segments that condition the appearance of each of the plural forms. (c) Finally, determine the phonetic features that characterize each class of conditioning segments.

1. šæb	9. bɛš
2. fowš	10. gæč
3. iyma	11. hɛs
4. šuwk	12. bɔrǰ
5. heyf	13. bɔz
6. lowž	14. fuw
7. biybiy	15. snæd
8. θæg	16. snʌp

*Problem F. The notion of rule is a central one in phonological theory. What evidence is there from child language acquisition that children acquire rules and don't simply memorize all the words. (Hint: What so-called mistakes do children typically make for the plural forms of *goose* and *child* or past tenses of verbs such as *take* and *go*?)

References

Chomsky, N., and M. Halle (1968) *The Sound Pattern of English,* Harper & Row, New York.

Cole, D. (1967) *Some Features of Ganda Linguistic Structure,* Witwatersrand University Press, Johannesburg, South Africa.

Denes, P., and E. Pinson (1963) *The Speech Chain,* Bell Telephone Laboratories.

Fodor, J., and J. J. Katz (1964) *The Structure of Language: Readings in the Philosophy of Language,* Prentice-Hall, Englewood Cliffs, N.J.

Goldman-Eisler, F. (1954) "On the variability of the speed of talking and on its relation to the length of utterances in conversations," *British Journal of Psychology 45,* 94–107.

Grønbech, K., and J. Krueger (1955) *An Introduction to Classical (Literary) Mongolian,* Harrassowitz, Wiesbaden, Germany.

Halle, M. (1962) "Phonology in a generative grammar," *Word* 18, 54–72. Reprinted in Fodor and Katz (1964).

Heffner, R-M. (1964) *General Phonetics,* University of Wisconsin Press, Madison.

Jakobson, R., and M. Halle (1956) *Fundamentals of Language,* Mouton, The Hague.

Lenneberg, E. (1967) *Biological Foundations of Language,* Wiley, New York.

Smalley, W. (1963) *A Manual of Articulatory Phonetics,* rev. ed., Practical Anthropology, Tarrytown, New York.

Chapter Seven

MORPHOLOGY:
THE STRUCTURE OF
WORDS

7.1 SOME SIMPLE CONCEPTS OF MORPHOLOGY

The central concern of morphology has traditionally been the study of the structure and content of words. Within the realm of morphology, it is possible to pose many questions about the nature of words but among the more persistent questions have been the following:

What are words and how are they formed?

How are complex words structured? What are the basic building blocks in the formation of complex words?

How is the meaning of a complex word related to the meaning of its parts?

How are individual words of a language related to other words of the language?

These are all complex questions, and linguists studying morphology have not yet arrived at completely satisfactory answers to any of them. Once we begin to construct answers, we quickly discover that interesting and subtle problems arise, and it turns out to be far from obvious how such problems are to be resolved.

It should be mentioned at the outset that there are traditional answers to each of the questions we have posed. It would be good to examine some of these answers, inasmuch as they present us with some seemingly basic and obvious principles of word formation.

It is traditionally held that a word is an arbitrary pairing of sound and meaning. For example, the word *horse* is a sound (albeit, a complex pattern of sounds) associated with a certain meaning (roughly "an equine mammal"). There is no necessary reason why the particular phonetic sequence represented by *horse* should mean what it does—

nothing in the sound dictates what the meaning ought to be—and hence we say that the pairing is *arbitrary*. It is true that every language contains *onomatopoeic* words—that is, words whose sounds mimic the objects to which they refer: *meow, bow-wow, splash, bang, hoot, crash,* and so on. But such words form a very limited subset of the words of any given language; for the vast majority of words the sound–meaning pairing is arbitrary.

Morphemes and Complex Words

It has long been recognized that words must be classed into at least two categories: *simple* and *complex*. A simple word such as *horse* seems to be a minimal unit: there seems to be no way to analyze it, or break it down further, into recognizable parts. On the other hand, the word *horses* is different. This seems to be made up of two parts: the noun *horse* and what we have come to call the plural ending, spelled -*s* in this case. A cursory examination of a list of simple English nouns will reveal that this is a general feature:

(1) Noun   Plural Form

Noun	Plural Form
boy	boys
rake	rakes
lip	lips
tree	trees
dog	dogs
bush	bushes

Not every noun in English forms its plural in this fashion, of course. However, for these particular nouns and others of this class we can say that complex words such as *trees* are made up of simple nouns such as *tree* followed by the plural ending -*s*. Traditionally, meaning-bearing parts of a complex word—that is, the different building blocks that make it up—are called *morphemes*. In this case we say that we have the plural morpheme -*s*; and in addition, we say that each of the simple nouns *boy, rake, tree,* and so forth, is itself a morpheme. It is held that morphemes are the minimal units of meaning in a language: they can be broken down no further into meaningful parts. This is only a rough-and-ready characterization of the term *morpheme,* but it will suffice for our purposes here.

The traditional view about the meaning of complex words is that it is a simple function of the meaning of the parts of the complex word.

Hence the meaning of *horses* is said to be a combination, in some vague and unspecified sense, of the meaning of *horse* and the meaning of the plural morpheme -*s*.

The issue of how words are related to each other in a language we will take up in section 7.2.

The traditional ideas just discussed are useful in that they provide a preliminary rudimentary framework in which to examine the processes of word formation. When we actually examine word formation, however, we see that the processes are more complex and subtle than we may have imagined.

7.2 HOW ARE NEW WORDS FORMED?

There are a number of equally valid ways to approach the questions and problems of morphology. One of the more revealing ways, perhaps, is to explore the question, How are new words formed?, That is, how do new words enter a language? By examining the processes of the creation and birth of new words, we may be able to discover basic and general principles of word formation.

New Words and New Uses of Words

First of all, entirely new, previously nonexistent words can and do enter a language. This often happens when speakers invent new words to name previously nonexistent objects that result from technological change. For example, words such as *radar, laser, kleenex,* and *xerox* are very recent additions to the English language.

The words *radar* and *laser* are *acronyms:* each of the letters that spell the word is the first letter (or letters) of some other complete word. Thus, *radar* derives from **ra**dio **d**etecting **a**nd **r**anging, and *laser* derives from **l**ight **a**mplification (by) **s**timulated **e**mission (*of*) **r**adiation. It is important to note that even though such words are created as acronyms, speakers quickly forget such origins and the words come to be viewed as simple, unanalysable items—as single morphemes.

The process of forming acronyms is just one of the processes of abbreviation that is becoming increasingly more powerful in American society (and perhaps internationally) as a means of word formation. For many Americans, one-time abbreviations such as *TV* have come to replace the longer word in most styles of casual speech—a new, previously nonexistent word has come into use. Various forms of identity cards are now simply called *ID*; venereal disease is widely referred to as *VD*; although it was once a joke to use *OJ* to refer to orange juice, the word is beginning to come into wider use.

No account of word formation would be complete, of course, without reference to possibly the most famous word in the English language, one that has become an international vocabulary item: *OK*. The theories that have been advanced to explain the origin of this word probably number in the dozens by now. One theory has it that *OK* stands for *Old Kinderhook,* the name of a Democratic party organization, abbreviated as the O. K. Club, which supported President Van Buren for reelection in 1840 (Kinderhook being Van Buren's birthplace in New York State). Another theory has it that *OK* stands for *oll korrect*, a parody spelling of *all correct*. The word *OK* is attested in American English as early as the 1830s, and there is some speculation that it may have been connected with another abbreviation, *D.K.,* for *don't know*. In any event the various theories for the origins of *OK* seem equally dubious and it would be foolish to attempt any new ones here. The point, however, is that words such as *OK* or *TV* are felt to be complete words, and not merely abbreviations, as evidenced by the fact that in casual styles of writing we see spellings such as *okay* and *teevee*.

The words *kleenex* and *xerox* represent another technique of creating previously nonexistent words (a technique restricted to technological societies), namely, using specific brand names of products as names for the products in general. Hence, *kleenex,* a brand name for facial tissue, has come to mean facial tissue in general. *Xerox* is the name of the corporation that produces the well-known photocopying machines, and much to the dismay of the company, the term *xerox* has lost its specific brand-name connotation and has come to be used to describe the process of photocopying in general. Hence, in casual speech we can commit the grave sin of talking about buying in IBM xerox machine.

Although the creation of entirely new words is certainly a significant part of word formation in a language, a much more pervasive and interesting process is the creation of new words from already existing words. For example, new words can quite literally be formed from existing ones by various *blending* processes. We have blends such as *motel* (from *motor hotel*), *selectric* (a blend of *select* and *electric*), *brunch* (a blend of *breakfast* and *lunch*), and so on.

A more interesting device of word formation is found in the use of an already existing word in a novel way. With this device the language does not gain a new word, per se, but since a word is being used in a new way, the language has become augmented, as though new words had been added. Let us consider an example. Even though space exploration is a new phenomenon in human history, it is interesting to note that speakers of English have adopted many existing terms from the realm of ocean navigation to speak of space exploration. We use the word *ship* to refer to space vehicles as well as to ocean-going vessels; we speak of a spaceship docking with another in a way related to the way an ocean-going ship docks; we speak of navigation in both types of transportation; it would not be anomalous to speak of a spaceship sailing through space, even though no sails are involved nor is there windpower; we speak òf certain objects as floating in space and of ships as floating on water; we speak of a captain and a crew for both kinds of ships; names of ship parts, such as hull, have been carried over (hence, both kinds of ships contain cabins and hatches; and, at least on television, spaceships are said to have decks). The reader can construct many more examples along these lines. It is striking that terms that basically derive from the historical epoch of wind-powered ocean navigation have with great ease been *extended* into the realm of space navigation. The technology is radically different in the two realms, yet we apparently perceive enough similarities to use already existing terms, in new ways, to describe the new phenomena. This is an important fact to notice; it shows that technological changes in a society will not necessarily result in the addition of previously nonexistent words to its language. Indeed, speakers of all human languages show great creativity and imaginative power in extending the existent language into new realms of experience.

The example we have just discussed is a case of *metaphorical extension,* in which certain objects, ideas, or events from one realm are described with words from a different realm of objects, ideas, and events. Another interesting case is the metaphorical extension of words from the physical realm of food and digestion into the mental realm of ideas and interpersonal exchange of ideas. For example, consider the following cases:

(2) a. Let me *chew on* these ideas for a while.
   b. They just wouldn't *swallow* that idea.
   c. She'll give us time to *digest* that idea.
   d. On the exam, please don't merely *regurgitate* what I've told you.

e. He *bit off* more that he could *chew*. (Speaking of someone's research project.)

f. Let's make them the offer and see if they *nibble* at it; after all, it is pretty good *bait*. (From the realm of fishing as well as food.)

g. Will you stop *feeding* me that old line!

h. You'd better *cook up* a good story this time!

i. He's such a hypocrite—I don't see how he can say those pious things without *gagging* on his words.

j. Her proposal left a *bad taste in my mouth*.

k. Let's start examining the really *meaty* ideas—something we can *sink our teeth* into.

l. She's really *hungry* for knowledge.

m. I think that *spicy* ideas are better than *bland* thoughts.

n. Let's *chew the fat*.

o. My lecture was pure nonsense, but they really *ate it up*.

p. What she says is *food for thought*, but it gives us only a *taste* of what she means.

q. Where were you last night? Come on, *spit it out!*

r. I wish they would stop *spoon-feeding* us these *predigested, half-baked* ideas.

The reader will be able to construct many similar examples in which one realm (roughly, a realm involving ideas) is described in terms of words from another realm (food and digestion). A feature of this particular case is that words from a physical realm are being extended into a mental realm, perhaps because the physical vocabulary provides a familiar and public frame of reference for discussing our private mental life.

Metaphorical extension is not the only mechanism by which already existing words can be put to new uses. Sometimes the meanings of existing words can simply be changed so that the word can be used in novel ways. Meanings of words can become broader. For example, the slang word *cool* was originally part of the professional jargon of jazz musicians and referred to a specific artistic style of jazz (a use that was itself an extension). With the passage of time the word has come to be applied to anything conceivable, not just music; and it no longer refers just to a certain genre or style but is a general term indicating approval of the thing talked about.

Conversely, meanings can narrow as well. A typical example is the word *meat*. At one time in English it meant any solid consumable food (a meaning that persists in words such as *nutmeat*), but it now refers only to the edible solid flesh of animals.

Finally, reversals of meanings can occur. In certain styles of American slang the word *bad* has come to have positive connotations, with roughly the meaning "emphatically good." Hollywood movies of the '30s and '40s reveal that the words *square* and *straight* had positive connotations, meaning "honest" and "upright," meanings that survive in the phrases *square deal* and *play it straight*. During the late '50s and into the '60s, the word *square* came to have a negative connotation, referring to anyone or anything hopelessly conventional and uncomprehending of "in" things. By the late '60s this use of *square* had itself come to be regarded as old-fashioned and the word dropped out of use (which, incidentally, illustrates the rapid rate at which slang terms enter and leave a language). In the same period the word *straight* came to be used in a wide range of areas, always with the general meaning of adhering to conventional norms: for example, a straight person is one who doesn't take drugs; who is heterosexual rather than homosexual; who is generally "out of it," and so on.

So far, we have discussed various kinds of extensions and modifications of meaning as a way to create new uses for already existing words. Although this is one of the most interesting areas of morphology, we unfortunately have very little understanding of the exact mechanisms of meaning change and extension. For one thing we have very little idea *what* the meaning of a word is: Is the meaning an abstract idea, a concept? Is it an image? When we describe the meaning of the word, are we describing the thing to which the word refers? Or is meaning best described neither as an idea nor as a referent but rather as the *use* of a word in some context? We discuss these possibilities in more detail in chapter 11, which deals with semantics. Suffice it to say here that because we do not know precisely *what* the meaning of a word is and because theories of the psychology of human thought are still at a rudimentary level, we can say very little about metaphorical extension or other meaning shifts. At the present time we can do no more than guess about why we can describe space travel but not, say, a tractor moving across a field, in terms of ocean-going vessels. This area, especially the study of so-called slang, will be extremely important for future research because it provides fundamental evidence about the linguistic creativity of speakers.

Word Formation Rules

Other means of word formation are much better understood. Complex words can be formed from simple words by means of various morphological processes that have traditionally been collected under the label of *derivational morphology*. As an illustration, consider what are called agentive nouns, formed by adding the suffix *-er* to verbs:

(3) Verb   Agentive Noun (V + er)

(to) write	writer
(to) kill	killer
(to) play	player
(to) win	winner
(to) run	runner
(to) farm	farmer
(to) till	tiller
(to) open	opener
(to) scrape	scraper
(to) roll	roller
(to) level	leveler

The derived noun form means roughly "one who does X," or "an instrument that does X," where X is the meaning of the verb. Suppose that a new verb enters the English language, such as the verb to *Xerox*. Native speakers of English will automatically know that this verb can be converted into an agentive noun, *Xeroxer*. This word would be perfectly natural in a sentence such as *If you want to get that copied, you'll have to see John, because he's our* Xeroxer *around here*. Hence the process of agentive noun formation (using the suffix *-er*) establishes a relationship between verbs and nouns and can be used to create new words from already existing ones.

It is important to understand that in discussing the formation of agentive nouns in English we have begun to examine the *interrelationships* among the words of a language, that is, how certain words are related to certain other words. The question of how more complex words are formed from simpler parts always involves examining words as members of morphological relationships. Indeed, the traditional term, *derivational morphology*, reflects this interest in morphological relationships in its concern with how words are derived.

There is good evidence from many languages of the world that word formation follows systematic morphological rules: rules by which complex words are built up from simpler words and morphemes and, conversely, by which complex words can be analysed into simpler ones. We will examine the general process of word formation by examining in detail one such process in English, namely the word formation rule associated with the suffix -*able* in English. Consider the following set of forms:

(4) (to) read   readable
    (to) wash   washable
    (to) break   breakable
    (to) think   .   thinkable
    (to) pay   payable
    (to) move   movable
    (to) excuse   excusable

In the left-hand column is a set of verbs; in the right-hand column those same verbs have the suffix -*able* attached to them. There is an obvious systematic relation between the words in the two columns. To native speakers of English who know the words listed in the left-hand column, many features of the words in the right-hand column will be completely predictable. If I know the verb *to read*, and if I know English morphology, I will automatically be able to predict that *readable* has certain well-defined properties. Hence, the relation between *read* and *readable* is not arbitrary—the suffix -*able* is a morpheme that is used in a highly systematic way. What are the various effects of the -*able* suffix? In what basic ways are the verbs changed when -*able* is added?

Obviously, there is a phonological change, which in this case is quite straightforward: the pronunciation of the verb must be augmented by the sound /əbl̩/ when the -*able* suffix is added. In other cases the phonological change is not so trivial. For example, when -*ion* is added to verbs, it causes phonological changes in the verb stem itself:

(5) deci*d*e   deci*s*ion   (d → ž)
    rela*t*e   rela*t*ion   (t → š)

However, -*able* does not cause such phonological changes.

Another obvious change introduced by -*able* is in the basic part of speech of the item to which it is added. Note that though -*able* attaches to verbs, it converts the verbs into adjectives; that is, the -*able* word is an adjective:

(6) This book is readable. (Compare: This book is red)

The suffix -*able* introduces a new element of meaning, roughly "able to be *X*'d," where *X* is the meaning of the verb. For example, *breakable* means roughly "able to be broken," *movable* means "able to be moved," and so on. So we can immediately detect at least three changes introduced by the suffix:

(7) a. a phonological change
    b. a change in the part of speech
    c. a meaning change

We don't have to look far to start finding interesting complications with -*able*. For example, if we wish to express the idea that man is mortal, we cannot say *Man is dieable*. Yet there is nothing wrong with the meaning of the hypothetical word *dieable*—the concept "able to die" is quite clear. If the car is able to go, we nevertheless cannot say that it is *goable*; if John and Mary are able to cry they are still not *cryable*. It is all too tempting to suppose that these cases are somehow exceptions or that no rule governs the data in question. But if we compare the columns in (8), a generalization emerges:

(8)

Verbs that take -*able*:	Verbs that don't take -*able*:
read	die
break	go
wash	cry
ply	sleep
mend	rest
debate	weep
use	sit
drive	run
spray	walk

The verbs on the left are transitive—they occur with object noun phrases—whereas the verbs on the right are intransitive—they do not occur with objects. For example,

(9)   John read the book.
      John broke the dish.
      John washed his clothes.

(10) John died.
      John went.
      John cried.

Indeed, it seems to be the case—as the reader should try to verify—that -*able* attaches only to transitive verbs, not to intransitive verbs.

Let us now examine another case in which *-able* cannot be used. If our friend Mary is able to read, we cannot describe this by saying *Mary is readable*. There would be nothing wrong with the meaning of this hypothetical usage of *readable,* since "able to read" is a perfectly well-formed concept. A comparison of the following examples will reveal what is going on here:

(11) a. We can read these books.

  b. These books are readable.

(12) a. We can wash these clothes.

  b. These clothes are washable.

(13) a. We can drive this car.

  b. This car is drivable.

The relation that emerges is this: the subject of the *-able* adjective must correspond to the direct object of the transitive verb to which *-able* is attached. In other words the subject of V + *able* is always understood as the logical object of V. For this reason if we say *Billie Jean King isn't beatable,* we mean that we aren't able to beat Billie Jean King (*Billie Jean King* is understood as the logical object of *beat*); we do not mean that Billie Jean King is unable to beat other players. For another example we can say *These books are readable,* where the phrase *these books* is understood as the object of the verb *read*. However, we cannot say *John is readable,* even if John is able to read, since a noun phrase such as *John* is not usually understood as the object of *read,* only as the subject of *read*.

We are now led to state the *-able* word formation rule as follows:

(14) a. Phonological change: when *-able* is attached to a word, its pronunciation is augmented by the phonetic sequence /əbl/.
  b. Category change: *-able* is attached to transitive verbs and converts them into adjectives.
  c. Syntactic usage change: the subject of the adjective with *-able* must correspond to the direct object of the transitive verb to which *-able* is attached.
  d. Meaning change: if X is the meaning of the verb, then *-able* adds the meaning "able to be X'd."

In general, then, whenever we postulate a systematic morphological relation between sets of words, we will describe (a) the systematic phonological changes, if any, (b) the category changes, if any, (c) the syntactic use changes, if any, and (d) the meaning changes that characterize the relationship.

It is important to note that the word formation rule (14) has more than one function. On the one hand, it describes a relation between already *existing* words: it tells us, for example, what the relation between *read* and *readable* is. On the other hand, the rule is followed by speakers of the language in creating *new* words for the language. Consider again the recently acquired verb *to xerox*. This is a transitive verb, and it would be perfectly possible for speakers of English to invent the word *xeroxable*. If, for example, one person claims that a certain page in a book is too light to be xeroxed, another person could answer, *No, that page is certainly xeroxable.*

If we look at these functions of word formation rules a bit more carefully, we see that they are in fact unified: a word formation rule serves to analyze complex words in such a way that it gives the predictable information about the complex word. Thus the word *readable*, even though it is an independent word, in fact contains information that is completely predictable. We can see this very clearly from a different point of view. Suppose someone invents a nonsense word, such as *glark*. Even though we know nothing about the meaning of this word, if we are told that *-able* can be added to *glark* to form *glarkable*, we in fact do know some very predictable things about this second word. For one thing we would all say that *glarkable* includes the meaning "be able," that is, it means "able to be glarked." Second, even though it was not mentioned in rule (14), all regular *-able* words can take the suffix *-ity* in forming nouns, as in *readable:readability*. Hence we can predict that *glarkability* is possible if *glarkable* is possible. Further, our word formation rule tells us that *-able* goes on transitive verbs and converts them into adjectives. Hence we can deduce that *glark* is a transitive verb and that *glarkable* is an adjective.

Thus, by telling us the predictable information about complex words, given the basic forms, word formation rules (a) specify the relations between pairs of existing words, and (b) are followed by speakers in creating new words. Recall that simple words are arbitrary pairings of sound and meaning. We now see that complex words are at least in part nonarbitrary in their makeup, and we posit word formation rules to account for this predictable, systematic part of the composition of words.

Problematic Aspects of Morphological Analysis

Now we must face one of the hard facts of life in doing morphological analysis, namely, the exceptions or apparent exceptions to many aspects of a given analysis. For example, we have claimed that the suffix *-able* is attached only to transitive verbs. Yet in English we can find a small set of nouns that seem to occur with the same suffix *-able*:

(15) peaceable   companionable
     marriageable   impressionable
     knowledgeable   actionable
     saleable   reasonable
     fashionable

Does this mean that the word formation rule given in (14) is wrong? The answer seems to be no. These nouns form a small, closed set, and as far as anyone can tell, no new words in which *-able* is attached to a noun are entering English. In more technical terminology we say that the attachment of *-able* to verbs is *productive*, but attachment to nouns is not productive. Productive morphological rules are living rules of a language, by which speakers make up new words. New V + *able* forms continually enter the language, but the nouns in (15) are now fixed, or dead, expressions that are learned by rote, not formed by rule.

Another general problem we must be sensitive to is the possibility of false analysis. Consider the following words:

(16) hospitable
     comfortable
     sizeable

Even though these words end in the phonetic sequence /əbl̩/, it is unlikely that we would want to analyze this sequence as the suffix *-able*. For one thing *able* in these words does not seem to have the meaning of "to be able," which is certainly a feature of regular (productive) *-able* words. For another thing recall that the regular *-able* suffix can itself take the suffix *-ity* to form a noun:

(17) readable   readability
     provable   provability
     breakable   breakability

But this is not possible with the words listed in (16): we do not seem to have the forms *hospitability, *comfortability, *sizability. We do not speak of the hospitability of our host, or the comfortability of the chair, or the sizeability of the crowd. In two respects, then, *able* in the words of (16) is significantly different from the productive suffix *-able*; hence it would seem to be a false analysis to claim that the words of (16) have the productive suffix *-able*.

Returning to our words in (15), we might make a reasonable case that these words end accidentally in the phonetic sequence /əbl/ and that it would be a false analysis to claim that it is the *-able* suffix. Against this idea we note that in some of the words, such as *marriageable*, we do seem to find the meaning of "be able" (as in *eligible to marry*), and we also seem to have the *-ity* noun form *marriageability* (although some speakers of English might well reject this word). Other words of (15), however, are not so regular. (For further discussion of (15) and (16) see the exercises at the end of this chapter.) In any event, in carrying out a morphological analysis we must always be careful to determine whether the processes in question are productive or not and whether a certain analysis might be a false analysis.

Closely related to these problems is another classic problem of morphology, namely, the problem of a complex word with a recogniz-able suffix or prefix, but with a stem that is not an existing word of the language. For example, among the *-able* words we have words such as *malleable*, and *feasible*. In both cases the suffix *-able* (spelled *ible* in the second case because of a different historical origin for the suffix) has the regular meaning "be able," and in both cases the *-ity* form is possible, as in *malleability* and *feasibility*. We have no reason to suspect that *able/ible* here is not the real suffix *-able*. Yet if it is, then that means that *malleable* is broken down as *malle+able* and *feasible* as *feas+ible*; but there are no existing words in the English language such as *malle* or *feas*, or even *malley* or *fease*. We thus have to allow for the existence of complex words whose stems exist only in those complex words.

This example shows that word formation rules cannot be viewed solely as relating pairs of existing words or of specifying how new words are formed. Sometimes a complex word is not paired with another word but exists by itself, only as a complex word (such as *malleable* or *feasible*). In spite of this lack of pairing, we can neverthe-less use our word formation rule (14) backwards, as it were, to deduce that the stem for *feasible* is *feas*: word formation rules can analyze single words into parts, even if some of those parts don't exist as words. Thus, though word formation rules serve a variety of purposes, these are all unified: the rules are always based on a single analysis of the predictable features of complex words.

The problems discussed so far can be summed up by saying that they are problems in isolating the base, or stem, of the complex word: (a) sometimes the base comes from a closed set of forms no longer productive as the base for the word formation rule; (b) sometimes one must beware of a completely false analysis of the base; and (c) sometimes the base may not be an existing word. All of these problems have to do with correctly analyzing how the complex word is broken down.

The problems of morphological analysis do not end here by any means. Another major problem is to analyze the meaning of complex words and to determine the relation between the meaning of an entire complex word and the meanings of its parts.

Let us begin by taking some cases that appear to have a regular meaning change. For example, *fixable* seems to mean nothing more than "able to be fixed," *mendable* means "able to be mended," and *inflatable* means "able to be inflated." The meaning of each of these -*able* words seems to be a regular composition of the meaning of the verb stem and the simplest meaning of the -*able* suffix. However, in other cases certain complications arise. Take, for example, the words *readable, payable, questionable,* and *washable.* The word *readable* doesn't mean simply "able to be read." In formal usage, when we say that a book is readable we usually mean that it is well written, has a good style, and in general is a good example of some type of literature. Obviously, a readable book is one that, strictly speaking, is able to be read, but it is much more. If a banker tells us that a bill is payable on October 1, he does not mean simply that the bill "can be paid" on that date—in normal use we would understand *payable* as meaning "should be paid." If a theory or an explanation is questionable, it is not merely the case that it can be questioned. After all, any statement at all can be questioned, even very well established theories. Rather, a questionable theory or explanation is one that is, in fact, dubious and suspect—not merely one that *can* be. Finally, the word *washable* doesn't mean merely "able to be washed"; we in fact use the word in a very specialized way, to refer to certain types of objects, notably fabrics. Hence, though we can talk about washing a car, it would be somewhat odd to say that the car is washable (even if this is, strictly speaking, true). It is perfectly natural, however, to say that a shirt is washable or that the plastic parts of a wooden table are washable (whereas the wooden parts are not).

These facts show us in a particularly clear way that the meanings of many complex words are not merely composites of the meanings of their parts. The word *washable* is more than a composite of *wash* and *-able*—rather, it has a life of its own, as an independent word, with additional elements of meaning of its own. When a word accrues some feature of meaning independent from its morphological origin, as *washable* has, we say that the word has undergone *semantic drift*.

A reasonable way to view this drift problem is to say that the word *washable* means at least "able to be washed," according to the word formation rule for *-able*. However, we will go on to say that the word has additional elements of meaning which restrict or narrow its basic meaning. A common dictionary will indicate such restrictions by stating that certain words or expressions are said of certain things. Hence, we can say that *washable* means "able to be washed, said of certain fabrics and water resistant objects." The reader can check that, at least for the cases we have given, the additional meaning, over and above the basic meaning of the complex word, always involves a narrowing or restricting of the more general meaning of the complex word.

We should point out that some of the elements of additional meaning that we have examined may not be additions in the strict meaning of the word itself; rather, they may involve purely pragmatic inferences from the context of the use of the words. For example, we have noted that *payable* does not mean merely "able to be paid" but means "should be paid" in the context of the banker talking about the due date of the bill. This additional meaning may come from the fact that we know certain things about bankers and about bills, and if a banker were to say *This bill can be paid on October 1*, we would invariably assume that he meant the bill should be paid on that date, despite what his words meant literally. Our interpretation of *can* as meaning "should" would be a matter of a pragmatic inference, on our part, from the actual situation. In support of this idea, notice that if I lend my best friend some money and he asks when it has to be paid back, I might well say *This loan is payable any time at all*. Here, in this particular context, *payable* indeed seems to mean nothing more than "able to be paid." For this reason, perhaps we should say that *payable* literally means "able to be paid" and that additional aspects of meaning will be derived from the context of the actual use of the word. This seems like a promising explanation for some cases, but we will not pursue the matter further here. (See chapters 11 and 12.)

Psychological Reality of Morphological Rules

We have seen that word formation rules can be used by speakers of a language to create new words. Given a newly created verb such as *to xerox*, we can create another new word, *xeroxable*, by using the word formation rule for *-able*. Hence, it is evident that word formation rules are not merely artificial creations of linguists; they have psychological reality in the minds of speakers.

A particularly interesting example illustrating the psychological reality of morphological rules is a process known as *backformation,* which is, in a sense, the process of using word formation rules backwards. We can illustrate backformation with the following examples, taken from Williams (1975). It is a historical fact about English that the nouns *pedlar, beggar, hawker, stoker, scavenger, swindler, editor, burglar, sculptor,* and *agressor* all existed in the language before the corresponding verbs *to peddle, to beg, to hawk, to stoke, to scavenge, to swindle, to edit, to burgle, to sculpt,* and *to aggress.* Since each of the nouns referred to a general profession or activity, and since each noun terminated in a phonetic sequence similar to the *-er* suffix, speakers simply assumed that the nouns ended in the agentive suffix *-er.* With this assumption the speakers could then subtract the *-er* ending and arrive at a new verb—just as one can subtract the *-er* ending on *writer* and arrive at the verb *write*. This process of factoring out some element of a word in order to arrive at a simpler form is called backformation.

An interesting modern example of backformation with the agentive suffix involves the word *laser*. Recall that this word is an acronym; it ends in *er* only because *e* stands for *emission* and *r* stands for *radiation* (*l*ight *a*mplification (by) *s*timulated *e*mission (of) *r*adiation). Recall, though, that speakers quickly forget such origins, and before long physicists had invented the verb *to lase,* used in sentences such as *This dye, under the appropriate laboratory conditions, will lase,* where *to lase* refers to emitting radiation of a certain sort. The *er* on *laser* accidentally resembles the agentive suffix *-er*, and the word itself refers to an instrument; hence, physicists took this *er* sequence to be the agentive suffix and subtracted it to form a new verb.

Other examples cited by Williams (1975) are as follows:

(18) Existed earlier   Formed later by backformation
      resurrection   to resurrect
      preemption   to preempt

vivisection	to vivisect
electrocution	to electrocute
television	to televise
emotion	to emote
donation	to donate

It is ironic that even the word *backformation* is becoming subject to processes of backformation. The technical linguistic term *backformation* existed in English first, and now one hears fellow linguists saying things such as, *Speakers backformed word X from word Y,* creating a new verb in English, *to backform.* What's going on in all these cases is that speakers recognize that the ending *-ion* is used to create abstract nouns from verbs (for example, *to instruct:instruction*). Hence, they can take nouns ending in *-ion*, factor out the ending, and arrive back at a verb, which has a simpler morphological shape (that is, it lacks the ending).

Finally, a slightly different sort of backformation has taken place with the word *cranberry*. Until very recently in the English language, the *cran-* of *cranberry* existed in that word alone. In fact, linguists coined the term *cranberry morpheme* for morphemes, such as *cran-*, that are said to occur in only one word of a language. Currently, however, even though the morpheme *cran-* is not yet an independent word, speakers of English have begun using it in other words besides *cranberry*. In particular, the fruit juice section of any supermarket will now reveal words such as *cranapple, cranicot,* and *cranprune* referring to juice mixtures. By substracting the recognizable morpheme *berry* from *cranberry*, speakers have created a new prefix *cran-* by backformation. (And consequently, we face the task of finding a new linguistic term to replace *cranberry morpheme*.)

In sum, all these cases show that morphological rules and analyses are not simply artifacts of morphological theory. Their reality in speakers' minds is demonstrated by the fact that speakers produce (and hearers understand) new words based on these rules and analyses.

7.3 THE SEARCH FOR MORPHOLOGICAL PRINCIPLES

At the current time in linguistics there are various promising ideas about how to formulate a theory of morphology, but as of yet we do not have many solid results. Exactly how a theory of morphology should be stated precisely and more formally is still a matter open to considerable debate; the reader can get an idea of the range of proposals from the references at the end of this chapter. Here we will give an idea of at least one aspect of morphology that is, and will continue to be, an important area of research, namely, the search for universal principles of morphology. Our examples will be drawn from English, but it must be stressed that all claims about word formation in general must be tested in many languages before we can take them as more than speculations. We offer here one example of the kind of hypothesis that deserves such testing.

Transitive and Intransitive Predicates

Recall the observation that, in general, the suffix -*able* is attached to transitive verbs, converting them into adjectives, for example, *read:readable*. Let us define the distinction between transitive and intransitive predicates as follows: transitive predicates occur with direct objects immediately following them, whereas intransitive predicates do not. By this simple definition, verbs such as *kill*, *read*, and *hit*, are transitive since they occur with direct objects (*kill the fly*, *read the book*, *hit the ball*), whereas verbs such as *vanish*, *grow*, and *change*, are intransitive since they do not occur with direct objects (*Mary vanished*, *Mary grew*, *Mary changed*). Note that intransitive predicates often occur with prepositional phrases and adverbs following them: *Mary vanished into thin air*, *Mary grew quickly*, *Mary changed into a bear*. By the definition we have set up, adjectives are intransitive predicates, inasmuch as they do not occur with direct objects: *The book is readable*, *Mary is tall*. We can now observe that in converting transitive verbs into adjectives, the -*able* suffix is actually causing a change in transitivity: transitive predicates (transitive verbs) are converted into intransitive predicates (adjectives).

Based on this observation, we offer a tentative candidate for a universal principle of morphology:

Transitivity Switch
When a word formation rule relates pairs of words where one member is transitive and the other member is intransitive, then the *subject* of the intransitive form must always correspond to the *direct object* of the transitive form.

We have already seen that this principle is true of the -*able* suffix. Given that we are proposing it as a general hypothesis about word formation, obviously we must present detailed evidence for it, especially detailed evidence from languages other than English. Here we will present additional evidence from English to establish that the Transitivity Switch is at least plausible as a candidate for a universal morphological principle, even if we will not be able to establish its truth.

Let us begin by examining another suffix of English, namely the suffix *-ize*. Its effect is just the opposite of that of the *-able* suffix in that it converts adjectives into transitive verbs:

(19) Adjective   Transitive Verb

    modern   (to) modernize
    equal   (to) equalize
    personal   (to) personalize
    federal   (to) federalize
    natural   (to) naturalize
    central   (to) centralize
    general   (to) generalize

In other words, intransitive predicates are being converted into transitive predicates; hence, according to our principle of Transitivity Switch, the subject of the intransitive should correspond to the object of the transitive. This is indeed true as we can see from the following examples:

(20) a. The house is modern.

    b. We modernized the house.

If we modernize the house, then the house ends up modern—*we* do not end up modern—which demonstrates that the phrase *the house* is the logical subject of *modern*. To put it another way, the logical, or semantic, relation of *house* to *modern* is just the same in the two sentences *The house is modern* and *We modernized the house*. The form *modernize,* of course, has additional elements of meaning—for example, the interpretation of a change in state and the interpretation that someone or something causes the change of state—and these extra elements of meaning are part of the meaning change associated with *-ize*. Leaving these extra elements aside, the correspondence of subject-of-intransitive to object-of-transitive holds in this case, consistent with our tentative principle of Transitivity Switch.

Another suffix that has the same effect as *-ize* is *-en*, as in the following examples:

(21)

Adjective	Transitive Verb
red	(to) redden
black	(to) blacken
mad	(to) madden
soft	(to) soften
hard	(to) harden
sweet	(to) sweeten
short	(to) shorten
wide	(to) widen
sharp	(to) sharpen

We can see from the following kind of example that the Transitivity Switch works here, too:

(22) a. The coffee is sweet.

b. We sweetened the coffee.

When we say that we sweetened the coffee, we understand it is the coffee that ended up being sweet; that is, *the coffee* is understood as the logical subject of *sweet*. Although the *-en* suffix no longer seems to be productive (see chapter 10), the direct object of the transitive form nevertheless corresponds to the subject of the intransitive form.

There is a process in English whereby transitive verbs are converted into intransitive verbs, called middle verbs. No suffix is involved in the process, and in fact there is no phonological change. Some examples of the intransitive verbs derived in this process are as follows:

(23) a. The books *read* well.
b. These apples have *sold* quickly.
c. The oranges from that tree *peel* with great difficulty.
d. The car *drives* badly.
e. The shirt doesn't *wash* well.

Normally, *read, sell, peel,* and so on, are transitive verbs, but here they are used intransitively—in these examples the verbs cannot occur with direct objects. Note that in their intransitive use, these verbs have as their subjects the kinds of noun phrases that normally function as their objects: normally, the object of *read* is a noun phrase like *the book* and the object of *sell* is a noun phrase like *the apples*. In (23) these phrases are the subjects. But when we say *The book reads well,* we understand *the book* as the logical object of *read*; this sentence does not mean that the book carries out some action well but rather that someone can read the book easily. Again, the change in transitivity has been governed by the Transitivity Switch, with object-of-transitive corresponding to subject-of-intransitive.

Still another process of English converts intransitive verbs into transitive verbs called causative verbs. Again no suffix is involved, and again there is no phonological change:

(24) a. John *grows* tomatoes. (Compare: Tomatoes grow.)
    b. John *galloped* the horse. (Compare: The horse galloped.)
    c. John *ran* the machine. (Compare: The machine ran.)
    d. John *walked* the dog. (Compare: The dog walked.)

If John galloped the horse, then we understand that the horse did the galloping—though John caused the horse to do it. So even though *the horse* is the object of the verb *gallop* in (24b), it is understood as the logical subject of the verb. Thus the semantic relation of *horse* to *gallop* is the same in *John galloped the horse* and in *The horse galloped.* Here, too, the object of the transitive form corresponds to the subject of the intransitive form.

We have now described five morphological processes that conform to the Transitivity Switch:

-able formation
-ize formation
-en formation
formation of middle verbs (no suffix)
formation of causative verbs (no suffix)

This by no means exhausts the evidence that must be found before we can accept the Transitivity Switch as a principle of morphology. In particular, we must examine quite carefully evidence from many other languages aside from English. Further, we must sharpen up the concept of subjects *corresponding to* objects—what does it mean, exactly, for subjects to correspond to objects? Here we have been using the term in an unanalyzed, intuitive way.

Finally, it may be useful to present an exception, or at least an apparent exception, to the principle as we have stated it. This will not only serve to illustrate areas in which future research must be carried out in morphology but will show what a counterexample to our analysis will look like. Consider the English suffix -ive, as in the following examples:

(25) Transitive Verb   Adjective

    (to) repress   repressive
    (to) oppress   oppressive
    (to) impress   impressive
    (to) elude   elusive
    (to) select   selective
    (to) express   expressive
    (to) permit   permissive
    (to) deceive   deceptive
    (to) produce   productive
    (to) prevent   preventive

Even though we have a change in transitivity here—a change of transitive verbs to adjectives—the Transitivity Switch does not hold. That is, the subject of the intransitive (adjective) form corresponds to the subject—not the object—of the transitive (verb) form:

(26) a. They permit many things.

    They are permissive.
   b. This measure prevents things.

    This measure is preventive.

If the Transitivity Switch were valid in these cases we would expect that the object of the transitive would correspond with the subject of the intransitive, but this never happens:

(27) a. They permit smoking.

    *Smoking is permissive.
   b. This measure prevents fires.

    *Fires are preventive.

Since the subject of the -ive form is understood as the same as the subject of the transitive verb form, we have a counterexample, or exception, to the Transitivity Switch.

    This possibly shows that the Transitivity Switch is wrong and that our attempted generalization is only apparent. Or perhaps it shows that the principle as stated is simply too broad and that we must narrow the claim somewhat. For example, notice that the *-ive* suffix goes on intransitive as well as transitive verbs:

(28) Intransitive Verbs   Adjective

    (to) progress   progressive
    (to) recede   recessive
    (to) submit (to)   submissive (to)
    (to) aggress   aggressive
    (to) compete   competitive
    (to) egress   egressive
    (to) regress   regressive

In contrast, notice that the morphological processes discussed previously pick out specific subclasses of predicates to operate on. For example, *-able* goes only on transitive verbs; *-ize* and *-en* go only on intransitive predicates (adjectives); middle verb formation occurs only with transitive verbs; and causative verb formation occurs only with intransitive verbs. All of these word formation processes are restricted to a specific subclass of predicates: they apply exclusively to transitive predicates or exclusively to intransitive predicates, but not to both types.

This suggests a refinement in our formulation of the Transitivity Switch principle:

Transitivity Switch II
When a word formation rule relates pairs of words where one member is transitive and the other member is intransitive, then the subject of the intransitive form must always correspond to the direct object of the transitive form. Condition: applies only to word formation rules that operate exclusively on transitive predicates or exclusively on intransitive predicates, and not to those that operate on both transitive and intransitive predicates.

With the added condition the Transitivity Switch principle again makes the correct predictions for the data we have looked at so far.

Only further research in morphology can ultimately determine whether the reformulated Transitivity Switch principle is correct or not. We offer the principle here as an illustrative example of the general kinds of principles one might propose in morphology. In any event our best hope of making progress in morphology, as well as in other areas of linguistics, is to state linguistic hypotheses (such as the Transitivity

Switch) as precisely as possible and then to test these hypotheses against the facts of human languages.

Exercises

*1. The following are all onomatopoeic words for the sound that roosters make:
English: cock-a-doodle-doo
German: Kikeriki
Spanish: quiquiriquí (*qu* = /k/)
Italian: chicchirichì (*ch* = /k/)
French: cocorico
Japanese: kokekokkoo (accent on final *oo*)
Hopi: kokoweʔeè
Navajo: ha'íí'áo (' = glottal stop; ą́ = high tone nasal /a/; í = high tone /i/)
What do these examples tell us about how closely onomatopoeic words mimic the natural sounds they refer to?

2. We stated that *radar* and *laser* are acronyms. List three other recent English words that are acronyms and state their origin.

3. List three additional recent words that, like TV or ID, are abbreviations of longer words and state their origin.

*4. Words referring to spending and finances (such as *cost, spend, invest, buy, sell*) also have abstract metaphorical uses, as in: *That mistake will cost you a lot, He invested a lot of time in the project, He paid dearly for his ways, You're only buying trouble if you do that.* List three additional examples of the metaphorical use of words from the realm of spending and finance and discuss how the metaphorical uses are related to the concrete (financial) meanings.

*5. What is the relation, if any, between the following uses of the word *hot*?
a. hot, said of a surface (sense of touch)
b. hot food (sense of taste)
c. hot temper
d. hot war
e. hot on the trail of something
f. hot ball (from baseball)
g. hot wire
h. hot news
i. hot car (stolen)
j. hot car (souped up)
k. hot idea (really good idea)
Discuss the ways in which *hot* in the above examples is used in contrast with the words *warm, cool,* or *cold*.

6. Suppose a speaker of English invents the following italicized English words, as a joke: "They're always causing a commotion. I tell them not to *commote*,

but they insist on being big *commoters.*'' What process of word creation does this example illustrate, and why? What do the new words mean?

*7. Discuss each of the words listed in example set (15) and state, for each case, whether the suffix *-able* is related to the true productive suffix *-able*, or whether that would be a false analysis of those words. Use concrete arguments and examples to back up your proposals.

*8. Discuss the meaning of the words *unthinkable* and *unbreakable.* The meaning of these complex words is more than the simple sum of the meaning of the parts. State how, and discuss the relation, if any, between these words and the words of a similar nature discussed in the chapter (*readable, questionable, payable, washable*).

9. The word *perishable* is a true exception to the word formation rule for *-able* stated in (14). Why? Cite another example like *perishable.*

*10. Use the following two lists for this exercise:

List A

redo	regain	restate	reshape
rewrite	reimport	recalculate	rethink
rework	reinterrogate	redraw	reuse
reexamine	rerelease	reset	redo
recook	rerefine	retool	re-create
rebroadcast	retake	relight	rearrange
reorganize	repaint	refreeze	rediscover
reenter	refinish	resharpen	redecorate
re-form	rebuild		

List B (impossible words)

*rego	*resit
*recry	*revanish
*resleep	*rechange

State the word formation rule for the prefix *re-*. Follow the format given for the *-able* rule in this chapter. In particular, answer the following questions:

a. What phonological changes, if any, does the prefix *re-* cause in the word or stem to which it is attached?

b. What part(s) of speech does the prefix *re-* attach to? Note the contrast between List A and List B. What is the difference between these sets of words?

c. When *re-* is attached to a word or stem, what part of speech does that word or stem become?

d. In general, what meaning change(s) will be caused by the suffix *re-*? In the ideal case, what will be the element(s) of meaning contributed by the prefix *re-*?

e. Can you find any words with *re-* that have erratic or unexpected meanings? Are there any *re-* words that systematically mean more than you would expect from the simple meaning of *re-* and the simple meaning of its base?

f. Why are the following *re-* words problematic? Discuss three of them: reduce, reflect, refine, refuse, repeat, relax, release, renew, replicate, revive, remember.

*11. Use the following word lists for this exercise:

List A

equalize	Italianize	Christianize
mobilize	actualize	animalize
personalize	familiarize	immortalize
legalize	fertilize	modernize
generalize	humanize	
centralize	constitutionalize	
naturalize		
federalize		
Americanize		

List B

symbolize
alphabetize
atomize
scandalize
revolutionize
magnetize
alcoholize
fossilize
crystallize

List C

dramatize
democratize
hypnotize
colonize
energize
harmonize

State the word formation rule for the suffix -*ize*, following the same format as in exercise 10. In particular, answer the following questions:

a. What phonological change(s), if any, does the suffix -*ize* cause in the word or stem to which it attaches? Compare lists A, B, and C to answer this.

b. What part(s) of speech does the suffix -*ize* attach to? Again, compare the above lists to answer this.

c. When -*ize* is attached to a word or stem, what part of speech does that word or stem become?

d. In general, what is the meaning change caused by the suffix -*ize*? That is, in the ideal case, what element(s) of meaning will be contributed by the -*ize* suffix?

e. Are any of the -*ize* words listed problematic for question (d)? That is, are there any -*ize* words that seem to deviate from the systematic cases referred to in (d)? Are there any -*ize* words with erratic or unexpected meanings?

f. Why are the following -*ize* words problematic? galvanize, moralize, organize, scrutinize, winterize, weatherize.

*12. In example (25) we discussed the suffix -*ive* in English. State the word formation rule for this suffix, using the format of exercises 10 and 11. Provide your word list(s) along with your answer.

*13. How does the word *elective*, as in the phrase *elective courses*, differ from the other -*ive* words listed in (25) in this chapter?

14. How does phonological information enter into morphology? Discuss this from the point of view of word formation rules in particular.

15. When new words are added to the English language, they must obey certain phonological constraints. Give a specific example of such constraints (recall chapter 6).

16. Which theories of the chart picturing human language structure given in the Note to the Student (at the beginning of this book) are reflected in morphology—in particular, complex word formation?

References

Aronoff, M. (1976) *Word Formation in Generative Grammar*, MIT Press, Cambridge, Mass.

Bloomfield, L. (1933) *Language*, Holt, Rinehart & Winston, New York. (See chaps. 13 and 14.)

Jackendoff, R. S. (1975) "Morphological and semantic regularities in the lexicon," *Language* 51, 639–671.

Jespersen, O. (1911) *A Modern English Grammar*, Allen and Unwin, London. (See vol. VI.)

Lehrer, A. (1974) *Semantic Fields and Lexical Structure*, North Holland Publishers, Amsterdam, Holland.

Marchand, H. (1969) *The Categories and Types of Present-Day English Word-Formation*, 2nd ed., Beck, Munchen.

Matthews, P. H. (1974) *Morphology: An Introduction to the Theory of Word Structure*, Cambridge University Press, Cambridge, England.

Sapir, E. (1921) *Language*, Harcourt, Brace & World, New York. (See chap. 4.)

Williams, J. M. (1975) *Origins of the English Language*, Free Press, New York.

Chapter Eight

SYNTAX: THE STUDY OF SENTENCE STRUCTURE

8.1 THE CONCEPT OF STRUCTURE

Syntax is the study of how sentences are structured, and this chapter will discuss and elaborate the notion of syntactic structure. As soon as we say this, we immediately raise the question: What is syntactic structure, and what does it mean to say that sentences are structured? Like many other questions one can pose about human language, it is difficult to answer this one in any direct fashion. In fact, it is impossible to answer the question What is structure? without actually constructing a theory of syntax, and indeed one of the central concerns of current theories of syntax is precisely to provide an answer to this question. Thus it must be stressed that we cannot define the concept of structure before we study syntax; rather, our study of syntax will be an attempt to find a definition (however elaborate) of this concept.

To begin our attempt to find such a definition we will adopt the following strategy: we will assume that sentences are merely unstructured strings of words. That is, given that we can recognize that sentences are made up of individual words (which we can isolate), it would seem that the absolutely minimal assumption we could make would be that sentences are nothing more than words strung out in linear order, one after the other. If we examine some of the formal properties of sentences in light of this strategy, we can quickly discover whether our unstructured string hypothesis is tenable or whether we will be forced to adopt a hypothesis that attributes greater complexity to sentences.

If we adopt the hypothesis that sentences are unstructured strings of words, then almost immediately we must add an important qualification. One of the first things we notice about the sentences of human languages is that the words in a sentence occur in a certain linear order. Although some languages display considerable freedom of word order (standard examples being Latin, Russian, and aboriginal Australian languages), in no human languages may the words of a sentence occur in any random order whatever. No matter how free a language is with respect to word order, it nonetheless imposes some constraints on word order. Further, in many languages linear order of words plays a crucial role in understanding sentences: in English, *The horse bit the dog* means something quite different from *The dog bit the horse* even though the very same words are used in both. Hence, we might say that sentences are unstructured strings of words, but we must insure that we specify at least a *linear order* for those words.

Structural Ambiguity

Even with the important qualification about word order, our unstructured string hypothesis runs up against an interesting puzzle. Consider a sentence such as the following:

(1) The mother of the boy and the girl will arrive soon.

This sentence is ambiguous. It is either about one person (the mother of both the boy and the girl), or else it is about two people (the mother of the boy, and, in addition, a second person, the girl). In sentences with verbs that require agreement with the subject, these two possibilities are brought out clearly:

(2) a. The mother of the boy and the girl *is* very talented.
    b. The mother of the boy and the girl *are* (both) very talented.

The interesting feature of sentence (1) is that the ambiguity cannot be attributed to an ambiguity in any of the words of the sentence. That is, we cannot attribute the ambiguity of the sentence to an ambiguity in *mother* or *boy* or *girl*. In contrast, consider a sentence such as the following:

(3) She's good at catching flies.

This, too, is an ambiguous sentence, but it seems clear that the ambiguity of the sentence is attributable to an ambiguity in the word *flies* (and possibly *catching*): it is referring either to baseball or to insects. For sentence (1), however, we cannot appeal to such an explanation.

At this point we are faced with a puzzle: how is it that a sentence consisting of unambiguous words can nonetheless be ambiguous? Our unstructured string hypothesis does not lead us to expect this sort of sentence ambiguity, nor does it provide any mechanism for explaining the phenomenon. In order to find an explanation, it would seem that we are forced to concede that sentences are not merely unstructured strings of words but that the words can be grouped together in various ways. If we make this assumption, we can provide an explanation for ambiguous sentences such as (1) by saying that although the sentence consists of a single set of unambiguous words, those words can in fact be grouped in two different ways:

(4) a. The mother (of the boy and the girl) will arrive soon.
b. (The mother of the boy) and (the girl) will arrive soon.

The parentheses indicate the intuitively natural groupings of the words which correspond to the two meanings we have isolated.

By saying that words in a sentence can be grouped together, we have started to define the concept of sentence structure. Notice that even with this simple example, by appealing to a notion of grouping we have already gone beyond the directly observable properties of a sentence and are postulating abstract or theoretical concepts. Although the linear order of words is something we can check by direct observation of some sentence, the grouping of words in that sentence is generally not directly observable. Rather, word grouping is a theoretical concept that we appeal to in order to account for certain abstract properties of sentences—such as structural ambiguity.

Given what we have said so far, it would appear that in specifying the structure of a sentence we specify (a) the linear order of words, and (b) the possible groupings of the words. Indeed, these are two important properties of the structure of sentences, but by no means are they the only important properties. Given that we have some initial evidence that we must attribute some kind of structuring to sentences, let us examine in more detail what will be involved in specifying the structure we have discovered.

8.2 AN INFORMAL THEORY OF SYNTAX

One of the most important ways of discovering why and how sentences must be structured is to try to state explicitly some grammatical rules for a given language. For example, consider the following set of sentences, which consist of English declarative sentences and their corresponding question forms:

(5) a. John can lift 500 pounds.
      Can John lift 500 pounds?
   b. Mathematicians are generally thought to be odd.
      Are mathematicians generally thought to be odd?
   c. They will want to reserve two rooms.
      Will they want to reserve two rooms?
   d. Mary has proven several theorems.
      Has Mary proven several theorems?

We will now engage in an apparently simple exercise: that is, to state as precisely as we can how such English questions are formed. We will disregard the evidence of section 8.1 and return to our earlier assumption that sentences are unstructured strings of words. Once again, we will soon be able to see whether this assumption is valid or whether we are forced into more complex assumptions about sentences.

The English Question Rule

How can we describe the way the questions in (5) are formed from the declarative sentences? Possibly the simplest way to begin would be to number each word of the declarative sentences:

(6) John can lift 500 pounds
     1   2   3   4   5

Now we can state a set of instructions for forming a question based on this sentence.

(7) Question Rule I
    To form a question from a declarative sentence, place word 2 at the beginning of the sentence.

This rule, as we will call it, instructs us in such a way that (8) would be produced as an output, given (6) as input.

(8) Can John lift 500 pounds
     2   1   3   4   5

Notice that this is the correct question form. A simple check will reveal that rule (7) also works for the other examples in (5), and nothing forces us to talk about sentence structure.

However, it should be clear that Question Rule I quickly runs into problems. Consider what would happen if we followed that rule faithfully with respect to the examples in (9).

(9) a. Yesterday John could lift 500 pounds.
    b. Many mathematicians are thought to be odd.
    c. Those people will want to reserve two rooms.

The second word in each of these sentences is *John, mathematicians,* and *people,* in that order. If we faithfully follow Question Rule I and place the second word at the beginning of the sentence, we derive the following:

(10) a. John yesterday could lift 500 pounds.
     b. *Mathematicians many are thought to be odd.
     c. *People those will want to reserve two rooms.

The rule has given the wrong results in each case. Though sentence (10a) might be a possible (though awkward) sentence, it is certainly not the question that corresponds to (9a)—which should be *Yesterday, could John lift 500 pounds?* As for sentences (10b) and (10c) not only are they not the questions corresponding to (9b) and (9c); they are ungrammatical, or ill-formed, sentences. (We have followed common practice by indicating ungrammatical sentences with a prefixed asterisk.)

It is clear that we have to reformulate Question Rule I so as to account for the counterexamples in (9). We see that English questions are not formed by simply moving the second word of the sentence to the beginning of the sentence. After all, the second word of an English sentence can be any type of word: a noun, a verb, an adjective, an article, and so on. However, the examples of (5) and (9) show us that in forming a question in English, it is always a verb that is moved to the front of the sentence, that is, a word such as *can, will,* and *are.*

In order to state our question rule more accurately, we are now forced to suppose that the words of a sentence are not only strung out in some linear order but are also classified into different morphological categories—what have traditionally been called parts of speech. (Recall from chapter 7 that in morphology we also need to classify words into parts of speech so that we can state word formation rules properly.) If we make this assumption, then we can restate the Question Rule so that it is sensitive to this morphological information:

(11) Question Rule II

> To form a question from a declarative sentence, place the first verb of the sentence at the beginning of the sentence.

In an example such as *John can lift 500 pounds,* the word *can* is the first verb of the sentence; by placing it at the beginning we get *Can John lift 500 pounds?* Similarly, in *Many mathematicians are thought to be odd* the first verb is *are* and by placing it at the beginning of the sentence we derive the question *Are many mathematicians thought to be odd?* Indeed, our reformulated rule gives us the right results for the examples in both (5) and (9), with one exception. For sentence (9a), *Yesterday John could lift 500 pounds,* the first verb is *could;* by placing it at the beginning of the sentence we would get *Could yesterday John lift 500 pounds?*—which seems to be ill-formed. We want to arrive at the form *Yesterday, could John lift 500 pounds?* We will return to this problem shortly.

We have now been forced to assume that the words in a sentence must at least be classified into *parts of speech.* It should be stressed that this classification is not a matter of convenience or conjecture; rather, it turns out to be impossible to state the Question Rule properly if we cannot appeal to such a classification. However, just as we found counterexamples to the first rule we postulated, it turns out that it is easy to find counterexamples to Question Rule II as well. Consider what would happen if we followed Question Rule II faithfully with respect to the next set of examples:

(12) a. The men who are standing in the room will leave soon.
    b. Many mathematicians who you will meet are thought to be odd.
    c. Anyone that can lift 500 pounds is eligible for our club.

Notice that in example (12a) the first verb we come to is the verb *are:*

(13) The men who <u>are</u> standing in the room will leave soon.

If we follow Question Rule II faithfully and place this first verb at the beginning of the sentence, we will derive the following ungrammatical sentence:

(14) *Are the men who standing in the room will leave soon?

It is pretty clear that in this example it is not the first verb that should be moved; instead, as it turns out, it is the second verb (or third, if we count *standing* as the second):

(15) a. The men who are standing in the room <u>will</u> leave soon.

   b. <u>Will</u> the men who are standing in the room‖leave soon?

But is it really the *second* verb, as such, that we're looking for in such cases? The answer is clearly no. In examples such as the following, the appropriate verb does not correspond to any particular number—it can be the third, or fourth, or fifth.

(16) a. The men who were saying that John is sick <u>will</u> leave soon.

              1   2   3   4

   b. The men who were saying that John told Mary to quit <u>will</u>

              1   2   3   4 5

     leave soon.

An important point to notice here is that such examples can be extended indefinitely—there is simply no limit on the length of the sentences we can construct or on the number of verbs we can place within them:

(16) c. The men who were saying that John told Mary to have Bill quit

              1   2   3   4   5

   trying to persuade David that many mathematicians are thought to

   6   7   8   9

   be odd <u>will</u> leave soon.

   10   11

Naturally, when sentences become this long they become difficult to understand and remember; consequently, they would normally not occur in everyday conversation as single uninterrupted sentences. However, this is a practical problem, a problem of the performance limitations on the mental and neural mechanisms underlying speech. The point is that there is in principle no limit on the length of sentences, and this means that in principle every language contains an infinite number of sentences. The problem that linguists (and language learners) face is that they must construct a finite set of rules—that is, a *grammar*—that will account for an infinite number of sentences.

In the particular case of the sentences of (16), we see that in each instance we must choose the verb *will* as the correct verb to move. However, as we see, that verb does not occupy any particular fixed slot in the linear order of words. Further, it is in principle impossible to specify exactly what can come between that verb and the beginning of the sentence—because there is no limitation on the length of the sentence between the beginning point and the point where the appropriate question verb is located. It should be clear that for each of the sentences of (16), Question Rule II will give the wrong results if we apply it faithfully. Clearly a more general rule is needed.

If we take a more careful look at the examples in (12) and (16), we see that the verb that must be moved to the front of the sentence is the verb that immediately follows an intuitively natural constituent of the sentence:

(17) a. *The men who are standing in the room* <u>will</u> leave soon.
   b. *Many mathematicians who you will meet* <u>are</u> thought to be odd.
   c. *Anyone that can lift 500 pounds* <u>is</u> eligible for our club.
   d. *The people who were saying that Mary is sick* <u>will</u> leave soon.
   e. *The people who were saying that John told Mary to quit* <u>will</u> leave soon.

In each case the appropriate verb to move to the front of the sentence is the verb that is underscored; in each case, this is the first verb following the structural grouping of words that has traditionally been referred to as the *subject* of the sentence (where the verb in question is part of what is called the *predicate*).

Notice that the subject of a sentence can be fairly long—as in (16)—but this does not affect the basic fact that the Question Rule must pick out the first verb following the subject. Given these considerations, we can reformulate our rule as follows:

(18) Question Rule III
   To form a question from a declarative sentence, find the first verb that follows the subject of the sentence and place it at the beginning of the sentence.

Notice that in our latest statement of the Question Rule, we must make reference to *linear order* and morphological labeling of *parts of speech* (by referring to the first verb), and to structural grouping, or *constituent structure* (by referring to the subject).

We began with the minimal assumption that sentences are unstructured strings of words and attempted to state an adequate rule for forming questions in English. Faced with a successive series of counterexamples, we were gradually forced to modify our assumption and to adopt increasingly more complex assumptions about how sentences are structured. It is important to point out that at each stage the increased complexity of our assumptions was not a matter of convenience; rather, we found that we simply could not state the Question Rule of English properly without making reference to notions such as part of speech and constituent structure. The exercise we have carried out illustrates that our conception of syntactic structure becomes more elaborate and sophisticated as we seek to account for an ever wider range of data. Hence, as we look at further data, our conception of what elements are involved in syntactic structure will also change.

Before moving on, we must note that even Question Rule III must be further modified before it can be adequate. For one thing, as we have already seen, it is not the case that the appropriate verb is in all instances moved to the front of the sentence. Recall the following examples:

(19) a. Yesterday John could lift 500 pounds.
    b. *Could yesterday John lift 500 pounds?
    c. Yesterday, could John lift 500 pounds?

These examples suggest that the appropriate verb of the sentence must be placed *immediately to the left of the subject*—not actually at the beginning of the sentence. This would lead to the following modification:

(20) Question Rule IV
    To form a question from a declarative sentence, find the first verb that follows the subject of the sentence and place it immediately to the left of the subject.

As the reader can check, this reformulation will cover all the cases we have so far examined.

However, further counterexamples will now arise. Consider a simple sentence such as the following:

(21) You know those women.

By faithfully applying Question Rule IV to (21), we arrive at:

(22) *Know you those women?

Although the English language once formed questions of this sort (one can find them in Shakespeare, for example), it is a fact that questions such as (22) are ill-formed for the present language. Instead, (23) is the proper form:

(23) Do you know those women?

What is going on here is that contemporary English makes a distinction between *auxiliary* verbs and main verbs, and it turns out that only auxiliary verbs (*can, will, should, are, have,* and so on) can be fronted to form questions. This would entail at least the following revision in our Question Rule:

(24) Question Rule V
   To form a question from a declarative sentence, find the first *auxiliary* verb that follows the subject of the sentence and place it immediately to the left of the subject.

Since example (21) contains no auxiliary verb, but only a main verb, Question Rule V will not apply to it, thus correctly excluding the possibility of forming questions such as (22). But, then, how do we actually account for the well-formed question in (23)? Where does the auxiliary verb *do* come from?

We will not pursue this question further here (the reader will find ample discussion of this point in works cited in the references); we raise the question only to show that we still have not arrived at a final analysis for question formation in English, despite the initial impression that the task seemed to be a rather simple one. Recall once again examples of the sort in (5), such as *John can lift 500 pounds*. It is interesting to note that *any* of our formulations of the Question Rule will adequately form questions from the declarative sentences of (5). If we restricted ourselves just to that data, and no other, we would have at least five ways of stating the Question Rule in English, without knowing which of the rules was correct. It is only when we test each rule against new data that we can determine how adequate it is.

Structural Concepts, Functional Concepts, and Tree Diagrams

Structural Concepts
We have now cited two kinds of evidence in favor of the hypothesis that sentences are structured. First, if we do not assume that sentences are structured—that words are grouped together into *constituents*—then we have no way to explain how a sentence consisting of a set of unambiguous words can nevertheless have an ambiguous meaning. Second, it is impossible to state certain grammatical rules such as the Question Rule for English without appealing to constituent structure. Not only can we say that sentences are indeed structured, but we can

also indicate at least partially how they must be structured. That is, we have found (at least) three important aspects of sentence structure:

linear order of words in a sentence

morphological categorization of words into *parts of speech*

grouping of words into *structural constituents* of the sentence

It turns out that these three types of structural information can be encoded into a diagram called a *tree diagram* (or *phrase marker*) of the sort illustrated in tree 8.1.

Tree 8.1 is in effect a coding of the structural properties of a sentence that we have found to be important. The various parts of the sentence are shown in a fixed linear order. Each word is assigned a part of speech: Art, N, Prep, and so on. And different elements in the sentence are shown as grouped into successively larger constituents of the sentence: NP, AUX, and VP make up a sentence (S); V, NP, and PP make up a verb phrase (VP), and so on. What is important about this diagram is the information that it encodes, and any system of diagramming that encoded the same information would be just as good for our purposes. The same thing is true for the symbols we have chosen; although we have used the traditional names for the parts of speech, note that any system of naming that made the same distinctions would

Tree 8.1

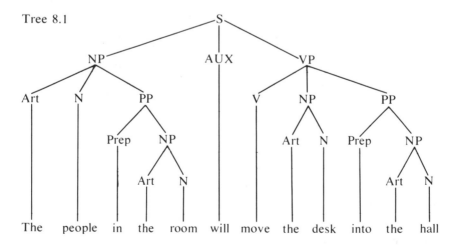

Symbols used: S—sentence; NP—noun phrase; AUX—auxiliary; VP—verb phrase; PP—prepositional phrase; Art—article; N—noun; V—verb; Prep—preposition.

be just as good for our purposes. Hence we could call articles Class 1 words, nouns might be Class 2 words, and so on. As long as the right distinctions were made and similar words were assigned to similar categories, this system of naming parts of speech would be perfectly adequate.

Functional (Relational) Concepts

So far we have not distinguished between *structural* concepts such as noun phrase (NP) and *functional* (or relational) notions such as subject or object, but this distinction reflects the fact that we can ask two questions about any given phrase: (a) What is its structure? (b) How does it function within a sentence? Diagrams such as tree 8.1 not only represent structural information, but we can also define on a tree the functional concepts (or grammatical relations) of subject and object. The *subject* of a sentence can be structurally defined in English as the noun phrase (NP) immediately under S which precedes AUX VP, as illustrated in tree 8.2. The *object* of a main verb can be structurally defined in English as the NP that immediately follows V under VP, as illustrated in tree 8.3.

For example, take the phrase *the people in the room*. Structurally, this phrase is a noun phrase, but this NP can function in different ways in different sentences. In tree 8.1 the NP *the people in the room* functions as the subject of the sentence. (With action verbs, such as *move* in tree 8.1, the subject of the sentence can be said to carry out the action.) However, in sentence (25) this same NP functions as the object of the main verb:

(25) The police arrested *the people in the room*.

Tree 8.2

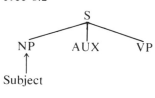

Tree 8.3

```
              VP
        _____|_____
       |             |
       V             NP
                     ↑
                     |
                   Object
```

(With action verbs, such as *arrested* in (25), the object of the verb can be said to undergo, or suffer, the action.) Hence the phrase *the people in the room* is structurally an NP and only an NP; but functionally this phrase can be either a subject or an object, depending on the particular sentence.

The distinction between structural and functional concepts is crucial in understanding a sentence, as can be illustrated by the fact that the sentences represented by trees 8.4 and 8.5 have exactly the same structural NP constituents, but those structural constituents have quite different functions, or grammatical relations, in the two sentences. (Following a common practice, we have used triangles in trees 8.4 and 8.5 to simplify the internal structure of the NPs.) These two sentences mean opposite things, and these opposite meanings result from the different grammatical relations borne by the NPs in the sentences.

An important distinction is often made between the *surface* subject (or object) and the *logical,* or understood subject (or object), a distinction we alluded to briefly in section 7.3 when we discussed sentences such as the following:

Tree 8.4

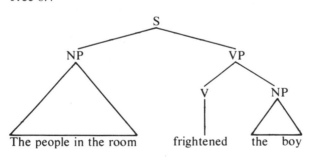

Tree 8.5

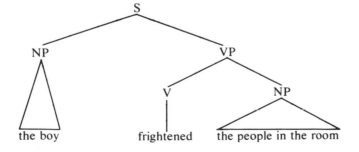

(26) a. *The book* reads well.
     b. We modernized *the house*.

We say that the NP *the book* in (26a) is the surface subject of the sentence (note that the verb, *reads,* agrees with this surface subject). However, the NP *the book* is the logical object or understood object of the verb *read*: the book does not carry out the action of reading but undergoes being read. In (26b) the NP *the house* is the surface object of the verb *modernize,* but it is the logical subject or understood subject of the adjective stem *modern*: as we pointed out in chapter 7, (26b) means that the house becomes modern, not that we become modern. As a final example, corresponding to the active sentence represented by tree 8.4 (*The people in the room frightened the boy*) we have the following passive sentence:

(27) The boy was frightened by the people in the room.

In this case, though the NP *the boy* becomes the surface subject of the sentence, it is still the understood object of the verb *frighten.* We have provided a structural definition of surface subject (as in tree 8.2) and surface object (as in tree 8.3), but we will not try to indicate how we might define logical subject and object in trees. Defining the latter notions is a fairly controversial matter, requiring much more argumentation than we have space for here.

So far, then, we have isolated the following structural and functional concepts and have shown how these concepts can be represented in, or defined on, tree diagrams:

(28) Structural Concepts
     a. linear order of elements
     b. labeling of elements into parts of speech
     c. grouping of elements into structural constituents.

(29) Functional Concepts
     a. (surface) subject (defined as in tree 8.2)
     b. (surface) object (defined as in tree 8.3)
     c. logical subject (not structurally defined here)
     d. logical object (not structurally defined here)

Tree Diagrams
So far we have shown that tree diagrams (phrase markers) can represent a certain variety of structural and functional concepts. Now we

must turn to the question of whether tree diagrams can be used to explain important linguistic phenomena. To address this issue, let us first recall the ambiguous sentence cited in (1), repeated here as (30):

(30) The mother of the boy and the girl will arrive soon.

In a theory of syntax using phrase markers to represent syntactic structure, the explanation of the phenomenon of structural ambiguity is straightforward: whereas an unambiguous sentence is associated with just one basic phrase marker, we can say that ambiguous sentences are associated with more than one basic phrase marker. For example, sentence (30) would be assigned two phrase markers which we could formulate as trees 8.6 and 8.7.

As before, we have simplified the structure in the diagrams by using triangles for certain phrases rather than indicating the internal structure of these phrases. But these trees suffice to show the difference in structure we postulate for the two phrase markers associated with sentence (30). In tree 8.6, the head noun of the subject, *mother,* is modified by a prepositional phrase that has a conjoined noun phrase in it: *of the boy and the girl.* In tree 8.7, on the other hand, the subject noun phrase is itself a conjoined noun phrase: *the mother of the boy* followed by *the girl.* We see, then, that a system of representation

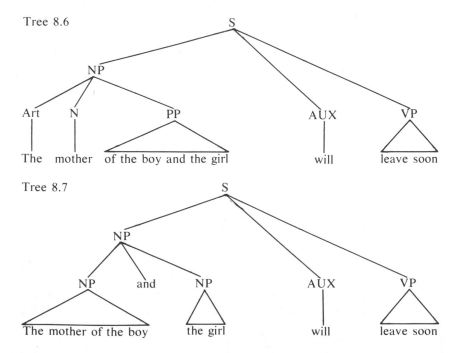

Tree 8.6

Tree 8.7

using phrase markers allows us to account for structurally ambiguous sentences by assigning more than one phrase marker for the ambiguous sentence. In this way the system of tree diagrams can be used to explain certain linguistic phenomena, not merely to represent them.

At this point a very natural question arises: Exactly how does one arrive at particular phrase markers such as tree 8.1, tree 8.6, and tree 8.7? How do we know that the sentences represented by those trees are structured as we have shown them? The answer to these questions may be a little surprising: the fact is that we do not know for certain how these sentences are structured. The structures we have shown here represent hypotheses, or guesses, about how the sentences might be structured. We have constructed these diagrams based on what we know about the sentences—and on *what we are trying to explain* about the sentences. In other words these phrase markers constitute hypotheses in our theory of syntax—they are not dictated by some sort of grammatical authority.

Let us illustrate what we are talking about by returning to tree 8.1. We have good reasons for supposing that the phrase *the people in the room* forms a single NP constituent and is not merely an unstructured string of words. One important reason (but by no means the only one) is that we define this single noun phrase constituent as the subject of the sentence and this in turn allows us to state the Question Rule in the simplest possible way: we can say simply that the auxiliary verb is to be moved to the left of the subject of the sentence, and not, for instance, that the auxiliary verb should be moved to the left of the string of words *the people in the room*. More to the point, however, recall that since there is no limit on the length of the subject of a sentence, it is impossible to state the Question Rule in terms of the linear string of words that make up a subject: we would never be able to list all the strings of words that could make up the subject of a sentence. Hence, we have good evidence for postulating an NP constituent as the subject of a sentence.

There are other aspects of the structure shown in tree 8.1 for which we have presented little or no evidence. For example, we show the auxiliary verb *will* as a constituent independent of the verb phrase. But another, quite conceivable, possibility is to consider the constituent AUX part of the verb phrase, as in tree 8.8. This structure may or may not be more adequate than the structure shown in tree 8.1—in the absence of any evidence bearing on the issue, we simply cannot say. We must stress that although the gross outline of the structure shown in

Tree 8.8

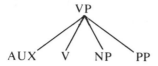

tree 8.1 is probably correct, many fine details of the structure are arbitrary at the moment.

We could use up a great deal of space attempting to justify the various features of the structure shown in tree 8.1; indeed much work in syntax has been concerned with this sort of issue. Nonetheless, this structure will give the reader a rough illustration of the general sort of structural diagrams used in current syntactic work, and that will suffice for our purposes at the moment. Even though the details of the structure may be arbitrary, there are certain important ideas about phrase markers in general that we have to deal with before we can profitably discuss details of sentence structure.

Transformational Rules

Discontinuous Dependencies
A natural assumption to make about phrase markers is that each sentence of a language is assigned exactly one phrase marker, except for those sentences that are structurally ambiguous. In the latter case, as we have seen, we assign more than one phrase marker—one for each particular meaning of the sentence, roughly speaking. But now let us examine some sentences that are not structurally ambiguous in the sense in which we have been using that term, but that nevertheless display interesting structural properties. Consider pairs of sentences such as the following:

(31) a. Mary stood up her date.
     b. Mary stood her date up.

These sentences contain a construction known as the verb–particle construction in English—in this particular case, the verb–particle construction *to stand up* (where *stand* is the verb, and *up* is the particle). The interesting feature of this construction is that the particle can occur separated from its verb, as in (31b). (Indeed, in many cases English speakers prefer the version in which the particle is separated from the verb.)

It is natural to suppose that *stood up* is a single constituent in sentence (31a). For one thing we have used the phrase *stood up* in its idiomatic sense, synonymous with *broke a social engagement without warning*, having ignored the literal meaning synonymous with *propped up*. In the idiomatic sense the combination *stood up* has a single meaning; neither part of the expression has the literal meaning it has in isolation. A good guess at the structure of (31a) would be that shown in tree 8.9.

When we turn to (31b), we now must ask what phrase marker we would assign to that sentence. The most obvious candidate, in terms of what we have done so far, would be tree 8.10. Because the particle *up* comes last in the linear order of words in (31b), we have shown it at the end of the VP in tree 8.10. (Keep in mind that we could just as easily have placed the particle at the end directly under S rather than under VP—again, we have presented no evidence for choosing between these detailed structures.)

Tree 8.10, though accurate in representing the linear order of words, is inadequate in other ways. Given the idiomatic use of *stood up* in *Mary stood her date up*, we know that the particle *up* goes with the verb *stand:* even though the particle is separated from the verb, it is nevertheless the case in this sentence as in (31a) that neither the verb nor the particle has the literal meaning it would have in isolation; it is still the combination of the two items that contributes the single meaning. Yet tree 8.10 does not represent this affinity in any way: there is no indication whatever in that diagram that *up* is to be associated with *stood*. Whenever a single constituent of a sentence is broken up in this way we say that we have a discontinuous constituent, or, more generally, a *discontinuous dependency*. It turns out that phrase markers, though very useful for representing certain kinds of information about

Tree 8.9

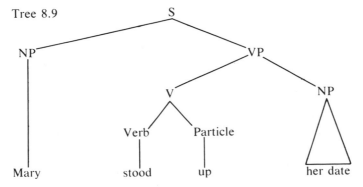

Tree 8.10

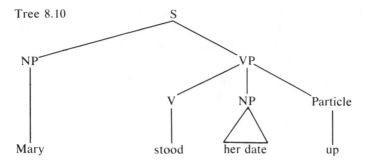

sentences, are completely inadequate in representing discontinuous dependencies.

For another illustration of the same phenomenon, consider sentences that contain modifying clauses in the subject:

(32) Several people *who were wearing hats* came in.

In this case we have a modifying clause, *who were wearing hats,* that serves to supply additional information about the head noun, *several people.* We would assign this sentence a phrase marker such as that in tree 8.11. (Here the symbol MOD indicates a modifying clause.)

It turns out that in English there is a rather general grammatical process known as *extraposition,* whereby modifying clauses (and other types of clauses that need not concern us) can be shifted to the end of the sentence. Therefore, sentence (32) also has the following version:

(33) *Several people* came in *who were wearing hats.*

This sentence is probably structured as in tree 8.12. This diagram correctly indicates that the linear position of the modifying clause is at the end of the sentence. However, tree 8.12 completely fails to show that the modifying clause goes with the subject NP, *several people.* This diagram does not indicate in any way that *who were wearing hats*

Tree 8.11

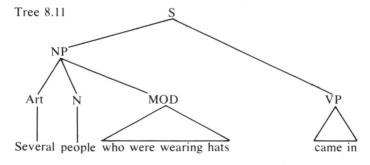

in fact modifies *several people*. In contrast, consider tree 8.11. There the head noun and the modifying clause are shown as a single syntactic constituent, indicating that the head noun and the modifier are related. It is not possible to show the relation between the two in tree 8.12, however, because the head noun and the modifier have been broken apart and separated by the verb phrase. Consequently, we have another case of a discontinuous dependency, and this dependency is not represented in any way by tree 8.12.

It turns out that discontinuous dependencies are quite common in human language; in fact, the complexity of such dependencies can be much greater than we have so far illustrated. To take just one example, note that the two processes just examined—separation of the verb particle and extraposition of the modifying clause—can interact in the same sentence. To see this, consider the following:

(34) She stood up all those men who had offered her diamonds.

Recall that the particle *up* can be shifted to the end of the verb phrase:

(35) She *stood* all those men who had offered her diamonds *up*.

As we see, this produces an awkward sentence that is difficult to understand: the particle and verb are separated by a constituent that is too long. But now recall that modifying clauses can be extraposed in English, and we can extrapose the clause here to produce the following perfectly natural sentence:

(36) She stood all those men up who had offered her diamonds.

In this example, the dependencies actually cross each other:

(37) She stood all those men up who had offered her diamonds.

As we see, *up* goes with *stood,* and *who had offered her diamonds* goes with *all those men;* both constituents are broken up in such a way that

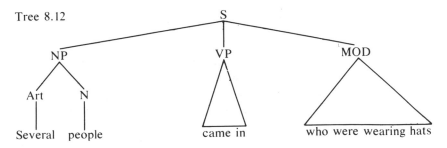

Tree 8.12

parts of one constituent intervene between parts of the other (in particular, *up* occurs between *all those men* and its modifying clause). This is a striking example of how sentences of natural language exhibit discontinuous dependencies.

Transformations as an Account of Discontinuities

The examples we have been discussing show that some properties of sentences in natural language cannot be accounted for in terms of single phrase markers, that is, in terms of relations between contiguous words. It turns out that we need to account for relations between those items in a sentence that are connected (in some sense), dependent, or related, but that are nonetheless not contiguous in the linear order of words. One way to account for discontinuous dependencies of this sort is to devise a means by which two or more phrase markers can themselves be related to each other in a special way—which is in fact the fundamental insight of the syntactic theory known as Transformational Grammar (TG).

To illustrate what we mean, consider again the pair of sentences in (31), repeated here:

(31) a. Mary stood up her date.
     b. Mary stood her date up.

With regard to sentence (31a), we will assume as before that it is assigned a single phrase marker, shown as tree 8.9. But what about sentence (31b)? This is the sentence with the discontinuous constituent, *stood . . . up*. In order to express the dependency between *stood* and *up* in (31b), let us suppose that this sentence derives from the same phrase marker as that for (31a): tree 8.13.Call this the underlying structure or *base structure* for sentence (31b), *Mary stood her date up*.

Now we will postulate a structural operation known as a transformation, which we can state informally as follows:

(38) Particle Movement Transformation
     Given a verb–particle construction, the particle may be shifted away from the verb, and moved to the immediate right of the object noun phrase.

When we apply the Particle Movement transformation to tree 8.13, the underlying structure, we get the derived phrase marker, or derived structure, shown in tree 8.14. This derived structure happens to correspond to what we will term the *surface structure* of sentence (31b), that

Tree 8.13 (= Tree 8.9)

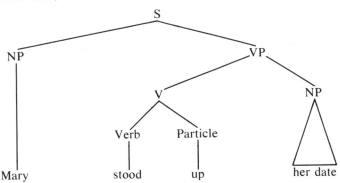

is, this phrase marker indicates the actually occurring order and structure for the elements of sentence (31b).

Notice now that there is a significant difference between the sentences of (31), given a transformational analysis of the sort we have
postulated. For the sentence *Mary stood up her date,* we are simply
postulating a single phrase marker, shown as tree 8.13. This phrase
marker expresses accurately the order and structure of the elements of
that sentence. However, for the sentence *Mary stood her date up,* we
are now postulating two phrase markers, not just one. The underlying
phrase marker, tree 8.13, contains a verb–particle construction, shown
as a single constituent; the derived phrase marker, on the other hand,
shown as tree 8.14, contains the particle separated from its verb, and
hence corresponds to the surface form of the sentence. In this way the
transformational rule we have called Particle Movement expresses a
relation between two phrase markers: it essentially says that for every
phrase marker that contains a verb-particle combination, there is a
corresponding phrase marker in which that particular particle has been
separated from the verb and placed after the object noun phrase.

Tree 8.14 (= Tree 8.10)

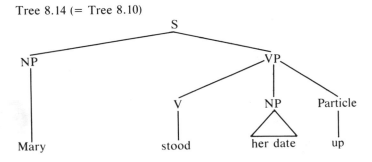

We now have a way of accounting for discontinuous dependencies. Tree 8.14 is the correct surface phrase marker for the sentence *Mary stood her date up,* and the particle is correctly represented as following the object NP. Nevertheless, we can account for the dependency between the particle and the verb because we are claiming that tree 8.14 derives from the underlying phrase marker, tree 8.13, and in that phrase marker the verb and its particle are in fact contiguous and form a single constituent. Thus the underlying structure of the sentence shows the basic constituency of the verb and its particle, but the surface structure of the sentence correctly shows the particle as separated from its verb.

The kind of analysis we have just sketched is illustrative of the transformational model of syntactic analysis. This particular model (and numerous variations on it) has dominated the field of syntax ever since the publication of Noam Chomsky's 1957 book *Syntactic Structures,* the first major work to propose this sort of model. Even though the transformational analysis we have presented is one means of accounting for discontinuous dependencies, the question remains whether there is any reason to suppose it is the best means, or the most insightful means. It is difficult to answer this question in any definitive way, but it is possible to give additional evidence for the model that will serve to illustrate its explanatory power.

Consider the transformational process alluded to earlier: extraposition. Recall pairs of sentences such as:

(39) a. Several people who were wearing hats came in.
  b. Several people came in who were wearing hats.

As before, we would assign to sentence (39a) the phrase marker 8.11, repeated here as tree 8.15. This phrase marker seems to represent

Tree 8.15 (= Tree 8.11)

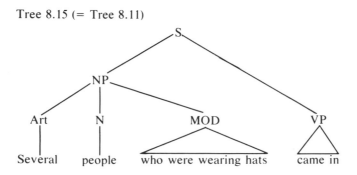

accurately the order and structure of the elements of sentence (39a).

But what about sentence (39b)? This is the sentence containing the discontinuous constituent *several people . . . who were wearing hats.* We will account for this sentence in a manner parallel to the case of Particle Movement, namely, by postulating that sentence (39b) derives from an underlying structure identical with tree 8.15. In the underlying structure, then, the head noun and the modifying clause form a single constituent. We will then propose the following transformational rule:

(40) Extraposition Transformation

Given a noun phrase containing a head noun directly followed by a modifying clause, the modifying clause may be shifted out of the noun phrase to the end of the sentence.

By applying this transformation to tree 8.15, we will get the derived structure shown in tree 8.16, which seems to be the correct surface structure for the sentence *Several people came in who were wearing hats.*

We have been able to account for the discontinuous dependency between the modifying clause and the head noun in tree 8.16 by claiming that tree 8.16 in fact derives from the underlying structure tree 8.15, in which the discontinuous elements of the surface are actually represented as a single constituent. This is another example of a transformational account of discontinuous dependency. The effect of the transformational rule of Extraposition, like that of Particle Movement, is to set up a relationship between phrase markers: it states, in effect, that for every phrase marker containing a noun phrase with a modifying clause directly following the head noun there is a corresponding phrase marker in which that same modifying clause has been shifted to the end of the sentence. (Although this is not strictly true—in certain cases

Tree 8.16 (= Tree 8.12)

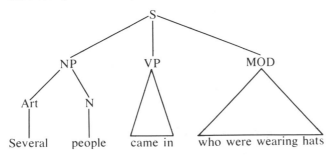

extraposition of the modifying clause is prohibited—it is nonetheless quite adequate for our purposes here, and we need not add any refinements.)

Interaction between Transformations

We have examined two cases in which a transformational analysis can account for discontinuities, but that in itself is not enough to indicate whether the transformational model is a particularly revealing account. It is time to turn to some rather striking evidence for this model. It turns out that individual transformational rules, established for independent reasons, can in fact interact with each other to account for a complex array of surface data in a straightforward and simple fashion.

Consider the structure shown in tree 8.17. One function of this phrase marker is to accurately represent the surface structure of the sentence,

(41) She stood up all those men who had offered her diamonds.

However, tree 8.17 also functions in a second way, that is, as an underlying structure from which we can derive another surface structure. Notice that in this structure we have both a verb–particle construction and a complex noun phrase composed of a head noun and a modifying clause. This is a structure to which the Particle Movement transformation (38) may apply. If we apply it we get the derived structure in tree 8.18. The particle has been placed after the object noun phrase, as dictated by the rule. This derived structure is not yet a well-formed surface structure, however (recall the awkwardness and difficulty of the sentence *She stood all those men who had offered her diamonds up*). It is, instead, an intermediate structure, to which we will

Tree 8.17

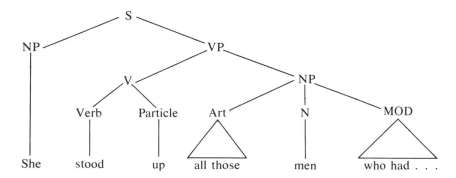

Tree 8.18

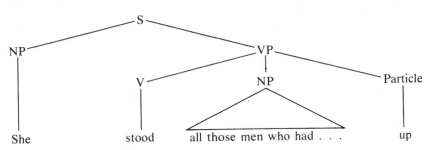

now apply the Extraposition transformation to get yet another derived structure, that of tree 8.19.

We have now arrived at the surface structure for the sentence *She stood all those men up who had offered her diamonds*. Recall that this sentence has two discontinuous dependencies, which actually cross each other, as shown in (37). Yet we can account for this complicated pattern of dependencies in a simple way: We have already postulated the Particle Movement and Extraposition transformations for independent reasons. If we simply allow both rules to apply in sequence, they will automatically interact to give tree 8.19. We can now specify precisely what elements of tree 8.19 are dependent upon each other, because we have claimed that it derives from the underlying structure tree 8.17, and that structure represents the surface discontinuities of sentence (37) as underlying constituents.

The important point here, then, is this: individual transformations are postulated to account for certain specific phenomena of dependency; but the strongest evidence for the transformational model comes in the interaction of the independently established transformations. In the case of sentence (37) a simple interaction—two transformations applying in sequence in the derivation of a sentence—

Tree 8.19

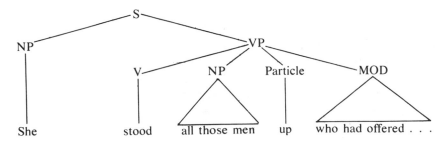

automatically leads to a simple account of a complex set of surface structure dependencies.

We began our investigation of syntax by posing the questions, What is structure, and how do we know that sentences are structured? As we have seen, there is no simple answer to these questions nor any way to answer them without actually constructing a theory of syntax. We have provided a partial answer, though, by arriving at the conclusion that sentence structure involves both structural and functional aspects: specification of the linear order of words, classification of words into parts of speech, grouping of words into structural constituents, and assignment of functions to certain constituents of the sentence (for example, by calling a certain NP in a sentence the subject of the sentence). We did not arrive at this view for the sake of convenience, nor because it was handed down to us by ancient grammatical authorities. Rather we found it impossible to state the most fundamental syntactic processes of a language—such as how to form questions—without appealing to these concepts. On further investigation we found that in order to account for the phenomenon of discontinuous dependencies, we needed to postulate not just structural properties of sentences but structural relations as well (represented by transformations). In this way our view of what constitutes syntactic structure is very much determined by what phenomena we are trying to explain, and there is no doubt that conceptions of syntactic structure will become increasingly subtle and complex as syntactic theorists are faced with an ever-expanding range of new and heretofore unexplained data about the formal properties of sentences.

Psychological Reality of Constituent Structure

Constituent structure of sentences is not merely an artifact of syntactic theory; there is reason to think that gross constituent structure has reality in the minds of speakers. In various experiments that have come to be known as the *click experiments,* Fodor, Bever, and Garrett (1974) have tried to show that test subjects utilize major constituent boundaries in their perception of sentences. Subjects wearing headphones were presented with a tape-recorded sentence in one ear while in the other ear they were presented with a click noise, which they heard simultaneously superimposed on some part of the sentence. They were asked to write down each sentence they had heard and to indicate at what point within the sentence they had heard the click sound. A typical sentence in this experiment is (42), where the dots underneath words indicate various locations of the superimposed click noises.

(42) That the girl was happy | was evident from the way she laughed.

The major constituent break in this sentence occurs between *happy* and *was*, and clicks were superimposed before, in, and after this major break. Under most conditions the subjects in the experiment showed a definite tendency to mis-hear the location of the click: when the click came before the major break, subjects reported hearing it later than it actually occurred, that is, closer to the break; when the click came after the major break, subjects reported hearing it earlier than it occurred, again closer to the break. When the click was located in the major break itself, there was much less of a tendency to mis-hear its location.

This experiment has been interpreted as showing that hearers process sentences in terms of major clauses of a sentence and that these major constituents resist interruption. When a click was placed within a major clause—say, in the word *was* in (42)—hearers tended to report its location as being in the break, not in the clause itself, suggesting that major clauses are perceived as integrated whole units that resist being broken up. If this is true, it appears that major constituent structure is not simply a theoretical device used by linguists to explain syntactic phenomena; it is a psychologically real basic unit of perception on the part of hearers.

The results of the click experiments are by no means uncontroversial, but this experiment illustrates the general sort of experimental work that is being done on the perception of the syntactic structure of sentences. The reader is referred to Fodor, Bever, and Garrett (1974) and Clark and Clark (1977) for a review of much of this work as well as for discussions of some problems and controversy in this area.

8.3 A MORE FORMAL ACCOUNT OF SYNTACTIC THEORY

The type of transformational analysis sketched informally in section 8.2 has, in fact, been given a more precise and formal description by theorists working on the transformational model. The references at the end of this chapter will give the reader a number of alternative accounts of the more formal theory (see Kimball 1973, and Wall 1972). In this section we will provide only a brief description to give the reader some idea of how transformational theory has been developed. It should be stressed that we will present here a description of some of the more basic features of standard, or classical, transformational theory; the reader should be aware that at present many linguists are working on significant modifications and variations on these basic concepts.

Phrase Structure Grammars

Within the standard transformational model it is assumed that basic phrase markers are generated by *phrase structure rules* (PS rules) of the following sort:

(43) a. S → NP AUX VP
  b. NP → Art N
  c. AUX → will
  d. VP →V NP

Each rule is essentially a formula, or specification, for how the con-stituent represented by a certain symbol—the symbol on the left of the arrow—can be constituted in a tree diagram. For example, PS rule (43a) tells us that S (sentence) can consist of, or can be expanded as, the sequence NP AUX VP. This is shown in tree form as tree 8.20. The rules also tell us that NP (noun phrase) can be expanded as Art N; that VP (verb phrase) can be expanded as V NP; and that AUX (auxiliary) can be expanded as *will*. These expansions are illustrated in tree 8.21. By inserting appropriate words, we get a structure like tree 8.22.

It is not the case that every noun phrase of English must contain an

Tree 8.20

Tree 8.21

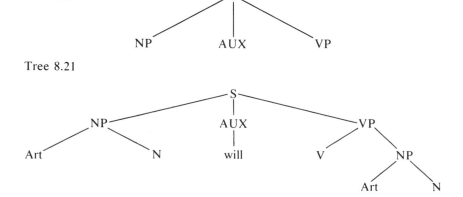

Tree 8.22

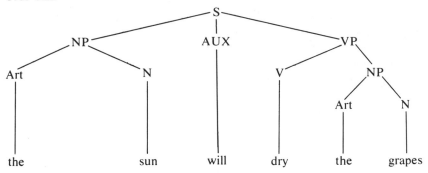

article, nor is it the case that every verb phrase must contain an object NP. We say that these are optional constituents of these phrases, and we represent optional constituents within parentheses:

(44) a. S   →NP AUX VP
     b. NP   → (Art) N
     c. AUX → will
     d. VP   → V (NP)

Items in parentheses *may* be chosen in generating a tree structure; other items *must* be chosen if a structure is to be well-formed. This allows us to generate structures such as tree 8.23.

Noun phrases in English may contain various sorts of modifiers after the head noun; we have already seen cases where head nouns are modified by clauses, as in *the men who offered her diamonds*. Nouns can also be followed by prepositional phrases (PP) as modifiers:

(45) a. the house *in the woods*
     b. the weather *in England*
     c. a portrait *of Mary*
     d. the prospects *for peace*

Tree 8.23

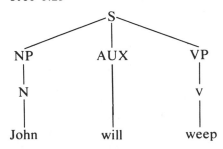

In order to form such phrases—to *generate* them as we say—we can modify our NP rule as follows:

(46) NP→(Art) N (PP)

We now add a PS rule to expand prepositional phrases:

(47) PP→Prep NP

Our set of PS rules, which we call a *phrase structure grammar,* now generates NPs such as that in tree 8.24.

Recursion

An interesting consequence of rules (46) and (47) is that we can generate a potentially infinite number of noun phrases. This is because the PS rule for NP allows a PP to follow the head noun and the prepositional phrase, in turn, contains an NP; this NP itself may in turn be expanded to contain a PP; and so on, indefinitely, as in tree 8.25. This is one of the ways in which a finite set of rules—in this case, the two rules (46) and (47)—can generate an infinite set of structures. PS grammars containing pairs of rules such as (46) and (47) are said to be *recursive.*

The Formal Statement of Transformations

Recall that a single phrase marker alone cannot account for a discontinuous dependency and that transformational rules are introduced into the theory in order to express syntactic relations between pairs of phrase markers. Transformational rules have been formalized in standard transformational theory; to illustrate the formalism used, we restate the Particle Movement transformation:

Tree 8.24

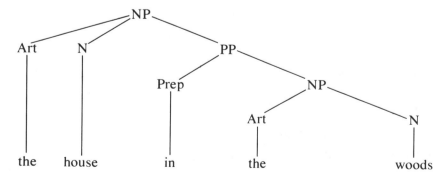

Tree 8.25

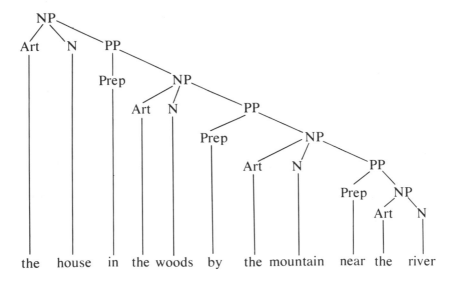

(48) Particle Movement
     SD: X - Verb - Particle - NP - Y
          1 - 2 - 3 - 4 - 5 ⇒
     SC: 1 - 2 - ∅ - 4+3 - 5

A transformational rule consists, first, of a *structural description* (SD), which is an instruction to analyze a phrase marker into a sequence of constituents, in this case, Verb followed by Particle followed by NP. The variables X and Y indicate that the constituents to the left of the verb and to the right of the NP are irrelevant to this transformation—they can represent anything at all. In order for a transformation to be applied, the analysis of a phrase marker must *satisfy* the SD of the particular transformation. As we can see, tree 8.26 can be analyzed—that is, can be cut up into chunks—in a way that matches exactly the sequence of constituents listed in the SD of the Particle Movement transformation. Hence, this phrase marker satisfies the SD of the rule.

The second part of a transformational rule is the *structural change* (SC), which in the case of (48) is an instruction to modify the structural description by shifting term 3 (Particle) immediately to the right of term 4 (NP), as illustrated in tree 8.27. The particle (term 3) has correctly been placed immediately after the NP (term 4), and the plus sign between them in the SC indicates that these two constituents are to be

Tree 8.26

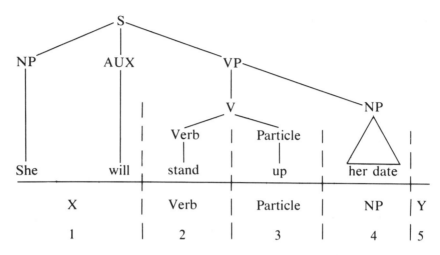

Tree 8.27

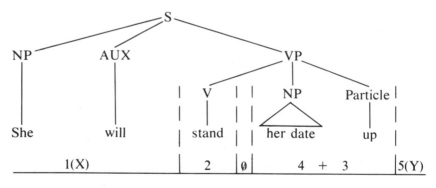

sisters; that is, they are to be immediately *dominated* by the same *node* (in this case, VP). The symbol Ø ("zero") indicates that nothing remains in the slot where the particle had been, and marks the spot from which the particle was moved. There are many other details of transformational formalism that we cannot go into here; the reader should consult the references.

The relation between phrase structure rules and transformations in the standard transformational model is summed up in figure 8.1. The syntactic component of a transformational grammar consists of a set of phrase structure rules, which generate a class of phrase markers called underlying structures. These underlying structures in turn form the

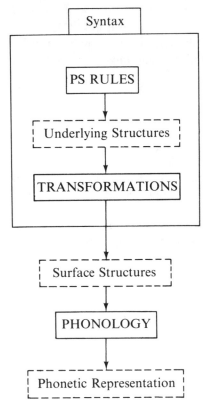

Figure 8.1
Relations between rules in a standard transformational model

input to the transformational rules, which transform them into a class of phrase markers called surface structures. The surface structures in turn are operated on by phonological rules, in particular, by stress assignment rules (see chapter 6), and phonetic representations for sentences are derived. We will see in chapter 11 that this conception of a grammar is not complete until we add a *semantic* component, which assigns representations of meaning to the underlying structures, and a *lexicon,* which lists the words of a language with their meanings.

Virtually no part of this overall picture of grammar has remained unchallenged in recent years. Linguists have been exploring different views about the correct nature of phonology, syntax, the lexicon, semantics, and the overall interrelations between them. Even though the standard theory of transformational grammar—roughly, the model presented in Noam Chomsky's 1965 work, *Aspects of the Theory of Syntax*—has been challenged at every level, it is still important for a student of linguistics to have some familiarity with this model in order to understand the many changes in linguistics that have occurred since the mid-sixties.

Exercises

*1. Word order can play a crucial role in understanding the functional relations of English sentences—*The horse bit the dog* does not mean the same thing as *The dog bit the horse*. But there are also cases in which a change in word order in a sentence will *not* change its functional relations or meaning. Cite three different examples of such cases.

2. We have noted that sentences such as *The mother of the boy and the girl will arrive soon* are structurally ambiguous: even though no word used in the sentence is ambiguous, the sentence itself is nonetheless ambiguous. List three different additional cases of structural ambiguity that do not involve conjunction (the word *and*). (To get started, see exercise 4.)

3. Show the structural groupings of words for the sentences you have cited in exercise 2. Do this in the manner of example (4) in this chapter, that is, by using parentheses.

4. The sequence of words *light house keeper* is structurally ambiguous. Show the different structural groupings, using parentheses as in exercise 3.

*5. In English we find many pairs of corresponding active and passive sentences:
a. Mary hit John (active sentence).
b. John was hit by Mary (passive sentence).
Hypothesis: To form a passive sentence from an active sentence,
(i) interchange the first and last words of the sentence (make the first word the last word and the last word the first word),
(ii) add *by* before the last word and insert the proper form of the verb *be* into second position of the sentence.

Why is the hypothesis wrong? Cite specific examples from English to support your answer. Show why it is necessary to refer to subject and object in the rule for forming passive sentences. (Hint: Review the discussion of the English Question rule in section 8.2.)

*6. The following sentences illustrate one type of tag question in English:
a. He can lift 500 lbs., *can he?*
b. They are generally thought to be odd, *are they?*
c. You will want to reserve two rooms, *will you?*
d. She has proved several theorems, *has she?*
Hypothesis: To form a tag question for a sentence of English, copy word #2, followed by word #1, at the end of the sentence:

He can lift 500 lbs., can he?

Why is this hypothesis wrong? Make up new example sentences from English to support your answer. In particular, show why the Tag Question rule must make reference to (a) linear order of words, (b) parts of speech, and (c) structural constituents and the notion "subject." (Hint: Review the discussion of the English Question rule in section 8.2.)

*7. The distinction between auxiliary verbs and main verbs is a basic one in English. We have already seen that auxiliary verbs are fronted to form questions whereas main verbs cannot be fronted in this fashion (see (22) and (23)). The following sentences illustrate three additional differences between main verbs and auxiliary verbs. What are these differences?

a. Mary will not know the answer. (placement of *not*)

b. John'll leave the room. (contraction)

c. He will eat supper, won't he? (tag question)

*8. In tree 8.1 we have structured the verb phrase *move.the desk into the hall* in such a way that we have three independent constituents: *move, the desk,* and *into the hall*. Why shouldn't we structure the verb phrase in such a way that *the desk into the hall* forms a single constituent? Cite specific evidence, using English examples, against this constituent structure. In doing this problem, contrast sentences containing the sequence *the desk into the hall* with sentences containing the sequence *the desk with the wooden drawers,* which actually is a single constituent:

a. Let's move the desk into the hall.

b. Let's move the desk with the wooden drawers.

The differences between these two sentences and others that you make up will reveal the answer to this problem.

*9. The subject of a sentence is not always interpreted as the "doer" of some action, nor is the object of a main verb always interpreted as the "recipient" of some action. In the following examples give the logical roles or meanings of the underlined subject or object. (Example: *John* received a book. — Subject = recipient)

a. *The garden* is swarming with bees.

b. They loaded *hay* onto the truck.

c. They loaded *the truck* with hay.

d. We gave *Mary* the book.

e. *The dog* died.

f. We kept *John* in Boston (for two days).

g. We kept *John* in mind (for the job).

h. *Noon* found us waiting at the railroad station.

*10. In the following sentence the NP *the chicken* is the surface subject of *ready*:

The chicken is ready to eat.

However, this sentence is ambiguous as to the *logical* relations of the NP *the chicken*. What is the ambiguity?

11. In example (31) we cited one instance of a verb–particle construction: *stood up*. Cite ten additional verb–particle constructions.

*12. The following sentence contains an example of a discontinuous dependency:
The students who need help have all left the room.
What is the discontinuous dependency? How would you account for the discontinuity using a transformational rule? (Hint: Recall Particle Movement and Extraposition.)

*13. The following sentences contain examples of a discontinuous dependency quite similar to a type we studied in this chapter:
a. A review will soon appear of the new book by Chomsky.
b. Several theories were presented last night about the structure of human language.
c. He took several recordings out of the famous Enrico Caruso.
What is the discontinuous dependency in these examples? How would you explain the discontinuity using a transformational rule?

*14. Consider the following ungrammatical sentence:
a. *You gave liquor to.
There is a gap—something is missing—after the preposition *to*, and this gap must apparently be filled in order for the sentence to be grammatical:
b. You gave liquor to the boy.
However, when a question word such as *which (boy)* is present, we can have a gap:
c. Which boy did you give liquor to ——?
In other words we understand that the phrase *which boy* in fact fills the gap at the end of the sentence; thus there is a dependency between the initial question word and the final gap.

Cite specific examples from English to show that there is in principle no limit on the length of the sentence that can intervene between the initial question word and the final gap. Second, propose a transformational analysis of such sentences that will explain the discontinuous dependency.

*15. In section 8.3, example (48) and trees 8.26 and 8.27, we showed how the Particle Movement rule can be written using transformational formalism. Formalize the Extraposition transformation (stated informally in (40)) in the same fashion as Particle Movement as stated in (48).

*16. The following sentences all show that Particle Movement is subject to a special condition in English:
a.   We wrote down the number.
     *We wrote down it.
b.   She stood up her friends.
     *She stood up them.
c.   The bartender kicked out Mary.
     *The bartender kicked out her.
What is the special condition on Particle Movement?

*17. How does morphological information enter syntax? In your answer discuss specifically the Question Rule examined in section 8.2.

*18. Which theories of the chart picturing human language structure given in the Note to the Student (at the beginning of the book) are reflected in the structural properties of sentences discussed in this chapter?

References

Akmajian, A., and F. W. Heny (1975) *An Introduction to the Principles of Transformational Syntax,* MIT Press, Cambridge, Mass.

Bach, E. (1974) *Syntactic Theory,* Holt, Rinehart & Winston, New York.

Baker, C. L. (1978) *Introduction to Generative-Transformational Syntax,* Prentice-Hall, Englewood Cliffs, N.J.

Chomsky, N. (1957) *Syntactic Structures,* Mouton, The Hague.

—— (1965) *Aspects of the Theory of Syntax,* MIT Press, Cambridge, Mass.

—— (1976) *Reflections on Language,* Pantheon Books, New York.

Clark, H. H., and E. V. Clark (1977) *Psychology and Language,* Harcourt Brace Jovanovich, New York.

Culicover, P. (1976) *Syntax,* Academic Press, New York.

Fodor, J. A., T. G. Bever, and M. F. Garrett (1974) *The Psychology of Language,* McGraw-Hill, New York.

Kimball, J. P. (1973) *The Formal Theory of Grammar,* Prentice-Hall, Englewood Cliffs, N.J.

Stockwell, R. P., P. Schachter, and B. H. Partee (1973), *The Major Syntactic Structures of English,* Holt, Rinehart & Winston, New York.

Wall, R. (1972) *Introduction to Mathematical Linguistics,* Prentice-Hall, Englewood Cliffs, N.J.

Chapter Nine

LANGUAGE
VARIATION

9.1 LANGUAGE STYLES AND DIALECTS

No human language can be said to be fixed, uniform, or unvarying: all languages, as far as anyone knows, show internal variation in that actual usage varies from speaker to speaker. For example, speakers of English differ in their pronunciation of the language, in their choice of vocabulary words and the meaning of those words, and even in their use of syntactic constructions. Further, not only are speakers of American English noticeably different from speakers of British English, but within American English itself there is considerable variation. When groups of speakers differ in noticeable ways in their use of a language, they are often said to speak different *dialects* of the language. It is notoriously difficult, however, to define with any precision exactly what a dialect is, even though many examples of dialectal differences can be given. Sometimes speakers are said to have *regional* dialects, as with the so-called Southern dialect or New England dialect. Sometimes we have occasion to speak of *social* or *ethnic* dialects—forms of the language used by members of some particular social or ethnic class, such as working class dialects in England or ghetto languages in the United States (which we will return to).

Variation in Pronunciation

It is almost impossible to label any dialect as being purely regional or purely social or ethnic, especially in a society as geographically and socially mobile as modern American society. A particular linguistic feature of a regional dialect might well be influenced by social factors. An interesting example of the effect of ''social prestige'' on a regional dialect is found in the pronunciation of /r/ in New York City speech. The so-called *r*-less dialect of New York City is so well known that it is often the subject of much humor, especially on the part of the New Yorkers who themselves have the *r*-less dialect. It is commonly thought that speakers of the dialect completely lack /r/ in words such as *car, card, four, fourth,* and so on, but this is a misconception, as an intriguing study by the sociolinguist William Labov (1972) reveals.

Labov began with the hypothesis that New York City speakers vary in their pronunciation of /r/ according to their social status. Labov interviewed salespeople at several New York City department stores that differed in price range and social prestige. Assuming that salespeople tend to "borrow prestige" from their customers, Labov predicted that the social stratification of customers at different department stores would be mirrored in a similar stratification of salespeople. These assumptions led him to hypothesize that "salespeople in the highest-ranked store will have the highest values of (r); those in the middle-ranked store will have intermediate values of (r); and those in the lowest-ranked store will show the lowest values" (1972, 45).

Labov chose three stores: Saks Fifth Avenue (high prestige), Macy's (middle level), and S. Klein (low prestige). He interviewed salespeople by asking them a question that would elicit the answer *fourth floor*:

The interviewer approached the informant in the role of a customer asking for directions to a particular department. The department was one which was located on the fourth floor. When the interviewer asked, "Excuse me, where are the women's shoes?" the answer would normally be, "Fourth floor."

The interviewer then leaned forward and said, "Excuse me?" He would usually then obtain another utterance, "*Fourth floor*," spoken in careful style under emphatic stress. (1972, 49)

The phrase *fourth floor* has two instances of /r/, both of which are subject to variation in the pronunciation of New York City speakers, and Labov was able to study both casual and careful pronunciations of this phrase.

The result turned out to correlate in an interesting way with the hypothesis. For example, Labov found that at Saks, 30 percent of the salespeople interviewed always pronounced both /r/'s in the test phrase; at Macy's 20 percent did so; and at Klein's only 4 percent did. In addition, Labov found that 32 percent of the interviewed salespeople at Saks had variable pronunciation of /r/ (sometimes /r/ was pronounced and sometimes not, depending on context); at Macy's 31 percent of the

interviewees had variable pronunciation; and at Klein's only 17 percent
did. These overall results do suggest that pronunciation of /r/ in New
York City is correlated, at least loosely, with social stratification of the
speakers.

What about the differences in pronunciation between the casual and
the emphatic styles? It turns out that in the casual response the /r/ of
floor was pronounced by 63 percent of the salespeople at Saks, 44
percent at Macy's, and only 8 percent at Klein's. In contrast, in the
careful, emphatic, response the /r/ of *floor* was pronounced by 64
percent at Saks, 61 percent at Macy's (note the jump from 44 percent),
and 18 percent at Klein's. In other words, at Saks there was very little
difference between casual and careful pronunciations, whereas at
Macy's and Klein's the difference between these styles was significantly
larger. This suggests that speakers at the middle and lower levels of the
New York City social scale are perfectly aware that a final /r/ occurs in
words such as *floor*. Even though they omit this /r/ in casual pronunciation, it reappears in careful speech:

In emphatic pronunciation of the final (r), Macy's employees come
very close to the mark set by Saks. It would seem that r-pronunciation
is the norm at which a majority of Macy employees aim, yet not the one
they use most often. In Saks, we see a shift between casual and
emphatic pronunciation, but it is much less marked. In other words,
Saks employees have more *security* in a linguistic sense. (1972, 51–52)

As we will see again in section 9.2, the difference between casual and
careful language styles is important in syntactic variation as well.

In our consideration of the pronunciation of New York City /r/, it is
interesting to note here that some New York City speakers insert /r/ in
words where it does not actually occur in spelling. One can find *Cuba*
pronounced [kyuwbər], *saw* pronounced [sɔr], *idea* pronounced
[aydiyr], and so on. It seems that the very speakers who drop out /r/ in
some words and positions will reinsert an /r/ in other words and
positions. The cause of this phenomenon is sometimes thought to be
hypercorrection (that is, overcorrection): speakers who have been
persuaded that it is "incorrect" to drop /r/ will overcompensate or
overcorrect for this by reinserting the sound where it does not actually
occur in spelling. (Overcompensation can be seen in syntax with
speakers who say *Between you and I* instead of *Between you and me* on
the grounds that *I* is more "correct" and "cultured" than *me*.)

However, we might question whether, for given speakers, reinserting /r/ involves only hypercorrection. For one thing even those speak-

ers who reinsert /r/ do not always pronounce words such as *idea* with a final /r/: the reinsertion of /r/ on such words happens only when the ensuing word begins with a vowel (hence, we could find phrases such as *the idear I heard about* but not *the idear John told me about*). The reinsertion of /r/ is thus at least partially governed by a phonological principle. In the second place, hypercorrection often involves imitating what is thought to be prestige language. For example, a hypercorrect phrase such as *It is I* is thought to sound more prestigious than *It's me*, even though there is nothing grammatically incorrect about the latter phrase. Returning to words such as *idear*, speakers who reinsert /r/ in *idear* may not think that such a pronunciation is prestigious. Since reinsertion of /r/ is governed partially by a phonological principle, and since it may not involve imitation of prestige language, for some speakers this reinsertion of /r/ is not strictly a case of hypercorrection.

To sum up, the Labov study illustrates that there is often no absolute or simple distinction between one dialect and another: we cannot simply say that the New York City dialect is *r*-less. Rather, the pronunciation of /r/ in that dialect is variable, and this variation seems to be correlated both with social factors and with the casual or careful context. Thus just as no language can be said to be unvarying or fixed, no dialect of a language can be said to be unvarying or fixed either. And, finally, not even the language of an individual speaker is unvarying: an individual New Yorker may well show variation in pronouncing /r/.

Variation in Vocabulary and Word Meaning

Just as the dialects of different speakers can vary phonologically (in pronunciation), they can also vary in vocabulary items and the meanings attached to those items, as illustrated by the following examples:

(1) a. *Dope* means "cola" in some parts of the South.
b. *Pocket book* means "purse" in Boston and in parts of the South.
c. *Fetch up* means "raise" (children) in the South.
d. *Pavement* means "sidewalk" in eastern Pennsylvania and in England.
e. *Happygrass* means "grasshopper" in eastern Virginia.
f. *Bubbler* means "water fountain" in Wisconsin.
g. *Knock up* means "phone up" in Scotland and "wake up" in England.

h. *Bonnet* means "hood" (of a car) in England.

i. *Fag* means "cigarette" in England.

As the last three examples indicate, vocabulary differences between American and British English are common and often amusing. Indeed, the Bell Telephone System publishes a pamphlet entitled "Getting Around the USA: Travel Tips for the British Visitor," which contains a section entitled "How to Say It." In this section we find the following correspondences:

(2) British   American

British	American
car park	parking lot
coach	bus
garage	service station
lay by	rest area
lift	elevator
lorry	truck
petrol	gasoline
underground (or tube)	subway
call box	telephone booth
telephonist	switchboard operator
gin and French	dry martini
minerals	soft drinks
suspenders	garters
vest	undershirt

These examples are typical of the sort of dialectal variation we find in the vocabulary of British and American English.

Variation in Syntax: "Standard" versus "Nonstandard" Language

Sometimes linguists use the term *dialect* to refer to variations that can't be defined as regional, social, or ethnic. Rather this use of *dialect* simply indicates that speakers show some variation in the way they use elements of the language. For example, some speakers of English are perfectly comfortable using the word *anymore* in sentences such as the following:

(3) a. Tools are expensive anymore.

Here, *anymore* means roughly the same as *nowadays* or *lately*. Other speakers of English can use *anymore* only if there is a negative element, such as *not*, in the sentence:

(3) b. Tools are not cheap anymore.

As far as we can tell, this difference between speakers cannot be linked to a particular region of the country or to a particular social class or ethnic group.

No doubt some people would characterize example (3a) as nonstandard or incorrect, or possibly as slang, while designating example (3b) as standard English, or as grammatical. Those who would label (3b) as correct and (3a) as incorrect, are usually speakers of the dialect that uses (3b) and not (3a)! And that illustrates an important point about social attitudes toward language: in most societies of the world there is a pervasive opinion that one dialect of the native language is what is called the standard language, whereas other dialects are nonstandard, inferior, incorrect. In America, Standard English is the form of the language used on the national media, especially in news programs; it is the language of legal and official functions; and it is the language used in schools as a vehicle of education.

In linguistic terms no one dialect of a language is any more correct, any better, or any more logical than any other dialect of the language: all dialects are equally effective forms of language, in that any idea or desire that can be expressed in one dialect can be expressed just as easily in any other dialect. The idea that Standard English is the correct form of the language is a social attitude—more precisely, a language prejudice—which is just as irrational as social prejudices toward race or sex. In America the so-called standard language is perhaps most widely identified with the educated white middle class; hence a good case can be made that the reverence toward the standard language in our schools and official functions is a reflection of the far more general bias in the United States toward considering the white middle-class value system the correct or best value system. It is important to realize at the outset that labeling one particular dialect as standard and others as inferior reflects a sociopolitical judgment, not a linguistic judgment.

A well-known example of a social dialect that has been labeled as nonstandard is Black English, a dialect (or group of similar dialects) spoken in Black ghettos in large urban areas of the United States. In recent years Black English, or BE for short, has attracted a good deal of attention from linguists (see references), whose investigations have shown quite clearly that BE is every bit as rule-governed and as logical as Standard English (henceforth, SE). In a series of important studies Labov (see references) has demonstrated that there are several important and highly systematic relationships between BE and SE. To take what is perhaps the best-known example, consider the often noted fact that in BE present tense forms of the verb *to be* are often dropped out in casual speech (examples taken from Labov 1969a).

(4) a. She the first one started us off.
   b. He fast in everything he do.
   c. I know, but he wild, though.
   d. You out the game.
   e. We on tape.
   f. But everybody not black.
   g. They not caught.
   h. Boot always comin' over my house to eat.
   i. He gon' try to get up.

The omission of the verb *to be* in BE can easily be misinterpreted by those untrained in linguistics as evidence that BE is a kind of defective dialect that violates rules of grammar or, worse yet, has no rules of grammar. As Labov (1969b) notes, this has even led to the mistaken view on the part of certain educators and psychologists that Black children entering school have a language deficit and are culturally deprived. Even though the omission of forms of the verb *to be* may at first appear to make BE quite distinct from SE, Labov (1969b, 203) points out that

The deletion of the *is* or *are* in [BE] is not the result of erratic or illogical behavior: it follows the same regular rules as standard English contraction. Wherever standard English can contract, [BE can] use either the contracted form or (more commonly) the deleted zero form. Thus, *They mine* corresponds to standard *They're mine,* not to the full form *They are mine.* On the other hand, no such deletion is possible in positions where standard English cannot contract: just as one cannot say *That's what they're* in standard English, *That's what they* is equally impossible in the vernacular we are considering.

In the examples already cited, the correspondence between SE and BE is as follows:

SE: Contraction	BE: Deletion
She's the first one . . .	She the first one . . .
He's fast . . .	He fast . . .
You're out . . .	You out . . .
They're not caught.	They not caught.

Both dialects have contraction, but only BE has the further option of deleting a contractible form of *to be*.

What appears at first to be a significant difference between SE and BE actually turns out to be rather minor. Indeed in both dialects the same general phenomenon is taking place: the verb *to be* (as well as other auxiliary verbs) becomes *reduced* in casual speech when it is unstressed. One dialect reflects this reduction process by contraction alone, the other dialect by contraction or deletion. On wider examination, in fact, the deletion of *to be,* and other auxiliary verbs, is by no means limited to BE but happens quite generally in casual speech in all dialects of American English.

Formal and Informal Language Styles

Before we go further, we must make a distinction between two language styles (or *registers,* as they are sometimes called), namely, the distinction between formal and informal speech. The clearest cases of formal speech occur in social contexts that are formal, serious, often official in some sense, in which you the speaker must watch your language and in which the *manner* of saying something is regarded as socially important. These contexts would include a formal job interview, meeting an important dignitary, and standing before a court of law. Informal speech in our use of that term occurs in casual, relaxed social settings in which speech is spontaneous, rapid, and uncensored by the speaker. Social settings for this style of speech would include chatting with close friends and interacting in an intimate or family environment or in similar relaxed settings.

Without being aware of it, each speaker of any language has mastered a number of language styles. To illustrate, in a formal setting we might offer coffee to a guest by saying *May I offer you some coffee?* or, perhaps, *Would you care for some coffee?* In an informal setting we might well say *Want some coffee?* or even *Coffee?* This shift in styles is completely unconscious and automatic; indeed, it takes some concentration and hard introspection for us to realize that we each use a formal and an informal style on different occasions. Once again we observe that an individual speaker of a language cannot be said to have a single, unvarying language: we each show internal variation in our language, whether in pronunciation (as with New York City /r/) or in syntactic constructions, as we will soon see.

Some speakers of English, notably self-styled educated speakers, often equate the formal language style with the so-called standard language; the informal style, if discussed at all, is dubbed a form of sloppy speech or even slang, especially in language classes in public schools. But on closer investigation of the actual details of informal language, it turns out that the informal style, far from being merely a sloppy form of language, is governed by rules every bit as precise, logical, and rigorous as the rules governing formal language. (Of course, the informal style also has idiosyncrasies and irregularities—but, then, the formal style does too.) In section 9.2 we will concentrate on some of the rules of the informal style because a detailed study of the syntactic differences between formal and informal language styles reveals a number of important ideas about language variation in general, and about the question of standard versus nonstandard language in particular.

9.2 SOME RULES OF THE GRAMMAR OF INFORMAL STYLE IN ENGLISH

A well-known difference between formal and informal language styles in English (and indeed in many other languages) is that the informal style can be characterized as having a greater amount of abbreviation, shortening, contraction, and deletion. Compare the formal *Would you care for some coffee?* with the informal *Want some coffee?* The formal style is often redundant and verbose, whereas the informal style is brief, to the point, and grammatically streamlined. In this section we will concentrate on two important grammatical features of the informal style, (a) the dropping of the subject of the sentence and (b) the dropping of the auxiliary verb, these being two central features of the *abbreviated* style of informal language.

The abbreviated style we will describe here is based on the language of the authors of this book, and all grammatical judgments will be based on our own speech. We have, however, tested and confirmed our judgments with those of numerous other speakers. Furthermore, it seems clear that the abbreviation processes we describe are quite general within American English. Some readers may find that their own judgments differ from ours at certain points, and this will be entirely natural; indeed there could be no better illustration of the topic of this chapter. The important point is that every speaker of English has an abbreviated style in casual speech. Consequently, readers will be able to judge for themselves how accurate we are in describing the abbreviated style in general.

Tag-controlled Deletion

To begin, let us consider sentences that end in tag questions:

(5) a. You've been hitting the bottle again, *haven't you*?
   b. He wants me to pay the bill, *does he*?
   c. She likes her new house, *does she*?
   d. He's failing his courses, *isn't he*?
   e. They'll steal my money, *will they*?
   f. You're getting pretty excited, *aren't you*?
   g. You're not ready to swim fifty laps, *are you*?

Tag questions—*haven't you, does he,* and so on—reflect at least two important properties of a sentence: (a) the tag contains the auxiliary verb found in the main sentence or (in the case of *do*) the auxiliary appropriate to the main sentence, and (b) the pronoun in the tag agrees with the subject of the sentence. The tag question thus contains, in part, a repetition of some of the information found in the main sentence.

In the informal, abbreviated style, the subject and the auxiliary of the main sentence can in fact be dropped out when these elements are identical with the pronoun and auxiliary of the tag:

(6) a. Been hitting the bottle again, haven't you?
   b. Wants me to pay the bill, does he?
   c. Likes her new house, does she?
   d. Failing his courses, isn't he?
   e. Steal my money, will they?
   f. Getting pretty excited, aren't you?
   g. Not ready to swim fifty laps, are you?

Let us refer to the process illustrated here as Tag-controlled Deletion, described as follows: given a sentence with a tag question, the subject and the auxiliary (if any) of the main sentence may be deleted if they are identical with the pronoun and the auxiliary of the tag question. Tag-controlled Deletion is a rule of the abbreviated style in informal language.

Notice that there is nothing incomplete about the sentences in (6). Even though the subjects and auxiliaries are missing from the main clauses, we can easily *recover* this information from the tag question. (Indeed, no matter how informal the style, we never delete from a sentence information that cannot be recovered in some manner.) No doubt some people would refer to sentences such as those in (6) as instances of sloppy speech. But notice that these sentences are formed by a regular rule. Further, these sentences show another regularity: if the subject is deleted, then the auxiliary must be deleted also. Consider the following examples which, as far as we know, are not possible for any speakers:

(7) a. *Have been hitting the bottle again, haven't you?
    b. *Is failing his courses, isn't he?
    c. *Will steal my money, will you?
    d. *Are getting pretty excited, aren't you?

We can make a firm judgment that these sentences are bad, indicating that there is a rule at work here which is being followed strictly. The abbreviation process is hardly sloppy.

How can we account for the fact that the auxiliary verb may not remain behind if the subject of the sentence has been deleted? Labov's observations on contraction suggest that we consider the fact that subjects and auxiliaries are often contracted. Along with *You have been hitting the bottle* (*have* uncontracted) we have *You've been hitting the bottle* (*have* contracted as *'ve*). If the rule is that the subject of the sentence can be deleted only if the auxiliary verb is contracted onto it, sentences such as those in (7) will never occur: the auxiliary will always be deleted along with the subject, since it is contracted onto the subject and forms a single unit with the subject. To form sentence (8),

(8) Been hitting the bottle again, haven't you?

we do not delete the two separate elements *you* and *have,* but the single contracted element *you've.*

What happens when the auxiliary verb of the sentence cannot be contracted onto the subject? For example, consider what happens when the auxiliary is negative:

(9) You haven't been hitting the bottle again, have you?

Even though the sequence *you have* can be contracted to *you've,* the sequence *you haven't* cannot be contracted to *you'ven't*—no such form exists in English. For a sequence such as *you have not been,* we can either contract the subject and auxiliary, as in *you've not been,* or we can contract the auxiliary and the negative, as in *you haven't been,* but we cannot contract both (*you'ven't*).

It is now striking to notice that negative auxiliaries, unlike positive auxiliaries, can remain behind if the subject is deleted:

(10) a. Haven't been hitting the bottle again, have you?
    b. Aren't getting too excited, are you?
    c. Doesn't like all these rules, does he?
    d. Won't take too much time, will it?

We now have an interesting explanation for the contrast in the following sentences:

(11) a. *Have been hitting the bottle again, haven't you?
    b. Haven't been hitting the bottle again, have you?

Example (11a) is not a possible sentence, but (11b) is. On the surface this might seem at first to indicate randomness, irregularity, or sloppiness in the abbreviated style. But a more careful consideration of the details reveals that *have* in (11a) is a contractible auxiliary whereas *haven't* cannot be contracted. This suggests the following revision in our Tag-controlled Deletion rule:

(12) Tag-controlled Deletion (revised)
    Given a sentence with a tag question, the subject of the main sentence may be deleted, under the following conditions:
    i. the subject must be identical with the pronoun in the tag, and
    ii. if the main sentence contains an auxiliary, it *must* be contracted onto the subject if it *can* be contracted onto the subject.

Since *have* in (11a) can be contracted onto the subject, it must be, before the subject can be deleted. Since this has not happened, (11a) is a bad sentence. However, in (11b) *haven't* cannot in any event be contracted onto the subject; thus condition ii of our rule is not relevant and the subject can be deleted.

Notice that the Tag-controlled Deletion rule, as stated in (12), has some interesting consequences. Auxiliary *will* has a contracted form, *'ll;* compare *It will get on your nerves* and *It'll get on your nerves.* In contrast, however, an auxiliary such as *could* has no such contracted form: from the sentence *It could get on your nerves* we cannot derive another in which *could* is contracted or shortened. Rule (12) now makes a prediction: since *will* can contract with the subject, it should not be possible to leave *will* behind if the subject is deleted; since *could* has no contracted form, it should be possible to leave *could* behind after the subject is deleted. This prediction seems to us to be true: it seems fine to say *Could get on your nerves, couldn't it?* but **Will get on your nerves, won't it?* seems bad. Further, negative *won't* (a contraction of *will* + *not*) differs from positive *will* in that it can remain behind, as in *Won't get on your nerves, will it?* But, then, *won't* has no further contracted form: the sequence *it won't* cannot be contracted in any way. Again, the uncontractible auxiliary can remain after the subject has been deleted.

We have now set up a system wherein the deletion of the subject is dependent upon contraction of the subject with the auxiliary, wherever this is possible. As we saw, in BE the link between contraction and deletion is crucial, and it turns out that this link is just as crucial in the abbreviated style.

We have by no means exhausted the topic of Tag-controlled Deletion. However, the tag cases are only one part of the general deletion processes that affect subject and auxiliary in abbreviated style. We will consider some other cases now.

Deletion in Abbreviated Questions

Deletion of Subject and Auxiliary *do*

Let us continue our study of informal language by noting again sentences of a sort discussed earlier:

(13) You want some coffee?

(14) Want some coffee?

We will refer to questions such as (13) and (14) as abbreviated questions, inasmuch as certain elements are missing or deleted. Such abbreviated questions occur quite commonly in the informal speech style and are one of the more interesting features of that style. In example (14) the subject of the sentence, *you*, has been dropped out. In example (13) another deletion process seems to be at work: the deletion of the auxiliary verb *do*. We propose that a sentence such as (13) derives from a sentence such as (15):

(15) Do you want some coffee?

When the auxiliary verb *do* is dropped out, we get the abbreviated question (13). Do we have further evidence for this hypothesis? After all, for these examples we need not assume that there is a deletion of *do*. We could just as easily say that *You want some coffee?* is the declarative sentence *You want some coffee* with a rising question intonation placed on it. Why should we assume any involvement of the verb *do* in this process?

When we examine a new set of examples drawn from a wider range of data, the *do*-deletion hypothesis is confirmed. Consider the following:

(16) Last night's party go well?

(17) She like her new house?

These are perfectly good examples of the informal speech style that we are discussing; the reader should take care to repeat such sentences (perhaps aloud) to get a feeling for how they would sound in rapid informal speech. The point to notice is the form of the verbs in (16) and (17): they are the uninflected infinitive forms *go* and *like*. Now examine the simple declarative sentences corresponding to these questions:

(18) Last night's party *went* well.

(19) She like*s* her new house.

In these examples the verbs reflect tense (*went*) and number (third-person *likes*). If we placed a question intonation on the declarative sentences in (18) and (19), we would simply get the questions *Last night's party went well?* and *She likes her new house?* We would *not* derive (16) and (17).

The verbs in (16) and (17) show no tense or number agreement. And this is precisely the form such verbs take in questions with *do*:

(20) Did last night's party *go* well?

(21) Does she *like* her new house?

If we now assume that in informal speech the verb *do* (*did, does*) can be dropped out, we will arrive at just the right verb form for abbreviated questions:

(22) *Did* last night's party go well → —— Last night's party go well?

(23) *Does* she like her new house → — She like her new house?

Hence, to account for the verb forms in (16) and (17), we must assume that *do* is deleted from these abbreviated questions and that they are not regular declarative sentences with rising intonation.

Of course, as already noted, along with (16) and (17) we do have such declarative sentences in the form of questions: *Last night's party went well?* and *She likes her new house?* It is interesting that these differ from (16) and (17) not only structurally in terms of the verb forms but also in terms of their use. For example, a declarative sentence with question intonation such as *Last night's party went well?* seems to be used in a conversation only if the situation referred to by the question is not a new topic of conversation for either the speaker or hearer: either it has already been mentioned or the overall *context* of the conversation makes it an obvious topic to bring up. In addition, there is the implication that the questioner expects that the party did go well and is asking for confirmation of that expectation. In other words the question *Last night's party went well?* is used in much the same way as the question *So, I take it that last night's party went well, right?*

In contrast, an abbreviated question such as *Last night's party go well?* could be used even if the situation referred to in the question is an entirely novel topic and hasn't been mentioned in the conversation. This question is a genuine request for information and does not imply that the questioner has any expectations either way about the party. It is striking that such subtle differences in use should be associated with the simple, and apparently trivial, difference between *go* and *went*. Given what we have said, it is interesting to note that (13)—*You want some coffee?*—could be either an abbreviated question from which *do* has been deleted or a simple declarative sentence with question intonation. Although it could be either, our concern here will be with its use as an abbreviated question with missing *do*.

Turning now to a second piece of evidence that auxiliary *do* drops out from questions in the abbreviated style, consider examples such as the following:

(24) Last night's party not go too well?

Let us concentrate here on the negative word, *not*. In a simple declarative sentence we cannot have *not* unless an auxiliary verb appears; that is, it is impossible to have (25). Rather, we get the verb *do* appearing in such examples, as in (26).

(25) *Last night's party not went too well.

(26) Last night's party *did* not go too well.

One question form of (26) is as follows:

(27) *Did* last night's party not go too well?

Given (27), again we see that by dropping out the verb *do* (*did*) we get just the right form for abbreviated questions such as (24). Thus there are at least two good reasons to assume that such informal questions as *You want some coffee?* and *Last night's party go well?* are derived by deleting the auxiliary verb, in this case *do*.

We have seen that two deletion processes are at work to produce abbreviated questions, (a) deletion of *do* and (b) deletion of the second person subject *you*. Hence, from *Do you want some coffee?* we can get *You want some coffee?* and *Want some coffee?* However, note the following restriction, already encountered in Tag-controlled Deletion: even though it is possible to delete the auxiliary verb without deleting the subject *you*, it is never possible to delete the subject *you* without also deleting the auxiliary verb *do*, as (28) illustrates.

(28) Do you want some coffee? →
    *Do want some coffee?

We have derived the impossible form **Do want some coffee?* by deleting the subject *you* but failing to delete the auxiliary verb as well. Again it is important to note that even in the abbreviated informal style precise grammatical rules must be followed.

At this point, what can we add to our account in order to guarantee that whenever the subject *you* is deleted, the auxiliary verb will be deleted too?

It is not only in declarative statements that auxiliary verbs in English undergo processes of reduction and contraction; contraction happens in questions as well. Consider the following facts:

(29) The sequence *do you* in a question is often pronounced *d'you* [dyuw] or *d'ya* [dyə] or *ja* [ǰə]; hence we have *D'you like dancing? D'ya like dancing?* or *Ja like dancing?*

(30) The sequence *did you* in a question is often pronounced *didja* [dIǰə] or *djou* [ǰuw]; hence we have *Didja like the party?* or *Djou like the party?*

These processes of reduction and contraction are common enough with speakers of English that we even have abbreviated exchanges such as

(31) a. Jeet?   (= Didja eat? = Did you eat?)
    b. No, djou?   (= No, did you?)

We can now make use of these contraction facts to explain the nonexistence of *Do want some coffee?* just as we did in the case of Tag-controlled Deletion.

Once again, suppose that we begin with the full question form, *Do you want some coffee?* At this point let us assume that either contraction of the auxiliary verb *do* with the subject *you* can occur, producing *d'you, d'ya,* or *ja*; or deletion of verb *do* can occur.

(32)   Do you want some coffee?
            Contraction: Deletion:

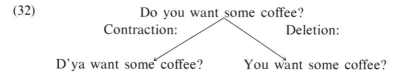

    D'ya want some coffee?   You want some coffee?

Notice that once the verb *do* is contracted with the subject *you* we get the form *d'ya* (or *ja* or *d'you*), which is a single word (inasmuch as contraction is the process of taking independent morphemes and fusing them into a single word unit). If we assume that *you* is deleted only if the auxiliary verb is contracted onto it, it will automatically be the case that whenever the subject is deleted the auxiliary verb is too: they are deleted together as a single contracted unit. Hence, it is not *you* that is deleted but some contracted form such as *d'you, d'ya, ja,* or *djou*. The undesirable case *Do want some coffee?* never arises because *you* won't delete if *do* is not contracted onto it.

At this point we have refined our account sufficiently to posit the following two rules in the grammar of the informal abbreviated style:

(33) Abbreviated Question Rules

Rule 1. To form an abbreviated question, the auxiliary verb (*do*) can be deleted, or else it can be contracted onto the subject *you*.

Rule 2. In forming an abbreviated question, the second-person subject *you* can be deleted as long as an auxiliary verb is contracted onto it.

These rules correctly describe the cases we have dealt with so far.

It is important to add a cautionary note at this point. The kind of process we have been examining involves the deletion of the subject and auxiliary verb (more accurately, contractible verb). This is not to say that other apparent abbreviations do not occur in informal English. For example, in a situation where we might use the abbreviated question *Want some coffee?* we might also be able to ask, simply, *Coffee?* To take another example, suppose we see a friend wearing shoes we haven't seen before. We might point to them and ask, *New?* These single-word utterances are quite common in casual styles and are perfectly appropriate and comprehensible. The point we want to make is that there is no reason whatsoever to suppose that such single-word utterances are derived from whole sentences from which all the other words have been deleted. It is simply that we can use many kinds of short expressions (including single words) as long as the context (linguistic or nonlinguistic) makes it clear what we're talking about.

In sharp contrast, the deletion of subjects and contractible verbs in abbreviated questions is a *systematic syntactic process,* governed by strict conditions. Not just any kind of deletion of subject and verb is possible, even if the context would make the abbreviation perfectly clear. For example, recall the impossible form in (28), **Do want some coffee?* There is nothing incomprehensible about this question: its meaning is clear and nothing in the context of conversation would rule it out. However, the expression has violated a systematic syntactic rule: if the subject has been deleted, the auxiliary must also be deleted. A very important point about syntactic rules is that expressions that violate those rules are ill-formed and cannot be rescued, or made good, by appealing to meaning or to pragmatic context. In other words syntactic rules do not have to have logical or commonsensical reasons for existing: it is a plain and simple fact that when syntactic rules are violated an ill-formed expression often results. For these various reasons, then, we say that an abbreviated question such as *Want some coffee?* is in fact the result of a systematic syntactic deletion, whereas expressions such as *Coffee?* are not.

Does all this mean that speakers actually go through the mental process of deleting subjects and verbs when they use abbreviated questions in real conversations? Are we claiming that a speaker's brain carries out an abbreviation operation just before the speaker utters an abbreviated question? The answer to both questions is no. Rules such as those in (33) are meant to be part of a description of a native speaker's *knowledge* of English. They are based on generalizations and regularities derived from the judgments we have made about the data we have examined. Such judgments are sometimes called grammaticality judgments: according to native speakers, some sentences are judged to be good, other sentences are judged to be bad. Rules such as those in (33), when made precise, predict which sentences (in this case, abbreviated questions) will be well-formed and which ill-formed. If such predictions match the grammaticality judgments of the native speaker, then the rules that make the predictions can be said to characterize, or match, the knowledge of the native speaker. The rules of (33) are in no way intended to be step-by-step directions that a speaker follows in producing sentences. Rules such as (33) may play a role in the actual production of sentences, but as yet we have little idea as to how directly they figure in sentence production. Hence, it is important to keep in mind the distinction between knowledge of language (sometimes referred to as *competence*) and the production of language (sometimes referred to as *performance*).

Recovering Deleted Information

Before elaborating on the rules we have formulated, let us mention two further regularities of abbreviated questions. Consider first examples such as

(34) Don't you want some coffee?

This is the negative question counterpart to examples we have looked at, and it is important to notice that we do not find deletion of the negative auxiliary. Hence, *(You) want some coffee?* is never interpreted as the negative question *Don't you want some coffee?* but only as a positive question, a fact we will return to. (Note that deletion of *you* in these cases is still possible: *Don't want coffee?*)

Second, consider the following contrast in time interpretation:

(35) a. Have any ideas about what to do?
  (= *Do* you have any . . .)
  b. Last night's party go well?
  (= *Did* last night's . . .)

We interpret the first example as present tense and the second as past tense, even though the verbs show no indication of tense. In the second case—*Last night's party go well?*—the expression *last night's* is an overt expression of past time, and so we interpret the question as in the past tense. We can thus infer, or recover, the information that the deleted auxiliary was *did*, as in *Did last night's party go well?* In the first example—*Have any ideas about what to do?*—there are no overt expressions of time or tense whatever; in this unmarked situation it seems that the present tense interpretation is preferred. In this respect the abbreviated questions of the informal style in English resemble very much the general picture in languages such as Chinese and the languages of Southeast Asia. In these languages verbs are never inflected for present or past tense; the interpretation of time and tense depends on overt expressions referring to time, such as *today, yesterday, last night*. Again there is nothing sloppy or incomplete about this system.

Given what we have said, notice that some abbreviated questions are bound to be ambiguous out of context. Consider:

(36) (You) meet any new people?

Here we can infer that either *do* or *did* is the deleted auxiliary verb, as shown by the following cases:

(37) a. How did you like your holiday? Meet any new people? I hope you did. (past tense)
b. When you take a holiday, do you relax? Meet any new people? (present tense)

As we see, both present and past interpretations are consistent with example (36).

The interpretation of tense in abbreviated questions, where the tensed auxiliary has been deleted, illustrates the problem of recovering deleted information. We have seen that with an overt element of past time (such as *last night*) we can infer that a past tense auxiliary has been deleted. But even if the sentence contains merely an indirect expression of past time, we can still infer that a past tense auxiliary has been deleted. For example, if someone asks *Your party go well?* we can infer that the deleted auxiliary is past tense *did* (as in *Did your party go well?*) because this particular question cannot be answered until the party has already happened. Hence pragmatic context plays a crucial role in interpreting such questions (see chapter 12).

To return to example (34), if we deleted *don't* from *Don't you want some coffee?* there would be no indication, or trace, left in the sentence to show that the negative had been present: *Want some coffee?* would not give even an indirect clue to help us infer that *don't*, rather than *do* or *did*, was the form that was deleted. In contrast, recall the cases of Tag-controlled Deletion, where deleted items must be identical with the items that remain in the tag; the tag always indicates what has been deleted. It seems reasonable to say, then, that the sort of deletion we are examining here—stylistic deletion for the abbreviated style— can take place only if the particular sentence or context provides clues that allow us to properly infer what was deleted.

Deletion of *have*

Returning again to rule 1 in (33), let us ask whether *do* is the only auxiliary verb that can be deleted in abbreviated questions. As it turns out, the following data indicate that the auxiliary verb *have* can be deleted as well:

(38) a. (You) seen John lately?
       (= Have you seen John lately?)
     b. (You) picked up your laundry yet?
       (= Have you picked . . .)
     c. She been sick these days?
       (= Has she been . . .)
     d. Your job been getting you down?
       (= Has your job been . . .)

In these cases auxiliary *have* has been deleted and, as before, *you* can be dropped out. Notice once again that even though *have* and *you* can both be deleted, it is impossible to delete *you* without also deleting *have*:

(39) a. *Have seen John lately?
     b. *Have picked up your laundry yet?

In this respect *have* behaves just as *do* does. And just as we found that *do* contracts with *you,* we also find that *have* contracts with you; that is, the sequence *have you* can be pronounced *'vyou* ([vyuw], rhyming with the word *view*), or *'vya* ([vyə]):

(40) a. 'vyou seen John lately?
     b. 'vyou picked up your laundry yet?

Once again, we will assume that *you* can drop out only if it is contracted with an auxiliary, in this case *have*; hence, it is not *you* that deletes, but rather *'vyou*. It will automatically follow that we cannot derive **Have seen John lately?* since *you* can delete only if *have* is contracted onto it and deleted also.

In English there is a distinction between auxiliary *have*, as in *I have seen him,* and main verb *have,* as in *I have some wool.* Stated simply, auxiliary *have* is followed by a verb (*seen*) and main verb *have* is followed by a noun phrase (*some wool*). Now consider the following question, made famous by a nursery rhyme:

(41) Have you any wool?

In our speech (that is, in the speech of the authors) this instance of main verb *have* cannot be deleted to form an abbreviated question:

(42) *You any wool?

Furthermore, in our speech the main verb *have* also lacks a contracted form with *you*. The following type of question is never found:

(43) *'vyou any wool?

This lends further plausibility to the idea that contraction is crucial for deletion: only a contractible verb can be deleted in an abbreviated question. This now leads to a prediction: if for some speakers of English it is possible to contract main verb *have,* as in (43), then for those speakers it should also be possible to delete main verb *have*, as in (42).

More on Contractible Auxiliaries (optional section)

The hypothesis that there is a relation between contraction and deletion gets further support when we turn our attention to the past tense form of auxiliary *have,* namely, *had*. Recall that past tense *did* can delete (*Last night's party go well?*). It turns out, however, that past tense *had* cannot. To see this, consider examples such as:

(44) a. Had you seen John back in those days?
     b. Had you done your own laundry back in those days?
     c. Had she been sick back in those days?
     d. Had your job been getting you down back in those days?

A phrase such as *back in those days* is typically used with past tense *had* but never with present tense *have*:

(45) *Have you seen John back in those days?

This phrase, then, would allow us to recover *had* if we were to delete it from the questions of (44), but in our speech any such deletion produces bad results:

(46) a. *Seen John back in those days?
     b. *Done your own laundry back in those days?
     c. *She been sick back in those days?
     d. *Your job been getting you down back in those days?

We cannot delete past tense *had,* even though we can delete past tense *did*.

There is an interesting difference between *had* and *did*: whereas *did* has two contracted forms with *you* (*didja* and *djou*), *had* has only one, namely *hadja* (as in *Hadja left the door open?*); it has no form corresponding to *djou*. The difference between the two contracted forms of *did* is the following: in *didja* the auxiliary *did* is preserved and the subject *you* reduces and contracts onto it; in *djou,* on the other hand, the subject *you* is preserved and the auxiliary *did* reduces and contracts onto the subject (as /ǰ/). It turns out that contractions of the *didja* sort—where the auxiliary is not reduced—can never be deleted. For example, we can never delete the forms *don'tcha* (recall example (34)), *won'tcha, can'tcha, couldja, wouldja, shouldja, willya*; nor can we delete *hadja*, as the examples in (46) show. In other words only when the auxiliary itself reduces and contracts onto the subject can the contracted combination be deleted; the combination cannot be deleted if the subject reduces and contracts onto the auxiliary. This leads us to infer that the form *didja* is in fact not deletable; but since the combination *did* + *you* has the other contracted form, *djou,* where *did* is reduced, we can assume that it is *djou* that deletes in abbreviated questions.

Now what about in questions where the subject is not *you,* such as *Had she been sick back in those days?* What is to prevent *had* from deleting, wrongly, in this case? The answer is that we must define a contractible auxiliary as one that can contract in at least some circumstances, though not necessarily all circumstances. Since the verb *had* never has a contracted form, even with the subject *you*—that is, no contracted form where *had* itself reduces and contracts—it can never be deleted. Compare this with the verb *did* in a question such as *Did last night's party go well?* Even though *did* cannot contract onto *last night's* in this particular case, there is, nonetheless, another type of sentence in which that auxiliary does contract, namely when the subject is *you* (as in *djou*). So we say that *did* is contractible since there is at least *one* environment where it can contract. We will therefore revise rule 1 as follows:

(47) Rule 1 (revised). To form an abbreviated question, the auxiliary verb can be deleted *if it is a contractible auxiliary*; or else it can be contracted onto the subject *you*.

Deletion of *be*

Continuing our exploration into which auxiliary verbs can be dropped in abbreviated questions, we find the following data indicating that the verb *be* can be deleted:

(48) a. (You) running a fever?
         (= Are you running . . .)
     b. (You) finally rich now?
         (= Are you finally rich . . .)
     c. Your car in the garage?
         (= Is your car . . .)
     d. Satisfied?
         (= Are you satisfied?)
     e. John a drug addict or something?
         (= Is John a drug addict . . .)
     f. (You) gonna leave soon?
         (= Are you going to leave soon?)
     g. (You) sposta do that?
         (= Are you supposed to . . .)

Our data show that deletion of auxiliary *be* and the subject *you* is possible, and by now it should not be surprising that once again the subject *you* cannot be deleted unless the auxiliary verb is deleted too:

(49) a. *Are running a fever?
     b. *Are finally rich now?

And, once again, the verb in question is a contractible verb. For example, the various forms of *be* can contract with various subjects:

(50) am I   =   'my [may]
     are you   =   'ryou [əryúw]
     is he   =   's he [ziy]
     is she   =   's she [žšiy]
     is it   =   's it [zIt]
     is John   =   's John [zǰan]
     are we   =   'r we [ərwíy]
     are they   =   'r they [ərðéy]

Am shortens and contracts as /m/, *are* contracts as /r/, and *is* as /z/, showing that *be* is a contractible verb and hence can delete. Since the subject *you* gets deleted only if *be* is contracted onto it, such ungrammatical cases as *Are running a fever?* can never arise. So far, our account of the verb *be* is completely parallel to our account of *do* and *have*.

There are some interesting differences, however. Recall the distinction between auxiliary *have* and main verb *have*. A similar distinction holds for the verb *be*:

(51) a. Auxiliary *be*:   You *are* running a fever.
    b. Main verb *be*:   The car *is* in the garage.
                                  John *is* a drug addict.

Stated simply, auxiliary *be* is followed by a verb, whereas main verb *be* is followed by a nonverb category: noun phrase, prepositional phrase, and so on. But main verb *be*—unlike main verb *have*—can be deleted in abbreviated questions, so we have cases such as *Your car in the garage?* and *John a drug addict?* This difference between main verb *have* and main verb *be* is matched by another difference between them: main verb *be* has contracted forms (those listed in (50)) whereas main verb *have* does not (recall (43)). Thus what appears on the surface to be an irregularity—main verb *be* can delete, but main verb *have* cannot— turns out to be a consequence of a regular principle governing the formation of abbreviated questions.

To complete our account of the verb *be,* let us ask whether *be* can delete in the past tense as well as the present tense. We have reported that in our speech (that is, in the speech of the authors) *do* can delete in the past tense (*did*) but *have* in the past tense (*had*) cannot delete. What about *be*? Readers are invited to judge for themselves how the following sentences compare:

(52) a. (You) going to school today?
       (= Are you . . .)
    b. (You) going to school back in those days?
       (= Were you . . .)

(53) a. John at home today?   (= Is John at home . . .)
    b. John at home yesterday?   (= Was John at home . . .)

In the judgment of the authors, the past tense forms are not as good as the present tense forms. Though it seems perfectly natural in the informal style to have an abbreviated question such as *You going to school today?* there is something odd about the question *You going to school back in those days?* On the basis of such judgments, we would conclude that the past tense of *be* is not deletable in these questions. But once again, we note the interesting correlation that, for us, the past tense forms of *be* do not have a contracted form. That is, in the speech of the authors, *were you* has no contracted form, nor does a sequence such as *was John*. For example, *were you* does not abbreviate to *'ryou* (which is the contraction of *are + you*), and *was John* does not abbreviate to *zJohn* (which is the contraction of *is + John*). Since *be* cannot contract in these cases, it follows that it cannot delete.

Given the hypothesis we have set up, we can make a clear prediction about abbreviated questions of the sort just cited: If there are speakers of English for whom the past tense of *be* does have a contracted form, then those speakers should be able to delete those forms. Imagine a speaker for whom the sequence *were you* can be pronounced *'ryou:*

(54) 'Ryou sick yesterday?   (= Were you sick . . .)

We predict that for such speakers it should be possible to delete *you*, which carries along the contracted verb *were*:

(55) Sick yesterday?

In other words our claim is that, for all speakers, in this abbreviated style the deletion of a verb will always be dependent on the contractibility of that verb. If speakers differ as to whether they can contract certain verbs, then they will also differ as to whether they can delete those verbs. A true problem for our theory (a counterexample) would be a case in which certain speakers of English could freely contract a certain verb in abbreviated questions but could not delete that verb. Although at the moment we know of no such cases, it is important to keep in mind how our theory can be tested by appropriate evidence.

We are now in a position to summarize our discussion of which verbs are affected in the formation of abbreviated questions. One can delete the contractible forms of the verbs *do, have,* and *be,* and these are the only verbs that can delete. Other auxiliary verbs may not. Consider the class of *modal* verbs:

$$
(56) \quad \left\{ \begin{array}{l} \text{Will} \\ \text{Must} \\ \text{Would} \\ \text{Can} \\ \text{Could} \\ \text{Should} \\ \text{etc.} \end{array} \right\} \quad \text{you leave tomorrow?}
$$

We generally cannot delete any of these verbs. For example, if we are asked *You leave tomorrow?* we interpret this strictly as *Do you leave tomorrow?* and never as *Will you leave tomorrow?* Conversely, if we were able to delete a verb such as *will,* we would expect to delete it in a question such as *Will you be leaving tomorrow?* But deleting *will* would produce the unacceptable question **You be leaving tomorrow?* Notice further that these modal verbs do not have contracted forms of the right sort—for example, a sequence such as *will you* has no contracted form **lyou.* (Recall that though we have the contracted forms *willya, couldja, shouldja,* and so on, in these forms the modal verb does not reduce and contract; it is the subject that does.) Finally, the modal verbs carry important information that would probably not be recoverable if they were deleted. It seems that in general only *do, have,* and *be* can delete in abbreviated questions. We will add only one qualification. The modal *would* can be deleted from questions that are not requests for information but are used as conventional offers, questions like *Like a drink?* from *Would you like a drink?* Such abbreviated questions are the only ones we are aware of that allow deletion of a modal verb.

Deletion of Subjects Other than *You* (optional section)
Having specified which auxiliary verbs can delete, let us ask whether *you* is the only subject that can delete. The answer, as far as we can determine, is that *you* is the only subject that can delete *systematically* in these abbreviated questions. This answer is not surprising, given that other important syntactic constructions in English involve systematic deletion of *you:*

(57) a. Imperatives
        Leave the room! (Understood: *You* leave . . .)
    b. Why (not)
        Why not study? (Understood: Why don't *you* . . .)
        Why study? (Understood: Why should *you* . . .)

Further, even when the context would make it absolutely clear what the missing subject was, it is very difficult to get a case of a non-second person understood subject. For example, suppose that we are discussing our friend John, and he is clearly the topic of our conversation. Imagine the dialogue:

(58) A: John is brilliant and can solve virtually any problem.
    B: Have any ideas about how to solve our problems?

Even though John is clearly the central topic and it would be perfectly natural to interpret John as the referent of the missing subject, we still interpret B's question in this dialogue as meaning, *Do you have any ideas . . . ?* There is nothing sloppy about the interpretation here. Thus, given that other constructions in English involve deletion of *you* specifically (see (57)) and that even a strongly biased context does not allow a second person interpretation of (58B), we conclude that the rule of subject-dropping for abbreviated questions is specific to *you* (but see exercise 9).

In this regard there is a significant difference between deletion in abbreviated questions and Tag-controlled Deletion. When a tag is present, subjects other than second person *you* can be deleted, as in the example *Wants me to pay the bill, does he?* where the deleted subject is third person *he*. This difference follows from the general nature of the two deletion processes. Tag-controlled Deletion is *deletion under identity:* we can delete any subject and any auxiliary if they are identical with the auxiliary and pronoun in the tag. Since identity is involved, the deletion is recoverable. On the other hand, the deletion in abbreviated questions involves no identity condition: we delete the specific items *do, have,* and *be* (and no others) and the specific subject *you*. It is not required that these items be identical with any other items in the sentence. However, since the deletion rules refer to specific verbs and to a specific subject, the deletion in abbreviated questions is recoverable.

Deletion in Declarative Sentences

So far, we have examined deletion processes only in questions. For simple declarative statements (without tag questions) the deletion possibilities are quite different from those in questions.

For example, in declarative statements the auxiliary *do* appears only when the sentences are negative or emphatic:

(59) a. I don't know that man.
   b. You DO know that man.

Neither emphatic nor negative *do* can delete, under any circumstances. And unemphatic positive *do* never appears: the unemphatic positive sentence is *I know that man,* with no overt auxiliary. Hence the question of the deletion of auxiliary *do* in statements is simply irrelevant.

Deletion of auxiliary *have* in declarative statements is possible, although some speakers have unclear judgments about *have*. The situation is variable in our own speech. We find the following deletions of *have* quite natural when *have* is followed by *been*:

(60) a. I been sick lately.
        (= I have been . . .)
    b. You sure been doin' good work these days.
        (= You sure have been . . .)

However, we find the following cases unacceptable:

(61) a. *I gone there many times.
        (= I have gone . . .)
    b. *I seen that film.
        (= I have seen . . .)

Some dialects of American English accept sentences such as those in (61). Hence, even though in questions *have* can delete quite generally (for all dialects), in declarative statements the deletion of *have* is more complicated, being variable for speakers in a single dialect and variable across different dialects.

What about the verb *be*? The answer is that for our own style of speech, deletion of *be* in statements is generally not possible (but see exercises for some examples of *be*-deletion in statements). We do not have sentences such as *He a doctor, Your car in the garage, You running a fever,* and so on, in contrast with the pattern cited for Black English.

We can summarize the results for our own speech as follows:

(62)	In Questions	In Statements
	Do: can delete	(irrelevant)
	Have: can delete	can delete, but variable
	Be: can delete	generally cannot delete

It is striking to realize, from (62), that the differences between Black English and other dialects and styles of American English are not really as great as some people think. Black English has the property of deleting forms of the verb *be*; the same deletion occurs in the informal abbreviated style—except that it is limited to questions. Hence, BE has simply generalized the process of *be*-deletion so that it occurs systematically in statements as well as questions. And the data we have been able to study indicate that BE has a more general deletion of *have* as well. It now becomes clear that the deletion properties of BE are hardly strange, unusual, or illogical. On the contrary, they are general exten-sions of widespread deletion processes in the abbreviated informal style of all speakers of American English.

Where Phonology, Morphology, Syntax, and Pragmatic Context Meet

The rules for the abbreviated informal style that we have discussed here not only give us some insight into the nature of language variation; they provide us with a concrete example of how different subfields of linguistics are integrated and unified at a broader level. The rules for the abbreviated style have to make reference to *phonological* informa-tion: the syntactic deletion process is dependent on the phonological process of contraction. *Morphological* information also plays a crucial role, since only certain kinds of morphemes can be (phonologically) contracted and (syntactically) deleted. For example, only contractible verbs can delete, other types of verbs may not; and the information about the part of speech, as well as the information about specific words are, both, types of morphological information. The deletion process itself is a *syntactic* process, having to do with the way sen-tences are formed in the abbreviated style. Finally, recall that in order to understand sentences that have undergone deletion, we have to be able to infer, or recover, the missing information. The pragmatic con-text in which the abbreviated sentences are actually used plays a crucial role in this inference process (recall examples such as (35)–(37), and hence *pragmatic* information is necessary in our overall account of the abbreviated style. In other words linguistic explanations are rarely purely syntactic, or purely morphological, or based on any single component of the grammar. More often than not, to account for linguistic phenomena we require diverse kinds of information from different components of a grammar. Even though various subfields of linguistics are presented in separate chapters in part II of this book— reflecting the need to break down the broad questions about language into more manageable questions—the reader should not forget that these areas are ultimately integrated when we seek to give complete explanations for linguistic phenomena.

Returning to the concerns of this chapter, we sum up by saying that dialects are related to other dialects and styles are related to other styles by *systematic rules*. In general, we can characterize the differences between various dialects and styles in terms of rules: certain dialects contain rules not found in other dialects, and certain styles are governed by rules not found in other styles. It is never the case that a dialect, or a style, has no rules, or "breaks the rules," or is sloppy. At the very most we can say only that one dialect or style has different rules from another. And those rules can always be discovered through careful study of the details of each dialect or style. For these reasons our brief study in this chapter should make it clear that labeling Standard English as a superior dialect, or formal English as a superior style, can only be the result of language prejudice, not of scientific fact.

Exercises

1. If you are acquainted with a regional, social, or ethnic dialect, list as many features as you can that distinguish this dialect from the so-called standard language. What are some significant differences in pronunciation, vocabulary words, and syntax?

*2. The following types of sentences (originally made famous by *Mad Magazine*) are frequently used in the informal style of English:
a. What, me worry?
b. What, John get a job? (Fat chance!)
c. My boss give me a raise? (Are you joking?)
d. Him wear a tuxedo? (He doesn't even own a clean shirt!)
How would you express each of these sentences in formal English? Do these informal sentences express any feeling or idea that is not expressed in the formal style?

*3. Several acquaintances who were raised in Brooklyn inform us that the following sentences are good Brooklyn slang:
a. Let's you and him fight—how about it?
b. Let's you guys shut up, all right?
How does this informal use of *let's* differ from the use in formal English?

*4. In the informal style it is quite common to hear sentences such as the following:
a. There's three cars in the garage.
b. There's a lot of problems with this car.
c. There's many ways to do this.
How would these sentences be expressed in formal English, and how do the formal and informal styles differ in the use of *there's*?

*5. Sports announcers on TV and radio use a style of English that is both colorful and unique. Listen to a variety of sports broadcasts, paying careful attention to the language, and try to characterize as precisely as you can how this language differs from the formal style or standard language. To get started, you might consider the following sample of sportscaster language: "Smith on third. Jones at bat. Mursky winding up for the pitch." (This language should be reminiscent of the informal style we studied in this chapter.) Don't forget to include differences (if any) in pronunciation and vocabulary words, as well as syntax.

*6. In this chapter we considered abbreviated questions of one type, namely, questions without question words (or Wh-words) such as *who, what, where,* etc. The following sets of sentences illustrate the differences between Wh-questions and the abbreviated questions we examined:

(i) a. Where have you been lately?
   b. Where've you been lately?
   c. *Where've been lately?
   d. Where ya been lately?
   e. *Where been lately?
(ii) a. Who are you taking to the prom?
   b. Who're you taking to the prom?
   c. *Who're taking to the prom?
   d. Who ya takin' to the prom?
   e. *Who takin' to the prom?
(iii) a. What do you want to do?
   b. Whattaya wanna do?
   c. *Whatta wanna do?
   d. Whatcha wanna do?
   e. *What want to do?

How do these abbreviated Wh-questions differ from the abbreviated questions studied in the chapter? That is, what are the differences in the rules for forming the two types of abbreviated questions? In answering, pay careful attention to (a) the fact that certain of the examples here are ungrammatical, and (b) the way contraction works in these cases.

*7. It is not quite true to say that *be* can never be deleted in declarative statements in the informal speech style of the authors, for the following sentences are good:
a. Odd that Mary never showed up.
b. Good thing you fixed your engine.
c. Too bad (that) she had to leave town so soon.
d. Amazing that he didn't spot that error.
What has been deleted from these sentences? Is this deletion general?

8. The following is the text of a letter to the editor of the (Tucson) *Arizona Daily Star,* written by a school principal:

To the editor:
   Your article in the Star June 1 left many of us smarting. The article implied that students cannot write because teachers and principals cannot write.
   Lest any more coprophagous critics take us to task, I have only one comment: Each day I read the Star, I find that it also contains spelling errors, poor syntax, excessive use of cliches, run-on sentences, and errors in punctuation. If reporters cain't rite, what do we do, jus' look at the pitchers?
a. Why does the writer include the final sentence of this letter? In what way does it reveal a language prejudice on the part of the writer?

b. In what way does the writer imply that formal English is correct but a dialect is incorrect? How would you correct this misconception?

c. Is the writer any less crude or vulgar for using the formal (and obscure) word *coprophagous* rather than an informal synonym of that word?

d. If students are said to write poorly, does this mean that their language is deficient? Is there any such thing as a deficient dialect?

*9. Questions typically come from a first-person speaker and are addressed to a second-person hearer. Can you relate this *use* of questions to the fact that *you* is deleted from abbreviated questions? Can *any* subject be deleted from abbreviated questions as long as use and context make the deletion recoverable?

References

Bailey, R. W., and J. L. Robinson, eds. (1973) *Varieties of Present-Day English,* Macmillan, New York.

Burling, R. (1973) *English in Black and White,* Holt, Rinehart & Winston, New York.

Dillard, J. L. (1972) *Black English: Its History and Usage in the United States,* Random House, New York.

Giglioli, P. O., ed. (1972) *Language and Social Context,* Penguin Books, Baltimore.

Glissmeyer, G. (1973) "Some characteristics of English in Hawaii," in Bailey and Robinson, *Varieties of Present-Day English.*

Hymes, D., ed. (1964) *Language in Culture and Society,* Harper & Row, New York.

Labov, W. (1966) *The Social Stratification of English in New York City,* Center for Applied Linguistics, Washington, D.C.

——— (1969a) "Contraction, deletion, and inherent variability of the English copula," *Language* 45, no. 4.

——— (1969b) "The logic of nonstandard English," in *Report of the Twentieth Annual Round Table Meeting on Linguistics and Language,* Georgetown University Press, Washington, D.C. Reprinted in Bailey and Robinson, *Varieties of Present-Day English*; and Giglioli, *Language and Social Context.*

——— (1972) "The social stratification of (r) in New York City department stores," in *Sociolinguistic Patterns,* University of Pennsylvania Press, Philadelphia.

——— (1973) "Some features of the English of Black Americans," in Bailey and Robinson, *Varieties of Present-Day English.*

Williams, F., ed. (1970) *Language and Poverty,* Markham, Chicago.

Chapter Ten

LANGUAGE CHANGE

10.1 SOME GENERAL QUESTIONS ABOUT LANGUAGE CHANGE

We will begin our study of language change by inviting the reader to consider the similarities and differences in the following lists of words from three different languages. Before reading on, try to discover as many correspondences as you can between the lists:

(1) | Language A | Language B | Language C |
|---|---|---|
| uno | łáá'ii | éka |
| dos | naaki | dvá |
| tres | táá' | trí |
| cuatro | dį́į' | catúr |
| cinco | ashdla' | páñca |
| seis | hastą́ą́ | ṣaṣ |
| siete | tsosts'id | saptá |
| ocho | tseebíí | aṣṭá |
| nueve | náhást'éí | náva |
| diez | neeznáá | dáça |

Some readers might know (or will be able to guess) that for each of the languages A–C words for the numbers one through ten are given. With a little study the reader will also notice that languages A and C have some phonological similarities: in seven instances out of ten, words for the same number begin with the same (or a similar) consonant; in both languages the words for *one* and *eight* are the only ones that begin with vowels; in nine cases the two words have the same number of syllables, and so forth. One might therefore surmise that languages A and C (Spanish and Sanskrit, respectively) are related in some way, but neither of these two is related to language B (Navajo). This brief exercise raises the central questions to be dealt with in this chapter: (a) How do we establish with a reasonable degree of certainty that two or more languages are related? (b) If languages are related but no longer the same in grammar and vocabulary, how and why did they change? (c) Does language change bring improvement or decay in expressive ability? In attempting to present some answers for these questions, we will be examining some of the important aspects of historical linguistics.

How Do Languages Change?

The central property of human languages that we have been developing, and will continue to develop, throughout part II is their rule-governed nature. Just as language itself is rule-governed, so too language change is rule-governed, and major changes in language can be viewed as *alterations in the set of rules of the grammars between generations of speakers of that language*. Given that a change has occurred between two generations, we find, in comparing the rules of the two successive grammars, that over time rules can be added, lost, or changed in structure. Language change is thus another source of evidence for our contention that language behavior is governed by abstract rules. We will illustrate this with some typical changes that occurred between Old and Modern English.

Changes between Old and Modern English

The English language has undergone extensive changes between the Old and Modern English period, although speakers of Modern English are still able to recognize Old English as a relative of Modern English. An example will illustrate this point:

(2) a. Old English: In þām tūne wǣron þæt hūs and
                             þæt būr þæs eorles.
   b. Modern English: In the town were the house and
                             the chamber of the chief.

In (2b), the word-for-word Modern English translation of (2a), many of the words show a strong similarity to the Old English words. Nevertheless, subsequent grammatical and vocabulary changes have made Old English no longer understandable to the speaker of Modern English.

Although the changes from Old to Modern English were continuous and gradual, linguists traditionally distinguish three major periods in the development of Modern English: the Old English period (fifth to eleventh centuries), the Middle English period (eleventh to fifteenth centuries), and Modern English (fifteenth century to the present). The changes between Old and Middle English were more extensive than the changes between Middle and Modern English for two basic reasons. First, the Norman invasion of England in the eleventh century brought the French language to England, and the vocabulary of English was greatly enriched through the acquisition of French (and therefore Greek and Latin) vocabulary items. Second, the loss of inflectional endings (suffixes indicating number, gender, and case on nouns, and number and person on verbs) had many effects on the grammar of Late Old English. For example, it is often said that because nouns lost the subject- and object-marking suffixes, word order came to play a much more important role in the later language in distinguishing subjects from objects.

Scholars studying the history of the English language are fortunate in that there exists a literary tradition spanning more than 1400 years, making it possible to trace many of the changes English has undergone during this period. These changes are representative of the types of changes all languages undergo. In our discussion of these changes we will concentrate on the four major components of a language we have studied so far: the vocabulary words (or *lexicon*), *phonology, morphology,* and *syntax.* Each of these four components can undergo the major types of changes mentioned earlier: addition, loss, and change in structure. To illustrate *how* languages change in these ways, we will discuss twelve representative changes that occurred between Old and Modern English.

Lexical Change

Addition
In the period since Old English (OE) was spoken, a large number of words have been added to the English language. Some recent additions are words such as *automobile, laser,* and *finalize,* and the reader will be able to think of many more examples. In chapter 7 we discussed in greater detail the addition of new words to the English language.

Loss

Conversely, a large number of words have been lost since the Old English period, but a surprising number of the lost words are still present in compound words. One example is *were*, which once meant "man." (This word is historically related to the Latin word *vir*, also meaning "man," which persists in our borrowed Latinate vocabulary in words such as *virile*.) The form *were*, even though lost as an independent word, still exists in *werewolf*, which used to mean "man-wolf."

Change

Many examples of meaning change in words have already been discussed in chapter 7, which focused on narrowing, broadening, and metaphorical extension of meaning. One example of semantic narrowing between Old and Modern English can be found in the word *hound* (OE *hund*), which once referred to any kind of dog, whereas in Modern English the meaning has been narrowed to a particular breed. The word *dog* (OE *docga*), on the other hand, in Old English referred to a particular type of dog; its meaning now has been broadened to include any dog.

Phonological Change

Rule Addition

There have been many phonological changes between Old and Modern English. For example, the Flap and Glottal Stop rules discussed in chapter 6 have been added to American English relatively recently. Of course, rules that are added to a language can later be lost as living rules, and only certain effects of the rules remain. An important set of extensive sound changes affecting the long (tense) vowels occurred in the Middle English period. This set of changes, known as the Great Vowel Shift, is the cause of one of the major discrepancies between the spelling of Modern English and its current pronunciation. The effects of the changes are shown in figure 10.1. (The arrows indicate the direction of the changes.)

We can represent the long (or tense) mid vowels of Middle English by /ē/ and /ō/ (where the bars over the vowels indicate length). Both were raised and diphthongized to yield the current high vowels /iy/ and /uw/, respectively. The earlier pronunciation of these long mid vowels is still reflected in the spelling of words such as *feet* (once pronounced

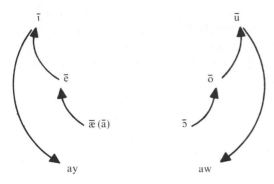

Figure 10.1
The Great Vowel Shift

/fēt/, now pronounced /fiyt/) and *mood* (once pronounced /mōd/, now pronounced /muwd/). The high vowels of Middle English, in turn, became diphthongs, the first part of the vowel moving down to become a low vowel. As part of the Great Vowel Shift, /ī/ became /ay/ and /ū/ became /aw/. Again the current orthography reflects the former pronunciation in spellings such as *five* (once pronounced /fīv/, now pronounced /fayv/). Note also the spelling of OE *tūne* for *town* in (2); the old spelling shows the pronunciation before the diphthong was created.

Two of the long low vowels, /æ/ and /ɔ/, were also raised to yield a new set of mid vowels, /ey/ and /ow/, respectively. Thus, Modern English *mate* /meyt/ was formerly pronounced as /mæt/, and the word *goat* /gowt/ was formerly pronounced as /gɔt/. The addition of these phonological rules caused a significant change in the pronunciation of English words, and even though the Vowel Shift has now been lost from Modern English as a purely phonological rule, its effects are still revealed in the discrepancy between the pronunciation of Modern English and its spelling system.

Rule Loss

English at one time had a rule called *i*-mutation (or *i*-umlaut) which turned back vowels into front vowels when they were followed by an /i/ or /y/ in the next syllable. For example, in a certain class of nouns in Old English the plural was formed not by adding -*s*, but rather by adding -*i*. Thus, the plural of *gōs* ("goose") was *gōsi* ("geese"). Later in time the *i*-ending of the plural conditioned the change of *gōsi* to *gǣsi* when the *i*-mutation rule applied. The /œ/ phoneme is a combination of the /o/ and /e/ phonemes; it is a front vowel like /e/ but has lip rounding like /o/. Hence, the effect of the *i*-mutation rule was to cause back vowels to move forward, but the newly fronted vowels kept the rounding they had when they were back vowels. Still later in time, rounding was lost, and the plural of *gōs* became *gēs(e)*. When *gōs* and *gēs* finally underwent the Great Vowel Shift, the current pronunciations of /guws/ (*goose*) and /giys/ (*geese*) resulted. Thus the *i*-mutation rule is an example of a rule that was present in Old English but has dropped out of the language; thanks to the Vowel Shift even the effects of *i*-mutation have become obscured.

Rule Change

In Old English, constrictives became voiced when they occurred between vowels; that is, /f/ → /v/, /θ/ → /ð/, /s/ → /z/. The rule causing this voicing is no longer present in Modern English, though its effects can still be observed in pairs such as singular *wife* /wayf/ and plural *wives* /wayvz/. This change of the stem in the plural is still the result of a rule, but the rule is different from its Old English counterpart. In Old English the rule was *phonologically conditioned:* it applied whenever constrictives occurred between vowels. In contrast, the alternation between voiced and voiceless constrictives in Modern English is not phonologically conditioned but *morphologically conditioned:* the voicing rule applies only to certain morphemes and not others. Thus a particular (and exceptional) class of nouns must undergo voicing of the final voiceless constrictive when used in the plural: *wife–wives, knife–knives, hoof–hooves, loaf–loaves.* Other nouns do not undergo the process: the plural of *proof,* which came into the language during the Middle English period, is *proofs* not *prooves.* The *v*-plural provides a clue to the history of a word—a clue that the word comes from Old English rather than having been added later, after the constrictive voicing rule had changed from a phonologically conditioned rule to a morphologically conditioned one. Thus, whereas *proof* is of French origin, *wife* is an Anglo-Saxon word.

Morphological Change

Rule Addition

The *-able* rule discussed in chapter 7 is an example of a rule that has been added to English since the Old English period. With the Norman invasion of England in 1066 came a great influx of French words into the English language. From these words English speakers were able to extract a rule that is still productive in current English. Words such as *doable* and *washable* have been formed by adding *-able* to the Germanic roots *do* and *wash*.

Rule Loss

An example of a morphological rule that has been lost is a causative verb formation rule of Old English. At one time causative verbs could be formed by adding the suffix *-yan* to adjectives. The verb *redden* meaning "to cause to become, or make, red," is a carry-over from the time when the causative verb formation rule was present in English: the final *-en* of *redden* is a residue of the earlier *-yan* causative suffix. However, the rule adding a suffix like *-en* to form new verbs has been lost, and we can no longer form new causative verbs such as **greenen* "to make green," or **bluen* "to make blue."

Rule Change

New nouns could be formed in Old English by adding *-ing* not only to verbs, as in Modern English (*sing+ing = singing*), but also to a large class of nouns. For example, the word *viking* was formed by adding *ing* to the noun *wic,* meaning "bay." (Why might the word for "bay" be used to describe the Vikings?) It turns out that the *ing* suffix can still be added to a highly restricted class of nouns and carries the meaning "material used for," as in nouns such as *roofing, carpeting,* and *flooring.* Thus the rule for creating new nouns with the *-ing* suffix has changed by becoming more restricted in application, in that a much smaller class of nouns can have an *-ing* attached.

Syntactic Change

Rule Addition

A syntactic rule that has been added since the Old English period is the Particle Movement rule discussed in chapter 8. Sentence pairs of the type *John threw out the fish* and *John threw the fish out* did not occur in Old English.

Rule Loss

An example of a syntactic rule that has been lost is the morphosyntactic rule of adjective agreement. At one time adjectives had inflectional endings and had to agree with the head noun in case, number, and gender. This rule is no longer found in English, since for the most part inflectional endings have been lost. A few relic expressions still in the language are carry-overs from the time when adjectives had endings. In the expression *olden days* the *-en* on *old* is a former adjective ending.

Rule Change

The Question Rule has changed slightly since the Old English period. The current form of the rule requires that the first auxiliary verb be moved to the left of the subject in order to form a yes/no question. In Old English the rule applied to the first *verb*, whether auxiliary or not. The effects of this OE rule can be illustrated with Modern English words: the OE question form for *John eats apples* was *Eats John apples?* Of course, Modern English requires the helping verb *do* in this case, to yield *Does John eat apples?*

These examples illustrate that language change is for the most part *rule change*. We have discussed a representative sample of the types of changes Old English underwent as it evolved into Modern English, kinds of changes that are typical in the history of the world's languages. In section 10.2 we will explore the question of why languages change and the mechanisms by which change spreads throughout a group of speakers.

10.2 WHY LANGUAGES CHANGE AND HOW LANGUAGE CHANGE SPREADS

The reader may be surprised to discover that linguists currently have little idea what causes language change. For purposes of discussion we can divide the topic of language change into two subtopics: internal change and external change. By internal change we mean spontaneous and individual change in a language on the part of a single speaker. External change may be defined as the transmission of changes among speakers in a linguistic community. The transmission of a change (external change) is somewhat better understood than the original cause of the change (internal change).

Internal Change

One source of internal change is grammar simplification. We have already discussed the small class of exceptional nouns in which the final voiceless constrictive must be voiced in the plural form (as in *leaf* and *leaves*). This change to a voiced spirant is an exception to the regular plural rule of English and represents a complication of the rule (see exercise E, chapter 6, section 6.3). In fact, many speakers of English are now regularizing these forms and use plurals such as *dwarfs* instead of *dwarves*. Furthermore, with words derived from the exceptional nouns, speakers will form the plural according to the regular rule if the derived word differs significantly in meaning. For example, the National Hockey League team located in Toronto is known as the Toronto Mapleleafs (not *Mapleleaves). The pressure to regularize is strong, and a great deal of the regularization of a language is probably carried out in language acquisition by children. But not all of it. Adults may also be a source of change, although very little is known at the present time about the possible contribution of adults (except in external change, discussed in the next section). At the present time we simply do not know why a rule such as the Flap Rule, or the Glottal Stop Rule, would be added to the grammar of English in the first place. But once a small group of speakers has changed their grammar, the change can spread to other speakers.

External Change

If a change begins in one area, it is possible to follow its progress, through time, as it moves wavelike through a community of speakers. Although some areas tend to be more active in innovating than others, changes will often spread in an overlapping fashion. For example, Joos (1942) reports a difference in the pronunciation of the word *typewriter* in two dialects of Canadian English: /tʌyprayDər/ and /tʌyprʌyDər/. The difference can be explained in terms of the interaction of two rules, the Flap Rule discussed in chapter 6 and the Vowel Centering rule found in problem A of the exercises for chapter 6, section 6.3. Vowel Centering applies in some dialects of American English: the diphthongs /ay/ and /aw/ become /ʌy/ and /ʌw/ before voiceless consonants. The pronunciation of the word *typewriter* in the two Canadian dialects can be accounted for by an interesting interaction of the following two rules:

(3) a. Flap Rule: $\begin{bmatrix} t \\ d \end{bmatrix} \rightarrow [D] \ / \ \acute{V}\text{——}V$

b. Vowel Centering: $\begin{bmatrix} ay \\ aw \end{bmatrix} \rightarrow \begin{bmatrix} \Lambda y \\ \Lambda w \end{bmatrix} / \underline{\quad} \begin{bmatrix} \text{voiceless} \\ \text{consonants} \end{bmatrix}$

Imagine two geographical areas, A and B. In area A, Canadian speakers have rule (3a) in their dialect but not rule (3b). In area B, on the other hand, speakers have rule (3b) but not (3a). What effect might this have on speakers who are located between these two groups? How might their pronunciation be influenced by their neighbors in areas A and B? Suppose that speakers are influenced, one after another, by neighboring speakers, so that a rule of pronunciation can be said to move or spread through successive groups of speakers located in close proximity. Given this, it turns out that two rules could originate in different areas, but as they gradually spread, they would eventually meet and cross, creating areas where their effects overlap, as illustrated in figure 10.2.

Figure 10.2 represents the general geographic spread of two rules. At point X, which is closer to area A than to area B, rule (3a) arrives first, before rule (3b) arrives. Point Y, however, is closer to area B, so rule (3b) arrives at Y before rule (3a) does. This difference in the order of arrival of the rules is responsible for the difference in the pronunciation of the word *typewriter* in the two Canadian dialects, as shown in (4):

(4)   X Dialect   Y Dialect
              taypraytər   taypraytər
First rule, 3a: tayprayDər   First rule, 3b: tʌyprʌytər
Next rule, 3b: tʌyprayDər   Next rule, 3a: tʌyprʌyDər

The example of the two Canadian dialects demonstrates how a change can move among dialects. The same type of overlapping occurs with lexical, morphological, and syntactic changes; thus a widespread language change can take place. If a group of speakers of a language becomes isolated from another group of speakers of the same language, each group will undergo its own set of changes, and after enough time

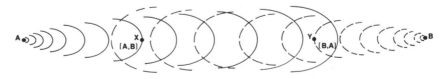

Figure 10.2
Geographic spread of two intersecting rules

has passed new languages will be created. We will explore this phenomenon in more detail in section 10.3.

Rule Ordering (optional)

In dialect X, an /ay/ diphthong will be pronounced as /ʌy/ before voiceless consonants, according to rule (3b), and alveolar stops will always be pronounced as voiced flaps when they occur between vowels, according to rule (3a). Therefore, one can argue that rules (3a) and (3b) are still phonological rules of dialect X. Now if one were to propose that the -*write* part of the word *typewriter* is phonologically related to the word *write,* and thus the flapped [D] in /tʌyprayDər/ is related to the /t/ in *write,* then to derive the proper phonetic forms as shown in (4) for Dialect X, rule (3a) must always apply before rule (3b) applies. Some linguists have therefore proposed that some phonological rules must be ordered with respect to each other. If ordering turns out to be a property of the internalized grammar of speakers of a language, the consequences for our understanding of how language (or knowledge of language) is stored and processed will be far-reaching.

Spread of Changes among Different Languages

An interesting feature of language change is that changes, especially phonological ones, can spread between adjacent but different languages. For example, the uvular *r* (an r-like sound pronounced in the uvular region of the vocal tract (see figure 6.2)) has been replacing the tongue-tip *r* in many of the languages of Europe. Uvular *r* is characteristic of French, but it is now common in many dialects of German; it is also replacing the tongue-tip *r* in dialects of southern Sweden, and a similar replacement is taking place in Italian dialects in northern Italy. There is much dispute about where this change started.

One of the more remarkable cases of the spread of a phonological change is found in the Native American languages of the northwestern United States. In Washington State, three distinct language groups were geographically adjacent before the European contact. These groups are represented by the Makah (a language of the Wakashan language family), the Quileute (a language of the Chemakuan family), and several members of the Salish language family. The relative geographic locations of these languages are indicated in figure 10.3, in which A is the Makah region, B is the Quileute region, and C is the Salish language area.

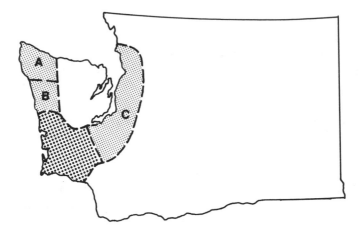

Figure 10.3
Geographical proximity of three language families in the Northwest. A. Makah (Wakashan family); B. Quileute (Chemakuan family); C. Salish family.

What is remarkable about these different languages is that all three of them lost their nasal consonants by changing them to voiced stops: /m/ became /b/, /n/ became /d/, and /ŋ/ became /g/. Although it is not possible to establish in which language the change began, it is noteworthy that this far-reaching change (indicated by shading in figure 10.3) spread throughout these distinct languages. Almost all of the world's languages have nasal consonants; these three languages are among the few exceptions. The reader may have noticed that the name *Makah* has a nasal consonant and thus appears to contradict the claim that these languages have no nasals. Another apparent contradiction is the nasalless Puget Sound Salish language, *Snohomish*, which has two nasals in its name. The solution is that *Makah* and *Snohomish* are names given by neighboring groups, which do have nasals. In fact, the *Snohomish* actually call themselves /sdəhobš/, in which the /d/ corresponds to the *n* and the /b/ corresponds to the *m*, according to the regular rule.

Our view of languages, then, is that they are constantly changing. In the past language change has been viewed as decay or, in some cases, as progress. But at the present time neither of these views seems appropriate or true. Languages seem to maintain a balance in expressibility and grammatical complexity, over time. If a particular grammatical feature is lost (say, because of a phonological change), some feature may be added in another component of the grammar (say, in the syntax). English provides an example of just such a pair of related changes. When English lost most of its inflectional endings through the deletion of certain final syllables by phonological rules, it was no longer possible to identify the functional roles of nouns (subject or object) by their inflectional endings. But the functional notions of subject and object are now indicated in part by the syntactic position of the nouns, that is, by their position in the word order. Another change in English was the loss of the morphological rule creating causative verbs from adjectives (*redden* from *red*). We did not thereby simultaneously lose the notion of causation, however, nor even the possibility of expressing a causative form of adjectives, since we can still say things like *to cause to be red* or *to cause to be blue*. Thus the expressive possibilities of a language do not seem limited by the lack of an overt grammatical structure to carry a particular notion. For example, although Chinese has no overt past tense marker, as we pointed out in chapter 9, this does not mean that the Chinese do not have a notion of past time. The idea of past time can be communicated quite clearly by either context or by the presence of a adverb referring to past time.

10.3 THE INDO-EUROPEAN LANGUAGE FAMILY

Establishing Historical Relations among Languages

Having examined some of the ways in which languages change, we are in a position to answer another question posed in section 10.1: How can one establish that two languages, such as Spanish and Sanskrit, are in fact related? It is not enough to discover the existence of a number of words that look and mean the same. Other explanations could account for similarities in vocabulary items—borrowing of words, for example. Many terms relating to Western technology have become part of the vocabulary of the world's languages, and if one were naively to study the vocabulary of present Japanese and English, the large technical vocabulary they share might suggest that English and Japanese were genetically related. (It may be that they are, but this is extremely unlikely, according to the present state of our knowledge.) Language contact with subsequent exchange of vocabulary in the past must be excluded if one is validly to establish a true historical relationship.

Another way that languages can be similar is through purely accidental correspondences. The fact that languages often have similarities in sound structure (languages usually have an /a/ vowel, /t/ and /s/ consonants, and so forth) and usually have a core of words referring to common entities such as water, baby, food, father, and so forth, yields a significant probability that there will be overlaps in sound–meaning correspondences among languages. In the Lummi language, a Native American language spoken in northwestern Washington State, the word for "father" is /mæn/. In Navajo the word for "mother" is /-má/, as in /shi-má/ "my mother." There is no additional evidence to support a claim that Lummi and English descended from a common ancestor, nor is there further evidence that Navajo and English are genetically related. Thus languages will share words similar in sound and meaning, based only on a statistically significant probability.

Given borrowing and accidental similarities between languages, how does one definitely establish that languages are related? The key to the solution to this problem lies in the fact that language is rule-governed behavior. One of the prime principles for establishing an historical relation between languages is given in (5):

(5) A group of languages can be said to be *genetically related* when individual sets of regular phonological rules can be written that derive each of the related languages from a common ancestor.

The languages of the Indo-European (IE) language family can all be shown to be related in that it is possible to write a set of regular phonological rules that will derive each of the languages in the family from a common language (or group of closely related dialects) spoken five or six thousand years ago. The original homeland of the Indo-European speakers is a subject of much dispute, but there is some evidence that it was in what is now southern Russia.

We follow here the traditional metaphorical terminology in describing the relations among related languages: each attested language is referred to as a *daughter* language descended from the *parent* language, Indo-European. No records of actual Indo-European exist; our knowledge of it can only be inferred from the structure of the daughter languages.

Languages of the Indo-European Family
Most of the languages of Europe belong to the Indo-European family. We have displayed the majority of these languages in figure 10.4. Languages on the same branch of the tree in the figure share certain changes not shared by languages on other branches of the tree. Hence,

figure 10.4 represents a classification system similar to the classification systems used by biologists for plants and animals.

One of the interesting sets of historical changes that figure 10.4 represents is the set of changes associated with the linguistic history of the Germanic languages.

Grimm's Law

A major discovery of the early nineteenth century was the set of sound changes that the Germanic languages underwent after their separation from the original IE family. These changes can be formulated as rules based on the correspondences shown in (6).

(6) Germanic (English)   Other IE Languages

    a. *f*ather   *p*ater (Latin) "father"

        *th*ree   *t*res (Latin) "three"

        *h*orn   *c*ornu (Latin) "horn"

    b. sli*pp*ery   lu*b*ricus   (Latin)   "slip-
                            pery"

        *t*en   *d*ecem (Latin) "ten"

        *k*nee   *g*enu (Latin) "knee"

    c. *b*rother   *bh*ratar (Sanskirt)
                            "brother"

        bin*d*   ban*dh* (Sanskrit) "bind"

        *g*uest   *h*ostis (Latin) "enemy"

The italicized portions of the words in (6) indicate critical consonants that correspond to each other in the languages in the two columns. The reader should keep in mind that Latin and Sanskrit are *not* the languages from which the Germanic languages descended; the Latin and Sanskrit forms in (6) are therefore not the original forms from which the Germanic forms descended. Rather, all are descended from a common source, but the consonants in Latin and Sanskrit are closer to the original IE pronunciation and thus are to a certain extent more conservative. The reader should also note that the /g/ in English *guest* is from an IE sound (spelled *gh*) which became /h/ in Latin. Ironically, through meaning shift, these two *cognate* (historically related) words in English

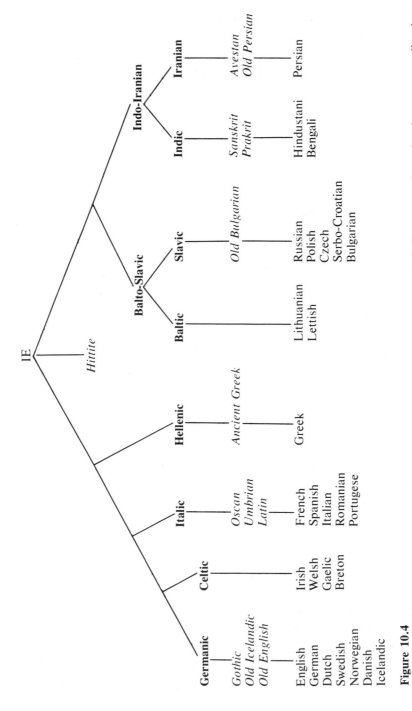

Figure 10.4
The Indo-European language family. Oldest attested forms of the language are in italics; currently spoken languages are listed at the end of each vertical branch.

and Latin are almost opposite in meaning. We display in (7) the set of changes that have been hypothesized, based on the correspondences exemplified in (6):

(7) (a) p → f
      t → θ
      k → x (h)
   (b) b → p
      d → t
      g → k
   (c) bh → b
      dh → d
      gh → g

The interrelated sets of changes in (7) are known collectively as Grimm's Law, because their systematic character was first stressed by Jacob Grimm (one of the Brothers Grimm, best known in this country for their collection of German fairy tales). There is some controversy over whether Grimm should be credited with discovering these laws, since the list of correspondences had already been published by a Dane, Erasmus Rask. Grimm, however, is usually given the credit because he emphasized the lawlike properties of the correspondences.

The changes are indeed lawlike in that all words containing these sounds underwent the changes, and all the changes applied to natural classes of phonemes, in the sense defined in chapter 6. For example, the class of phonemes that underwent the changes in (7a) is the class of voiceless stops. Thus, after the Germanic languages split off from the other IE languages, a rule was added that changed all voiceless stops into voiceless constrictives (with some minor restrictions that are not important here). This rule would presumably have had the following form:

(8) $\begin{bmatrix} +\text{stop} \\ -\text{voice} \end{bmatrix} \rightarrow [-\text{stop}]$

After rule (8) was added to the grammar of the Germanic dialect of Indo-European, a fundamental change in the language occurred, referred to as a *restructuring*. After rule (8) had applied, words that formerly had /p, t, k/ came to have /f, θ, x/ respectively. For a child acquiring the language *after* rule (8) applied, there would be no evidence for the earlier /p/, /t/, and /k/ sounds and the child would simply learn the new consonants. Once children have learned words that have a different basic phonological shape from words in the language of older generations, we say that the language has been phonologically *restructured* in the grammar of the children.

Language change, then, offers important evidence about the nature of human language—namely, that it is rule-governed. We have seen that the major changes the English language underwent between Old and Modern English are best viewed as changes in the sets of rules characterizing the two stages of English. Over time, grammatical rules can be added, lost, or changed, and unless there are conscious efforts on the part of a community of speakers to preserve the grammatical features of a language, it will continually change. Why languages change is not known for certain; however, once changes occur, they propagate, wavelike, through communities of speakers.

Exercises

1. What are the primary types of language change? Give examples.

2. What was the Great Vowel Shift? What consequences did this sound change have on contemporary English? Give examples in your answer.

3. What does it mean to say that some language changes move wavelike through a community of speakers?

4. What is the Indo-European language family? What is one way to establish that languages are genetically related?

5. What is Grimm's Law? Illustrate its effects with some comparisons between English and Latin or Greek.

*6. How can knowledge of Grimm's Law help one remember that a podiatrist is a foot doctor?

*7. Barry Fell, in his book *America B.C.*, argues that there was extensive contact between the people of the European and North American continents long before the Viking sailings. As part of the evidence, he cites (1977, 283) the following correspondences between Northeastern Algonquian, a Native American language of the northeastern United States, and Gaelic, the Scottish dialect of Celtic:

Algonquian	Gaelic	meaning
bhanem	ban	"woman"
alnoba	allaban	"person," "immigrant," (respectively)
lhab	lion-obhair	"netting"
odana	dun	"town"
na'lwiwi	na h-uile	"everywhere"
kladen	claden	"frost" or "snowflake"
pados	bata	"boat"

monaden	monadh	"mountain"
aden	ard	"height"
cuiche	cuithe	"gorge"

Discuss these examples in terms of the following questions: Do these correspondences prove that Northeastern Algonquian and Gaelic are historically related? Can we exclude the possibility that the similarities are accidental? Are these words the kinds of words that would be likely to be borrowed by one group from the other? Finally, what kind of further evidence would we need to establish a true historical relation?

References

Bloomfield, L. (1933) *Language* (especially Chap. 18), Holt, Rinehart & Winston, New York.

Bynon, T. (1977) *Historical Linguistics,* Cambridge University Press, Cambridge, England.

Fell, B. (1977) *America B.C.: Ancient Settlers in the New World,* Demeter Press Book, New York Times Book Company.

Joos, M. (1942) "A phonological dilemma in Canadian English," *Language* 2, 141–144.

Lehmann, W. (1962) *Historical Linguistics: An Introduction,* Holt, Rinehart & Winston, New York.

Moore, S., and T. Knott (1963) *The Elements of Old English,* George Wahr, Ann Arbor, Mich.

Williams, J. (1975) *Origins of the English Language,* Macmillan, New York.

Chapter Eleven

SEMANTICS: THE STUDY OF MEANING AND REFERENCE

Is Semantics Part of a Grammar?

In linguistics, semantics is generally considered to be the study of *meaning* (and related notions) in languages, while in logic semantics is generally considered to be the study of *reference* (and related notions) in languages. Other disciplines, such as philosophy, psychology, and computer science, sample freely from both traditions. Although there is sometimes tension between these conceptions of semantics, the dispute really is one of emphasis: in the end an adequate semantic description of natural languages must record both facts of meaning and facts of reference. But which facts of meaning and which facts of reference are relevant to semantics? What are meaning and reference? And finally, just what do theories of meaning and reference look like? To ask such questions is to take the first step into semantics. To attempt to answer them is to take the rest. But let the reader be forewarned that semantics is in a greater state of diversification than phonology or syntax and much that we will say is a selection from among possible alternatives. The reader is strongly advised to consult works listed in the reference section at the end of this chapter.

Semantics has not always enjoyed a prominent role in modern linguistics. From World War II to the early 1960s semantics was viewed, especially in America, as not quite respectable; its intrusion into a grammar was considered by many as either a sort of methodological impurity or an objective to be reached only in the distant future. But as Katz and Fodor (1963) pointed out in their influential article, there is as much reason to consider semantics a part of grammar as syntax or phonology are. It is often said that a grammar describes what fluent speakers know of their language—their *linguistic competence*. If that is so, we can argue that whatever fluent speakers know of their language is a proper part of a description of that language. And if that is the case, then it is easy to motivate the description of meaning as a necessary part of the description of a speaker's linguistic knowledge. Consider the following claims:

(1) a. The sequence of sounds in *desk* is meaningful, but its reverse *ksed* is not.

b. The sequence of words *room the leave* is not meaningful, but its reverse *leave the room!* is.

c. The words *bank* and *fly* are ambiguous.

Would we say that a person who did not know *any* facts such as (1a)–(1c) spoke fluent English? Probably not, since such a person would not even be capable of distinguishing meaningless sequences of sounds from meaningful ones. Thus, the description of a language must contain a component that describes what speakers know about the semantics of their language. In other words, if appealing to what fluent speakers know about their language counts as motivation for including a phonological fact or syntactic fact in the grammar of that language, then the same sort of consideration motivates the inclusion of semantic facts in the grammar of that language.

But a more general consideration also motivates us to include semantics in the grammar of a language. A language is often defined to be a conventional system for communication, a system for conveying messages. Moreover, communication can be accomplished (in the system) only because certain sounds (or shapes) have certain meanings, and so to characterize this system—the language—it is necessary to describe these meanings. Hence, if a grammar describes a language, part of it must describe meaning, and thus it must contain a semantics.

Taking these two considerations together, it seems reasonable to conclude that semantic information is an integral part of a grammar.

11.1 AIMS AND CLAIMS OF A SEMANTIC THEORY

Once we recognize that there are facts for a semantic theory to describe, the natural question to ask is what facts? What kinds of information are central to the description of the semantics of a language? Since in semantics the decision to include a certain phenomenon within the scope of one's theory can affect the whole character of that theory, we will illustrate a wide variety of phenomena commonly cited as semantic and allow readers to ponder which are necessary.

Meaning

In everyday English we use the word *mean* in a number of different ways:

(2) a. That was no mean (insignificant) accomplishment.
 b. They are so mean (cruel) to me.
 c. This will mean (result in) the end of second-class citizenship.
 d. Without ice cream, life wouldn't mean anything (have any purpose).
 e. I mean (intend) to help if I can.
 f. Keep off the grass, this means (refers to) you.
 g. His losing his job means (implies) that he will have to look again.
 h. Lucky Strike means (indicates) fine tobacco.
 i. Those clouds mean (are a sign of) rain.
 j. She doesn't mean (believe) what she said.
 k. *Procrastinate* means (?) to put things off.
 l. In saying that, she meant (?) that we should leave.

Since each of these uses, except for (2k) and (2l), has a paraphrase using words other than *mean*, we will reserve *mean* for these last two cases, which exemplify two importantly different sorts of meaning—speaker-meaning and linguistic-meaning.

Speaker-Meaning and Linguistic-Meaning

Speaker-meaning is what a speaker means in producing an utterance. Now, if we are speaking *literally* and mean what our words mean, there will be no important difference between the linguistic-meaning and the speaker-meaning. But if we are speaking *nonliterally*, then we will mean something different from what our words mean.

There are a number of different ways one can speak nonliterally. One can speak facetiously (ironically, sarcastically) and thereby mean the opposite of what one says. If we say, in the appropriate way, *That movie was a real winner* we would be (and would intend to be) taken as meaning that it was a real flop. One can exaggerate: In the right circumstances one can utter *She was ten feet tall!* and mean that she was very tall One can speak figuratively. Saying that someone has raven hair, ruby lips, emerald eyes, and teeth of pearl normally would not commit one to meaning that this person was some sort of inorganic monstrosity; rather, one would be taken (and intend to be taken) as speaking metaphorically (see chapter 7). Similarly, the adman who writes *Put a tiger in your tank* or *The future is now* is not proposing the impossible, just speaking metaphorically. We will return to speaker-meaning and the nature of nonliteral utterances in chapter 12. Our purpose in mentioning speaker-meaning here is mainly to set it aside. Clearly, a grammar of a language cannot predict when speakers will be speaking nonliterally (that is, not meaning by their words what the words mean in the language); thus the description of speaker-meaning is beyond the scope of a grammar. This is an important point, one to keep in mind as we proceed to investigate the domain of a semantic theory.

In general, the linguistic-meaning of an expression is simply the meaning or meanings of that expression in some form of language. For example, in one form of language, known as Standard English, we say that *run* means something different in each of the sentences of (3):

(3) a. I like to *run*.
    b. The engines *run* well.
    c. They *run* a mail-order house.
    d. He scored a *run* in the third inning.

But recall that an expression can mean something in one dialect of English that it does not mean in another. The matter is further complicated in that an expression can mean different things to different people within the same dialect. The version of the language that a particular person speaks is sometimes called that person's *idiolect*, and the idiolect-meaning of a word can differ from one person to another. Figure 11.1 should help the reader organize these distinctions.

Although an expression can mean something distinctive in a dialect or an idiolect, one cannot tell from looking just at a grammar whether it is a grammar describing one person's idiolect, a group's dialect, or the language in general, because the same kinds of facts are present in each case. Despite the importance that these different kinds of meaning have for communication, we may ignore these differences when surveying the various kinds of information that should be recorded in a semantic theory. What are these kinds of information?

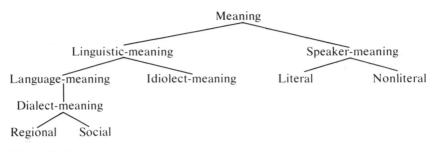

Figure 11.1
Some varieties of meaning

Meaning Properties and Relations

Recall that in motivating the inclusion of semantics in a grammar we noted some facts that must be accounted for. We now want to expand our list of examples as well as our list of meaning properties and relations that an adequate semantics must describe.

Probably the most central meaning property of expressions to be described is *meaningfulness* versus *meaninglessness*. An adequate semantic theory of a language must say which expressions are meaningful (and which are not), and for the meaningful ones an adequate theory must specify or represent their meaning. For example, in addition to (1) we have (4):

(4) a. *procrastinate* means "put things off"
   b. *bachelor* means "unmarried adult male"
   c. *father* means "male parent"

Another important meaning property of expressions is *ambiguity*. There are three sources of ambiguity in natural language: lexical and surface structural ambiguity (see chapter 8) and underlying structural ambiguity. A *lexical ambiguity* can be disambiguated by paraphrasing the relevant expression:

(5) a. He found a *bat*. (baseball bat; flying rodent)
   b. She couldn't *bear* children. (stand; give birth to)
   c. He *took her picture*. (removed her picture; photographed her)

As a rule an ambiguity is a *surface ambiguity* if the expression can be disambiguated by grouping the words appropriately (see chapter 8). For example, (6a) can be grouped as in (6b) and (6c):

(6) a. He visited a little girls' school.
    b. He visited a (little girls') school.
    c. He visited a little (girls' school).

Finally, we will consider an ambiguity to be an *underlying ambiguity* if it cannot be disambiguated lexically or by surface grouping. Notice that in none of the following are the words relevantly ambiguous:

(7) a. The chicken is ready to eat. (to feed; to be eaten)
    b. The whole band didn't show up for the concert. (some did not; none did)
    c. She knows a richer man than Rockefeller. (than Rockefeller is; than Rockefeller knows)

Still another meaning property of expressions is *redundancy:*

(8) a. female sister
    b. illegal murder
    c. She killed him dead.

A final meaning property of expressions is *anomaly*. An expression is anomalous when there is an incompatibility of meaning between constituent expressions:

(9) a. strawberry truth
    b. colorless green idea
    c. dream diagonally

Of course, it is almost always possible to impose a meaning on such expressions, in part because they are syntactically well-formed. Thus, to dream diagonally might be taken to mean "to lie diagonally in a bed while dreaming," but this is not what expression (9c) means in English.

Not only do expressions have meaning *properties* like those just surveyed, they also bear various meaning *relations* to one another. One central meaning relation is *synonymy* or sameness (in at least one sense) of meaning:

(10) a. *Automobile* is synonymous with *car*.
    b. *Sister* is synonymous with *female sibling*.
    c. *Intentionally kill oneself* is synonymous with *commit suicide*.

Notice that synonymy is a *symmetric* relation: if one expression is synonymous with a second expression, then the second is synonymous with the first. However, not all semantic relations are symmetrical, as we will see.

Another meaning relation is *meaning inclusion:*

(11) a. The meaning of *sister* includes the meaning of *female.*
b. The meaning of *to chase* includes the meaning of *move.*
c. The meaning of *is rectangular* includes the meaning of *has sides.*

This meaning relation is nonsymmetrical in that, for instance, the meaning of *female* does not include the meaning of *sister.*

Even if two expressions are not synonymous and one does not include the other, they still may be related in that they *overlap*, or *share* some aspect of meaning:

(12) a. *Father, uncle, bull,* and *stallion* all express the property "male."
b. To *say, speak, whisper, yell, shout,* and *scream* all express the property "vocalization."
c. *Fortunately, luckily, happily,* and *fortuitously* all express the property "good for" something or someone.

This meaning relation is symmetric in that if one expression shares or overlaps in meaning with a second expression, then the second shares or overlaps in meaning with the first.

Finally, expressions can be *antonymous*, that is, they can share an aspect of meaning but be opposite or incompatible in some other aspect of meaning:

(13) a. *Red, blue, green, yellow,* and so on, share the notion "color" but differ in shade (hue).
b. *small, medium-sized,* and *large* share the notion "size" but differ in degree.
Freezing, cold, cool, tepid, warm, and *hot* share the notion "temperature" but differ in degree.

This completes our initial survey of meaning properties and relations that have been proposed as being within the domain of a semantic theory of natural language. Not all practicing semanticists agree that every one of these properties and relations must be explained, or explained away. There is no doubt, however, that they form the core of a tradition in semantics that has been emphasized in transformational analyses of language. We turn now to some semantic properties and relations that have not received as much attention in the transformational tradition.

Reference and Related Phenomena

Speaker-Reference and Linguistic-Reference

As with meaning, we can distinguish speaker-reference from linguistic-reference. There is a variety of terminology here. Sometimes *refer* is reserved for what speakers do and *denote* is used for what words or phrases do. Under this terminology the object(s) referred to by a person can be called the referent(s) and the object(s) denoted by a word or phrase can be called the denotation of that word or phrase, though we will not follow this terminology here.

Speaker-reference is what the speaker is referring to in uttering an expression. As is the case with meaning, speakers may be referring to what their words refer to, as when one refers to George Washington by using the phrase *the first president*. However, it can happen that what the speaker is referring to is at variance with the conventional linguistic reference of the words used. For instance, suppose Jones believes himself to be the world's most famous linguist—much to the amusement of his friends. We might well refer to Jones in saying "Well, here comes *the world's most famous linguist*," even though our words refer to, say, Noam Chomsky. We will defer further discussion of speaker-reference to chapter 12.

Linguistic-reference is simply the reference of the expression as a part of the language. Here it is customary to distinguish *singular* expressions from *general* expressions. Singular referring expressions include proper names such as *Julius Caesar, The Eiffel Tower,* and *Paris;* pronouns such as *she, he,* and *they;* phrases such as *The present president of the United States,* and *the dents on the fender,* which are used to refer to some definite single thing or single collection of things. On the other hand, general referring expressions such as verbs, adjectives, and common nouns, apply correctly to many individuals or combinations of individuals. *Red* applies to any red thing, *table* applies to any table, and so forth. The difference in referential function between the sentences in (14) reflects a difference in the referential structure of the language;

(14) a. *The first table* had one leg. (singular expression)
  b. Each *table* has at least one leg. (general expression)

Referential relations have in general not received as much attention as referential properties in semantic theory. One relation that has received attention, though, is *coreference* between expressions in the same sentence, as in *"The first president of the United States was George Washington."* In the field of syntax a phenomenon similar to coreference has been studied, referred to as *anaphora*. This phenomenon has to do with the circumstances under which a pronoun can be taken as being linked to some noun phrase. For example, the pronoun *he* can be linked to the noun *John* in (15a) but not in (15b):

(15) a. *John* said that *he* was tired.

    b. *He* said that *John* was tired.

However, adding *as for himself* to (15a), forces *he* to be linked to *John*:

(16) *John* said that, as for himself, *he* was tired.

Some cases of anaphora similar to (15a) are not cases of coreference. Although in (17) *they* can be linked to *who*, these two expressions are clearly not coreferential, because *who* is not being used to refer:

(17) *Who* thinks *they* have been cheated?

Truth Properties

Not only do expressions in a language have meaning and often reference, they are also used to say things that are true or false. Of course, no semantic theory can predict which sentences are used to say something true and which are used to say something false, in part because truth and falsity depend upon what is being referred to, and the same words can be used in identical sentences to refer to different things. For instance, if two speakers utter the sentence *"I took your picture last night,"* then what one of them says may be true while what the other says may be false. Furthermore, if the sentence is ambiguous it may be used to say something true when taken one way but false when taken another way:

(18) a. I removed your painting last night.
    b. I photographed you last night.

Does this mean that the semantics of natural language cannot deal with truth and falsity? The answer is no, because some truth properties and truth relations hold regardless of reference, provided meaning is held constant.

Consider first the property of being *linguistically true* or *linguistically false* (the latter is also called *contradictory*). A sentence is linguistically true (or linguistically false) if its truth (or falsehood) is determined solely by the semantics of the language and it is not necessary to check any facts about the nonlinguistic world in order to determine its truth or falsity. A sentence is *empirically true* (or *empirically false*) if it is not linguistically true or false—that is, if it is necessary to check the world in order to verify or falsify it. Most of the claims of common sense and science are of this latter sort. If someone says that the glottis was discovered last year, this claim is true (or false) just in case the glottis was, as a matter of fact, discovered (or not discovered) last year; knowledge of the language alone does not settle the matter. Semantics is not concerned with empirical truths and falsehoods but with those sentences that are linguistically true or false. In each of the groups (19)–(21) it is possible to determine truth values (true = T, false = F) without regard to the actual state of the world.

(19) a. Either it is raining here or it is not raining here. (T)
 b. If John is sick and Mary is sick, then John is sick. (T)
 c. It is raining here and it is not raining here. (F)
 d. If John is sick and Mary is sick, then John is not sick. (F)

(20) a. All people that are sick are people. (T)
 b. If every person is sick, then it is not true that no person is sick. (T)
 c. Some people that are sick are not people. (F)
 d. Every person is sick, but some person is not (sick). (F)

(21) a. If John is a bachelor, then John is unmarried. (T)
 b. If John killed the bear, the bear died. (T)
 c. If the car is red, then it has a color. (T)
 d. John is a bachelor, but he is married. (F)
 e. John killed the bear and it's (still) alive. (F)
 f. The car is red, but it has no color. (F)

Again, knowing the language seems to be sufficient for knowing the truth or falsity of these sentences, and this being so, the semantics of these sorts of sentences will be relevant to a semantic theory.

Logical Form and Analytic Sentences (optional section)
There are some important differences between examples (19), (20), and (21). In (19) the truth value (T or F) is determined solely by the connectives *or, and, if . . . then,* and the word *not* (where this sometimes abbreviates *it is not the case that*). Since these sorts of words are often dubbed logical words, these sentences are also called *logical*

truths (of English). It can be seen that the *form* of these sentences makes them true regardless of how the world is. For instance, the logical form of (19a) and (19b) in terms of the logical words is:

(22) a. Either *S* or not-*S*. (T)
     b. If *S* and *S'*, then *S*. (T)

No matter what (grammatical) declarative sentences we may pick for *S* and *S'*, the resulting compound sentence will be true. The same holds for the falsity of (19c) and (19d), which also is attributable to their logical form:

(22) c. *S* and not-*S*. (F)
     d. If *S* and S', then not-*S*. (F)

The same remarks go for (20) except that the relevant logical words are *some, every,* and *no.* The first two of these sentences are true in virtue of their logical form; the last two are false in virtue of their logical form:

(23) a. All *X*'s that are *P* are *X*'s. (T)
     b. If every *X* is *P*, then it is not true that no *X* is *P*. (T)
     c. Some *X*'s that are *P* are not *X*'s. (F)
     d. Every *X* is *P*, but some *X* is not *P*. (F)

This procedure of getting the logical form of a sentence yields very different results when applied to the sentences in (21). This is because the words relevant to the linguistic truth or falsehood of these sentences are not logical words, which can be used in discussing any subject matter, but descriptive words such as *bachelor, kill,* and *red* used in discussing certain kinds of subject matter—bachelors, killings, colors, and so on. If we follow the procedure of replacing descriptive words with letters in (21a)–(21c), thereby converting them into their logical forms, we get (24a)–(24c) as a result:

(24) a. If John is a *B*, then John is *U*.
     b. If John *K*-ed the bear, then the bear *D*-ed.
     c. If the car is *R*, then the car has a *C*.

It is easy to see that such forms as those in (24) need not always result in sentences that are true, as was the case with previous examples of linguistic truth, since these forms can yield sentences that are false:

(25) a. If John is a bachelor, then John is unhappy. (F)
     b. If John kicked the bear, then the bear died. (F)
     c. If the car is repossessed, then the car has a carburetor. (F)

Even if such sentences as (25a)–(25c) are not true by virtue of their logical form, sometimes they can be converted into logical truths by substituting into the sentences definitions for these descriptive words. For instance, suppose that the following definition is correct:

(Def. 1) *bachelor* = Def. "unmarried and adult and male and human"

If we replace the word *bachelor* in (21a) with the right-hand side of Def. 1, we get sentence (26):

(26) If John is unmarried and adult and male, then John is unmarried.

What is interesting about (26) is that it has the form of a logical truth, and that form is (27):

(27) If John is U and A and M, then John is U.

Thus, certain sentences that are not logical truths can be converted into logical truths by replacing the crucial descriptive words with their definitions. Sentences that can be converted into logical truths by this sort of substitution are often called *analytic* sentences, and since they are true by virtue of their semantic structure, they are considered to fall within the scope of a semantic theory.

   In summary, we have seen that there are a variety of truth properties that a semantic theory should account for, including those of being a linguistic truth or a linguistic falsehood and, among these, of being logically and even analytically true (or false).

Truth Relations
We said earlier that there were truth relations as well as truth properties that fall within the scope of semantics. The most central truth relation for semantics is *entailment*. One sentence S is said to entail another sentence S' when the truth of the first guarantees the truth of the second and the falsity of the second sentence S' guarantees the falsity of the first, as in (28):

(28) a. *The car is red* entails *The car has a color.*
     b. *The needle is too short* entails *The needle is not long enough.*

We can see that the first sentence in each example, if true, guarantees the truth of the second; and the falsity of the second sentences guarantees the falsity of the first.

   Closely related to entailment is another truth relation, *semantic presupposition*. The basic idea behind semantic presupposition is that the falsity of the presupposed sentence causes the presupposing sentence not to have a truth value (T or F). Furthermore, both a sentence and its denial have the same semantic presupposiition. Although this truth relation is somewhat controversial, (29) and (30) show typical examples of semantic presupposition in which both the positive (a) and negative (b) sentences have the same presupposition (c):

(29) a. The present King of France is bald.
    b. The present King of France is not bald.
    c. There is a present King of France.

(30) a. John realizes that his car has been stolen.
    b. John does not realize that his car has been stolen.
    c. John's car has been stolen.

In sum, there are at least two truth relations that an adequate semantic theory must explain, or explain away, entailment and semantic presupposition, and these must be added to the truth properties we already have.

Goals of a Semantic Theory

We now come to the question of the goals of a semantic theory. What should a semantic theory do, and how should it do it?

The short answer to the first question is that a semantic theory should attribute to each expression e in the language the semantic properties and relations it has and it should define those properties and relations. Thus, if an expression e is meaningful, the semantic theory should say so. If the expression e has a specific set of meanings, the semantic theory should specify them. If the expression e is ambiguous, the semantic theory should record that fact, and so on. Moreover, if two expressions are synonymous, or one entails the other, the semantic theory should mark these semantic relations. We can organize these demands on a semantic theory by saying that an adequate semantic theory of a language must generate every true instance of the following schemes:

(31) a. Meaning Properties and Relations
    e means————.
    e is meaningful.
    e is ambiguous.
    e is anomalous (nonsense).

e is redundant.

e and *e'* are synonymous.

e includes the meaning of *e'*.

e and *e'* overlap in meaning.

e and *e'* are antonyms.

b. Referential Properties and Relations

e is a singular referring expression.

e is a general referring expression.

e and *e'* are coreferential.

c. Truth Properties and Relations

e is logically true (*or* false).

e is analytic.

e is contradictory.

e entails *e'*.

e semantically presupposes *e'*.

We can say in sum that the domain of a semantic theory is at least the set of properties and relations we have just set out and we should not be satisfied with a semantic theory of English that failed to say, for instance, the following:

1. *Bachelors are unmarried* means "unmarried adult human males are unmarried."

2. *Bachelors are unmarried* is meaningful.

3. *Bachelors are unmarried* is ambiguous. (men; academic degree holders)

4. *Bachelors are unmarried* and *Unmarried men are unmarried* are synonymous.

5. *Bachelor* is a general referring expression.

6. *Bachelor* and *unmarried man* refer to the same things.

7. *Bachelors are unmarried* is analytic.

8. *Bachelors are unmarried* entails *Bachelors are not married, Bachelors are adults, Bachelors are male*.

The second question concerning the goals of a semantic theory is, How should the theory handle all these semantic properties and relations? What kinds of constraints on a semantic theory are reasonable to impose? We will mention just two. First, it is generally conceded that even though a natural language contains an infinite number of phrases and sentences (recall chapter 8), a semantic theory of a natural language should be finite: people are capable of storing only a finite amount of information but they nevertheless learn the semantics of natural languages. The second constraint on a semantic theory of a natural language is that it should reflect the fact that, except for idioms, expressions are *compositional*. This means that the meaning of a syntactically complex expression is determined by the meaning of its constituents and their grammatical relations. Compositionality rests on the fact that a finite number of familiar words and expressions can be combined and recombined to form an infinite number of novel phrases and sentences; hence, a finite semantic theory that reflects compositionality can describe meanings for an infinite number of complex expressions.

The existence of compositionality is most dramatic when compositional expressions are contrasted with expressions that lack compositionality. In (32a) the expression *kick the bucket* has two meanings:

(32) a. John kicked the bucket.
    b. John kicked the wooden pail.
    c. John died.

One of the meanings of (32a) is compositional: it is determined on the basis of the meaning of its constituent words and is synonymous with (32b). The other meaning of (32a) is idiomatic and is paraphrasable as (32c). Idiomatic meanings are not compositional in the sense of being determined from the meaning of the constituent words and their grammatical relations. One could not determine the idiomatic meaning of (32a) by knowing just the meaning of the words and recognizing familiar grammatical structure—an idiomatic meaning must be learned separately as a unit. Idioms behave as though they were syntactically complex words whose meaning cannot be predicted, since their syntactic structure is doing no semantic work.

It would be a mistake to think of the compositionality of a complex expression as simply adding up the meanings and references of its parts. For adjective + noun constructions like that in (33a), adding up sometimes works:

(33) a. He was a *bearded Russian soldier*. =
    b. He was Russian and bearded and a soldier.

But even in such constructions the contribution of syntax can be devious, as in (34), where we cannot simply add up the meanings of *occasional* and *sailor*:

(34) a. An occasional sailor walked by. ≠
    b. *Someone who is a sailor and occasional walked by.

Modifiers can create other complexities for compositionality, and those complexities must be reflected in a semantic theory of the language. Contrast the arguments in (35) and (36):

(35) a. That is a *gray* elephant. (T)
     b. All elephants are animals. (T)
     c. So, that is a *gray* animal. (T)

(36) a. That is a *small* elephant. (T)
     b. All elephants are animals. (T)
     c. So, that is a *small* animal. (F)

In (35), (a) and (b) jointly entail the truth of (c), but in (36) the premises (a) and (b) do not jointly entail (36c). The only difference between (35) and (36) is the occurrence of *gray* in (35) and *small* in (36), so clearly there is some difference in the semantics of these two words.

More complicated and interesting examples of the interaction of semantics and syntax come from the functional relations of subject and object in a sentence. In sentences like (37a) and (37c) the words are the same, but the entailments (37b) and (37d) are importantly different.

(37) a. John killed the snake.
     b. The snake died.
     c. The snake killed John.
     d. John died.

This further illustrates the degree that a semantic theory must be integrated with a syntactic theory in an adequate description of a natural language.

11.2 WHAT ARE MEANING AND REFERENCE?

At the outset of this chapter we asked which facts about meaning and reference are relevant to semantics, and we have just concluded our preliminary answer. We also posed the question, What are meaning and reference? Of course, it would take a whole semantic theory to fully answer these questions, but there have been in the history of semantics a few "leading ideas" about the nature of meaning and reference, and a brief look at some of these conceptions is instructive.

What Is Meaning?

Historically, the most compelling notion concerning meaning has been that it is some sort of entity or thing. After all, we do speak of words as "having" a meaning, as meaning "something", as having the "same" meaning, as meaning the same "thing", as "sharing" a meaning, as having many "meanings", and so forth.

What sort of entity or thing is meaning? Different answers to this question give us a selection of different conceptions of meaning, and a selection of different types of semantic theory.

The Referential Theory of Meaning

If one focuses on just some of the expressions in a language—for instance, proper names such as *De Gaulle, Chris Evert, Italy,* or definite descriptive noun phrases such as *the present president of the United States, the first person to step onto the moon,* and so forth—one is liable to conclude that their meaning is the thing they refer to. For convenience we will formulate this conception of meaning as the slogan:

(R) The meaning of each expression *e* is the (actual) object it refers to, its *referent.*

Although (R) does reflect the fact that we use language to talk about the world, there are serious problems with the identification of meaning as reference.

For instance, if we believe that the meaning of an expression is its referent, we are committed to at least the following additional claims:

(38) a. If an expression *e* has a meaning, then it must have a referent.
b. If two expressions have the same reference, then they have the same meaning.
c. Anything that is true of the referent of an expression is true of its meaning.

Each of these consequences of (R) is false, and so the Referential Theory of meaning must be modified.

For instance, (38a) requires that for any expression having a meaning there is an actual object that it refers to. But this is surely wrong. What, for instance, is the (actual) object referred to by such expressions as: *Pegasus, the, empty, and, hello, very,* and *Leave the room?* Next, consider (38b). This says that if two expressions refer to the same object, then they mean the same thing, that is, they are synonymous. But many expressions that can be correctly used to refer to a single object do not mean the same thing. For instance, *The morning star, The evening star,* and *Venus* all can refer to the same planet, but they are not synonymous. Nor are the expressions *The first person to walk on the moon* and *Neil Armstrong* synonymous, but they refer to the same person. Finally, consider (38c). As far as we know, Sir Edmund Hilary was the first European to climb Mt. Everest, and as a consequence he was knighted by the Queen. But by (38c) one must conclude that it is the meaning of the words *Edmund Hilary* that climbed Mt. Everest and got knighted by the Queen. We conclude that the Referential Theory will either have to be rejected or modified in some significant way.

Mentalist theories of meaning
Well, one might say, if meanings are not actual objects, perhaps they are mental objects; even if there is no real flying horse for *Pegasus* to refer to, there is surely such an *idea,* and maybe this idea is the meaning of *Pegasus*. A typical example of this view can be seen in the following quotation from Glucksberg and Danks (1975, 50): "The set of possible meanings of any given word is the set of possible feelings, images, ideas, concepts, thoughts, and inferences that a person might produce when that word is heard and processed." As with the Referential Theory, this conception of meaning can be formulated as a slogan:

(M) The meaning of each expression *e* is an idea, *I,* associated with *e* in the minds of speakers.

This sort of theory has a number of problems, but the most serious one can be put in the form of a dilemma: either the notion of an idea is too vague to allow the theory to predict anything specific and thus the theory is not testable; or if the notion of an idea is made precise enough to test, the theory turns out to make false predictions. The above quotation from Glucksberg and Danks illustrates the first problem. How, in such a view of meaning, could one ever determine what an expression means? In such a view, could two expressions be synonymous, or would there always be feelings and thoughts associated with one expression that are not associated with the other?

Turning to the second problem, suppose we sharpen up the notion of an idea by saying that ideas are *mental images*. While this might work for words like *Pegasus* and perhaps *The Eiffel Tower,* it is not obvious how it would work for nouns such as *dog* and *triangle*, or a verb such as *kick*. For instance, if one really does form an image of a dog or a triangle, more than likely the dog will be of some particular species and will not comprise both a Chihuahua and a Saint Bernard; the triangle will be isosceles or equilateral but will not comprise all triangles. Similar problems arise with *kick*. If one really forms an image of *X* kicking *Y,* then that image probably will have properties not essential to kicking, such as the sex of the kicker, which leg was used, the kind of thing being kicked, and so forth. In general, mental images are just not abstract enough to be the meanings of even common nouns and verbs. But suppose for the moment that appropriate images could be found for these nouns and verbs. What about other kinds of words? What images are the meanings of words such as *only, and, hello,* and *not*? Worse still, can the theory apply to units larger than words, such as the sentence *She speaks French and Navajo*? How, for instance, does an Image Theory of meaning differentiate this sentence from *She speaks French or Navajo*?

One way around this problem of the excessive specificity of images is to make the relevant notion of an idea be a *concept*. Even though this way of making the theory testable has promise, there is as yet no theory in cognitive psychology that is detailed enough to test as a theory of meaning. To succeed, such a theory must be capable of identifying and distinguishing concepts independently of meaning, which they at present fail to do. In short, theories of meaning as entities, whether they be objects referred to, images in the mind, or concepts, are all in trouble for various reasons. Perhaps the trouble lies with the initial assumption that meaning is an entity.

The use theory of meaning
One of the last theories of meaning to emerge has been the (non-entitative) Use Theory of meaning. Advanced by Wittgenstein in the 1930s, it has more or less taken over Anglo-American theorizing about meaning for the past forty years. Properly construed, it is, we think, a promising theory. Like the previous theories of meaning, this one can be formulated as a slogan:

(U) The meaning of an expression *e* is determined by its use in the language community.

Notice that this theory does not suffer all the weaknesses of entitative theories. We can just as easily speak of the use of *hello* as of the use of *table* or *Pegasus*. The main problem with the Use Theory of meaning is that the relevant conception of *use* must be made precise, and the theory must say how, exactly, meaning is connected to use. Such a theory is being developed by various authors (see Grice and Schiffer, cited in the references) and we will say more about language use in chapter 12.

In conclusion, it is fair to say that we do not have a very good idea about what meaning is and all of the theories we have surveyed are in various states of disarray. The situation is not hopeless, as there are still promising avenues for future research. The student should not be deterred by this limitation on our present understanding, but should consider it an opportunity to make a contribution. Roughly the same situation holds for the theory of reference.

What Is Reference?

At present there are two major competing theories of reference; the Description Theory, and the Historical Chain theory. The basic idea behind the Description Theory is that an expression refers to its referent because it describes the referent, either uniquely or uniquely enough to be identified. For instance, the phrase *The first person to set foot on the moon* refers to Neil Armstrong by virtue of the fact that the description fits him uniquely. What about other kinds of referring expressions, such as the pronouns *he, she, that,* or proper names such as *Charles de Gaulle, America,* or *Fido?* These do not seem to describe anything uniquely, so how does the Description Theory handle them? It handles them by saying that people using these expressions have *in mind* some description of the object they intend to refer to. At this point the theory becomes one of speaker-reference, not linguistic-reference, and we will treat this subject in chapter 12.

The Historical Chain Theory, says, in effect, that an expression refers to its referent by virtue of there being a certain historical relation between the words uttered and some initial dubbing or christening of the object with that name. For instance, when a speaker uses the name *Charles de Gaulle,* it refers, in this view, to the person christened by that name, provided there is a chain of uses linking the current speaker's reference with the original christening. This view proposes no unique description to pick out the proper referent; rather, it proposes that referential uses are handed down from speaker to speaker, generation to generation, from the original dubbing or christening. Clearly, this theory works best for the kinds of referring expressions that function as names, which can be given to persons, places, and things.

Both theories of reference have strengths and weaknesses. The Description Theory works best for various uses of such descriptions as *the first person to walk on the moon* and perhaps also for most common nouns and adjectives. However, the Historical Chain Theory seems to work best for proper names, and is extendable to expressions such as *he, she, that,* and so forth. There is no reason to think that some mixture of these two views might not turn out to be correct, but much work needs to be done in the area of the theory of reference.

11.3 AN INFORMAL SEMANTIC THEORY

At the beginning of this chapter we asked what facts about meaning and reference were relevant to a semantic theory and we then schematized a number of them in (31). We said that the goal of a semantic theory was to correctly describe the semantic properties and relations of every expression in the language. The theory must also define what these semantic properties and relations are, and we surveyed some initial attempts in that direction. Furthermore, since a semantic theory must be finite though its scope must be infinite (there being an unlimited number of phrases and sentences in the language), we concluded that a semantic theory must be compositional and thus must be sensitive to the syntactic categories and structure of the expressions being described.

We turn now to the problem of outlining a semantic theory that begins to satisfy the goals just described. It is traditional to do this in two stages: first, to represent the semantics of words and idioms; second, to represent the semantics of phrases and sentences. The reason for this division is that syntactic relations such as subject and object are used in the second stage of representation but not in the first.

Words and Idioms

Semantic representation and decomposition
Most semantic theories have one component that represents the semantics of the syntactically unstructured expressions of the language, the words, as well as the semantics of those expressions whose syntactic structure is semantically irrelevant, the idioms. It also describes the semantic relations between words and idioms. This component is variously called the *dictionary* or the *lexicon*. We shall first look at the sorts of information that are represented at this level. We will call whatever information is recorded at this point the *lexical entry* for a word or idiom.

Beginning with syntactic information associated with words, note that we need to represent the part of speech of each expression. For instance, the word *run* can be either a verb or a noun:

(39) a. Run on now, I run this place. (verb)
   b. He scored nine runs in one inning and got a run in his sock. (noun)

Since a semantic theory must represent the meaning of each (meaningful) expression and represent nonsynonymous expressions as different in meaning, a lexical entry will have to associate the verb *run* with its verbal meanings while associating the noun *run* with its nominal meanings. Each occurrence of *run* in (39) means something different and the syntactic categories noun and verb distinguish the first two from the last two. Thus, the first piece of information we need for the semantics of a word is its syntactic category.

The situation is similar for idioms, some of which correspond to intransitive verbs (40a), some to transitive verbs (40b), and some to noun phrases (40c):

(40) a. NP kicks the bucket: NP dies
   b. NP reads the riot act to NP: NP bawls out NP
   c. That stick-in-the-mud: that old fogy

Though the syntactic category is necessary for correctly representing the semantics of an expression, it is not sufficient; many nonsynonymous expressions have the same syntactic categorization, as we witnessed earlier in the case of *run*. To account for the full range of semantic properties and relations set out in section 11.1, lexical entries for words and idioms will have to represent enough semantic information to predict these properties and relations at the lexical level. How can this be accomplished? First, by the representation of meaning (and occasionally reference) of words and idioms; and second, by the representation of various semantic relations between words and idioms.

The problem of how to represent the semantics of words and idioms is complicated by our inability to say exactly what meaning is, but the representation problem is not, thereby, made impossible. For instance, in mathematics one is able to describe various properties and relations between numbers as in (41):

(41) a. The number 2 is an even prime.
   b. For any number there is a larger number.

Yet we have no generally accepted theory of what numbers are. Similarly, it can be argued that in semantics one can represent meaning and reference without committing oneself to stating exactly what meaning and reference are. In order to do this, though, semantics must be fairly abstract and formal. We will not attempt a detailed discussion of semantic representation here. In spite of this, the student can gain insight into the nature of semantic representation from our informal presentation.

Consider some typical descriptive words and idioms such as *boy, girl, father, mother, kill,* and *kick the bucket.* It has seemed clear to many theorists that such words are not the most basic semantic units but are actually semantically complex items, composed or made up of more primitive semantic components. Semantic theories that decompose lexical items into more basic semantic components are called *decompositional* (or sometimes *componential*) semantic theories. In effect, a decompositional theory of word meaning extends compositionality to the level of the internal structure of lexical items. Let us consider, as an example of lexical decomposition, the following definition:

(Def. 2) boy: HUMAN(X) AND MALE(X) AND NOT-ADULT(X)

The basic idea in such a representation is that the symbols in capital letters represent the semantic components in the meaning of the word and the variable X stands for whoever is being spoken of. According to Def. 2, saying (42a) amounts to saying (42b):

(42) a.   That's a boy.
     b.   That's a human male who is nonadult.

A lexical entry for *girl* would look like Def. 2 except for having FEMALE(X) instead of MALE(X).

The word *father,* unlike *boy,* is a relational noun. To be a father is to be a male parent of someone—it is to bear a special relation to another person, the relation of fathering or begetting. Relations are usually represented with variables standing for the objects that are related. For instance, *father* is understood as "X is the father of Y," where X represents the father, Y the child. We can represent *father* at this level as Def. 3:

(Def. 3) father: MALE(X) AND X PARENT OF Y

Clearly, *mother* is like Def. 3 but with FEMALE(X) instead of MALE(X).

Transitive verbs are like relational nouns in requiring variables to indicate the various roles of the participants. Thus, *kill* is understood as "*X* kill *Y*." This is indicated by the fact that if there was a killing, then someone or something did the killing, and someone or something was killed; that is, if *X* killed *Y*, then *Y* died, and *X* caused this. We can represent this as in Def. 4, letting X_s indicate the subject and X_o indicate the direct object:

(Def. 4) kill: X_s CAUSE (X_o CHANGE TO (NOT-ALIVE(X_o)))

Thus at this level we can be said to have represented the meaning structure of these words.

It is easy to get the hang of doing decompositional semantics, though the details can get complicated (see Katz 1972 and Kempson 1977). The question now arises, What is the evidence for positing these semantic components out of which meaning representations are constructed? Probably the central form of linguistic argument in favor of lexical decomposition is from simplicity of predictions concerning the various semantic properties and relations. Just as transformational rules capture syntactic generalizations that would otherwise be missed, so it could be claimed that systems of semantics without decomposition fail to reflect certain generalizations concerning semantic properties and relations.

To see this, consider some additional kinship terms such as *mother, brother,* and *sister,* with their decompositional definitions:

(Def. 5) mother: FEMALE(X) AND X PARENT OF Y

(Def. 6) brother: MALE(X) AND X SIBLING OF Y

(Def. 7) sister: FEMALE(X) AND X SIBLING OF Y

On the basis of these representations we can predict a number of semantic properties and relations concerning these and related words. For instance, one can predict that *father* and *brother* (as well as the potentially infinite set including *son, uncle, nephew, grandfather, great-grandfather, great-great-grandfather,* and so on) all share the aspect of meaning, MALE, and so are similar in meaning in expressing the property of being male. The same goes for the analogous set containing FEMALE. That is, the decompositional representation of this potentially infinite set of kinship words can be given in terms of a very small number of repeatable semantic primitives. If we then add a general definition of *similarity in meaning* (in terms of repeated semantic primitives), it is possible to predict that each of these sets contains words that are similar (in meaning) with respect to maleness and femaleness.

Moreover, given a definition of *contradictory* (in terms of incompatible semantic primitives) it is possible to make certain predictions as automatic consequences of decompositional representation. For instance, we can predict that each of the examples in (43) is contradictory:

(43) X is a $\left\{ \begin{array}{l} \text{father} \\ \text{uncle} \\ \text{grandfather} \\ \text{great-grandfather} \\ \text{. . . great-grandfather} \end{array} \right\}$ and female

But with *male* substituted for *female,* each example is noncontradictory. Furthermore, such a theory can predict simply and directly that the members of each pair in the following potentially infinite list of pairs are *synonyms* (both members having identical semantic representations):

(44)   father: male parent
                         mother: female parent
            grandparent (of): parent of parent (of)
      great-grandparent (of): parent of parent of parent (of)

This form of prediction can be carried out for each semantic property and relation, covering huge parts of the vocabulary of a language. Without lexical decomposition each of these semantic predictions would have to be made separately for each of these words. Analogously in syntax, grammars without transformations could deal only clumsily, or not at all, with discontinuous constitutents and other dependency relations at the cost of adding many separate but clearly related rules. It might be concluded, then, that grammars excluding decomposition as well as grammars excluding transformations miss obvious generalizations in their respective domains.

As we said at the outset, the basic argument in favor of decomposition is simplicity of semantic prediction. Such theoretical elegance requires stronger conditions of adequacy on a semantic theory in that decompositional theories demand definitions of meaningful words. These definitions must provide not only necessary and sufficient conditions for correct application, but must be identical for synonyms and nonidentical for nonsynonyms. Some theorists have found such constraints highly desirable in principle but too strong in fact, a contention we will return to at the end of section 11.3.

Semantic restrictions and relations

Words and idioms combine with, and bear various semantic relations to, other words and idioms. So far our dictionary represents intrinsic meaning, but it does not represent semantic restrictions between words. For instance, it can be claimed that there is something anomalous about (45) taken literally:

(45) The table is a parent of the chair.

This could be accounted for by saying that the variables X and Y in the analysis of *parent* are restricted to animate objects. Ordinary dictionaries often put such restrictions in terms of what such words are "said of":

(Def. 8) addled: confused, *said of* minds; rotten, *said of* eggs.

In decompositional semantics, we can represent these semantic restrictions by using angle brackets, $\langle \rangle$, as in the complete definition of *father*:

(Def. 9) father: MALE(X) AND X PARENT OF Y AND $\langle$ANIMATE(X) AND ANIMATE(Y)$\rangle$

The angles enclosing ANIMATE(X) AND ANIMATE(Y) in Def. 9 restrict the application of *father* to animate things when it is used literally. The same device can be used to represent the semantic restrictions on *kill:*

(Def. 10) kill: X_s CAUSE (X_0 CHANGE TO (NOT-ALIVE(X_0))) AND $\langle$ANIMATE(X_0)$\rangle$

This representation makes the claim that whatever is killed must be animate and so predicts that when this restriction is violated, the compound expression will be (literally) anomalous, as in (46):

(46) John killed the table.

Since none of these definitions is more than a first approximation to a correct one, the reader should be thinking of ways they can be improved (see exercises).

If we consider again the meaning representation of *boy,* we can see that there are semantic relations that the dictionary entry alone does not represent. For instance, if X is a boy, then X is not female, and if X is a boy, X is animate, and so forth. How can we supplement the lexicon so as to account for these and similar facts?

One way would be to add such components as NOT-FEMALE(X) and ANIMATE(X) to our lexical entries for *boy* (as well as for other words such as *father, brother,* and *grandfather*). However, this would seem to miss the generalization that if a word contains MALE as one of its components, then that in itself guarantees that it will also contain ANIMATE and will not contain FEMALE, and so forth. How can each of these conditions be stated once as a single fact? Theorists all agree that what is needed here is some kind of a meaning rule connecting these semantic components, but they do not agree on the exact nature of such devices, which have been called redundancy rules by Katz (1972), and meaning postulates by Carnap (1956). For neutrality, we will call such principles *inference rules*, and they will be added to the lexicon as information concerning semantic relations between words and idioms, separate from any particular lexical entry. For example, the following rules by which one can infer what is on the right-hand side of the arrow from what is on the left-hand side would account for the facts we have mentioned about *boy*:

(IR 1) MALE(X) $\rightarrow$ NOT-FEMALE(X) ("Infer NOT-FEMALE(X) from MALE(X)")

(IR 2) MALE(X) $\rightarrow$ ANIMATE(X) ("Infer ANIMATE(X) from MALE(X)")

So far it may seem that the addition of inference rules to the lexicon is a matter of theoretical simplicity and that their job of recording certain semantic relations between words could be done, albeit less economically, by decomposition. However, there are semantic relations between words suggesting that inference rules are not simply elegant ways of stating certain facts, but are required. Some semantic relations between words cannot plausibly be represented by decomposition:

(47) a. John likes pizza and Mary likes pizza.
    b. John likes pizza.
    c. Mary likes pizza.

Although (47b) and (47c) can be inferred from (47a), it makes no sense to speak of the decomposition of *and*. Similarly, in the following examples the second member of each pair does not seem to be the result of decomposing the first:

(48) a. *Someone* likes ice cream.

    b. It is *not* true that *everyone* does *not* like ice cream.

(49) a. It is *possible* that someone likes okra.

    b. It is *not necessarily* true that *not* anyone likes okra.

(50) a. His window is *red*.

    b. His window has a *color*.

Examples (48)–(50) suggest that inference rules such as the following must be a part of the lexicon:

(IR 3) X AND $Y \rightarrow \begin{Bmatrix} X \\ Y \end{Bmatrix}$ ("From (X and Y) one may infer X and one may infer Y")

(IR 4) $RED(X) \rightarrow COLORED(X)$

With both lexical entries and inference rules, our semantic theory can account for a number of semantic properties and relations, for example, that (51a) entails (51b):

(51) a. Someone is a boy.

    b. Someone is not female.

This entailment can be accounted for by our semantic theory in the following way:

(52) a. According to Def. 2, *Someone is a boy* means something like: $SOME(X)$ IS $HUMAN(X)$ AND $MALE(X)$ AND NOT-$ADULT(X)$

    b. Then, according to IR 3, we may infer that $MALE(X)$.

    c. Then, according to IR 1, we may infer that NOT-$FEMALE(X)$.

    d. Since the English expression *not female* can be represented as NOT-$FEMALE(X)$, we may conclude that $SOME(X)$ IS NOT-$FEMALE(X)$.

According to this explanation, we show that one sentence entails another sentence when the second can be inferred from the first by decomposition and inference rules.

So far, then, we can represent the following three kinds of information in our semantics:

meaning (lexical entry)
semantic restrictions (lexical entry)
some entailments (inference rules)

We certainly have not shown that *all* semantic properties and relations can be represented in this format (see exercises). Indeed, it is still an open question in the field of semantics what a descriptively adequate format will look like.

Phrases and Sentences

So far we can account for the semantics of only words and idioms. We have not yet attempted to account for the semantics of syntactically *complex expressions*. For this we need a syntactic description of the strings of words which involves more than the parts of speech. We need to know the linear order of the words, the grouping of the words, and the grammatical relations that the various expressions in the phrase or sentence bear to each other. Since the effect of transformations is often to change the linear order of words, effect new groupings, and disguise grammatical relations such as subject and object, it has been thought that most if not all of the contribution syntax makes to semantics should be at the underlying or deep structure level. Thus, on the conception known as the Standard Theory, the grammar diagrammed in figure 8.1 would be supplemented by a semantic component at the level of underlying structure, as in figure 11.2.

Composition

We said at the end of section 11.1 that an adequate semantic theory must reflect the compositionality of natural language and to do this it must contain rules that are sensitive to the syntactic structure of phrases and sentences. We call these *composition rules* (also called projection rules). To illustrate them and their mode of operation, we consider a simple sentence such as (53):

(53) A boy kills a dog.

The syntax of (53) will be simplified somewhat and represented as tree 11.1, which reflects only semantically relevant structure. Given the meaning of (53), we want to be sure that in the semantic representation of this sentence it is the case that the dog dies, not the boy; whereas in the sentence *A dog kills a boy*, it is the boy who dies and not the dog. How can this be accomplished? The first thing that the semantic com-

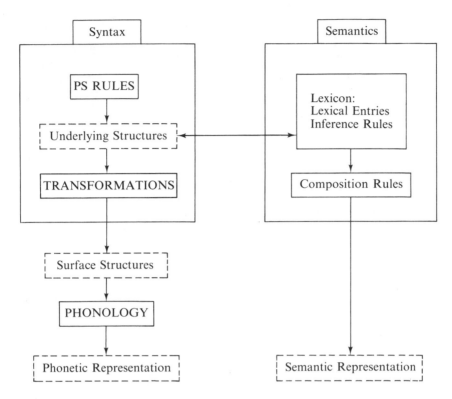

Figure 11.2
Model of the Standard Theory of transformational grammar

ponent does is to represent the meaning of each word by simply inserting its semantic representation from the lexicon—where *dog* is represented as CANINE(X) AND ANIMATE(X)—as illustrated in tree 11.2. This completes the semantic representation of the sentence for meaning at the lexical level.

We turn now to the phrase level and then to the whole sentence. The basic idea is to start combining, or composing semantic representations of different words that are grouped together under a single node in the tree, starting at the bottom and working our way up to the S node. But to compose semantic representations, we need rules of composition to get representations of complex expressions from representations of simpler ones. The nature and full variety of composition rules is still unsettled, so we will merely illustrate the process with the following three composition rules:

Tree 11.1

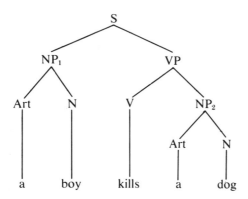

Tree 11.2

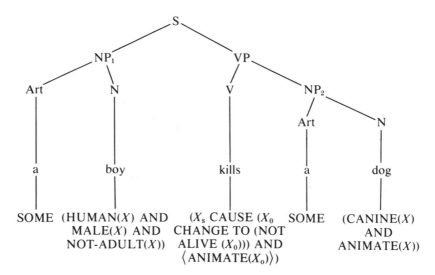

(CR 1) Variables in lexical entries that are not categorized for subject or object are given the number index from their dominating NP.

(CR 2) Lexical variables that are categorized for subject or object get the number of the NP they are categorized for.

(CR 3) Semantic components are joined with AND, provided semantic restrictions are not violated.

Let us see how these rules work. Recall that we apply the rules from the bottom of the tree up, starting with CR 1, then CR 2, and finally CR

3. Both NP_1 and NP_2 are at the bottom of tree 11.2, but we will begin with the most deeply embedded one. So the first step is to apply CR 1 to the phrase *a dog* under NP_2. The result is to subscript the lexical variable X with a 2 (see tree 11.3). Since CR 2 and CR 3 cannot apply, we move on to the next highest node, which is NP_1. The result of applying CR 1 here is illustrated in tree 11.4. Again, since CR 2 and CR 3 cannot apply, we move to the next highest node, VP.

The last two composition rules apply at VP; we will illustrate their application in order. First, notice that in the semantic representation for *kill,* the variable X is categorized for subject X_s, and then for direct object, X_0. However, tree 11.5 shows that only the direct object is a constituent at the VP node, so only it, NP_2, can be composed at this point. Since CR 1 does not apply and CR 2 does, we get the result shown in tree 11.5. Note that the semantic representation of NP_2 meets the semantic restriction on *kill,* and for simplicity we will henceforth omit the restriction $\langle$ANIMATE $(X_0)\rangle$ in the representation of *kill.*

Now all we need to do is to connect the semantic representation of *kill* to the semantic representation of *a dog* to get the semantic representation of the VP *kills a dog* (see tree 11.6).

Tree 11.3

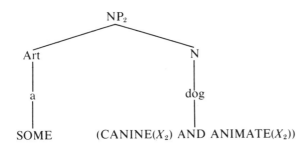

Tree 11.4

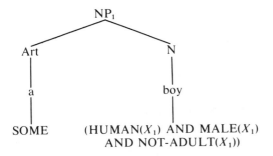

Tree 11.5

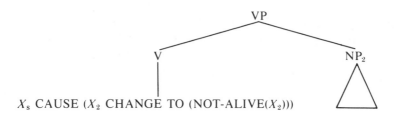

X_s CAUSE $(X_2$ CHANGE TO (NOT-ALIVE$(X_2)))$

Tree 11.6

X_s CAUSE $(X_2$ CHANGE TO (NOT-ALIVE$(X_2)))$ AND SOME CANINE(X_2)
AND ANIMATE(X_2)

Tree 11.7

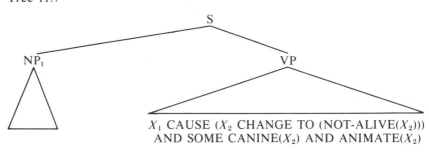

X_1 CAUSE $(X_2$ CHANGE TO (NOT-ALIVE$(X_2)))$
AND SOME CANINE(X_2) AND ANIMATE(X_2)

Finally, we move to the highest node in the sentence, the S node. So far our semantic representations have been at the word or phrase level. To compose at the S node is to say how the meaning of the whole sentence is determined by the meaning of its constituent phrases and their grammatical relations. Since CR 1 does not apply and CR 2 does, we get tree 11.7, where the subject variable in *kill* is indexed as X_1. This leaves only CR 3 to apply to connect the semantic representation of NP$_1$ with the semantic representation of VP within the sentence, producing tree 11.8.

Although tree 11.8 is not perfect as a semantic representation of the original sentence *A boy kills a dog,* further refinements are not necessary for our purposes here (see Bierwisch 1969; 1971). As we can see, some desired semantic properties and relations are captured. For

Tree 11.8

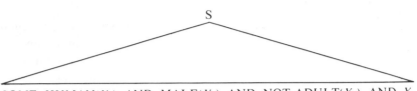

SOME HUMAN(X_1) AND MALE(X_1) AND NOT-ADULT(X_1) AND X_1
CAUSE (X_2 CHANGE TO (NOT ALIVE(X_2))) AND SOME
CANINE(X_2) AND ANIMATE(X_2)

instance, the fact that sentence (53) receives a semantic representation
at all predicts that the expression is meaningful, and tree 11.8 represents (imperfectly) its meaning. Also note that the component NOT-
ALIVE(X_2) in tree 11.8 is attached to the same variable, X_2, that the
reading for *dog* is: CANINE(X_2) AND ANIMATE(X_2), indicating that
the dog, not the boy, died. However, had the sentence been (54), then *a
boy* would have been the direct object:

(54) A dog kills a boy.

So *a boy* would have been NP$_2$ and the reading for *boy* would have
been attached to X_2, thereby representing the fact that if (54) were true,
it would be a boy who dies, not a dog. Other semantic properties and
relations are captured as well (see exercises). But, more importantly,
we can see how a semantic theory can be *compositional*: how the
semantic representation of a syntactically complex expression can be
determined by the semantic representation of its constituent words and
their grammatical relations by means of rules of composition.

   Finally, we might ask ourselves how this compositional theory might
define some of the semantic properties and relations set out earlier.
First of all, the theory will, if adequate, generate a semantic representation for every well-formed expression in the language: if the expression
is a word or idiom, its meaning is represented in the lexicon; if the
expression is a phrase or sentence, its meaning is represented on the
basis of syntactic structure plus composition rules. Since one way or
another every meaningful expression will receive a semantic representation in an adequate theory, we can say that an expression is
meaningful if it has a semantic representation; an expression is ambiguous if it is given more than one semantic representation; two
expressions are synonymous if they are given the same semantic representation; two expressions overlap in meaning if they share a semantic
component; and, finally, one expression entails another if the second

can be inferred from the first on the basis of decomposition and inference rules.

Notice that although these definitions do capture something essential to the notions of ambiguity, synonymy, overlap of meaning, and so forth, they in effect reduce these notions to the nature and number of semantic representations given by the lexicon and composition rules. But the question Why does expression e mean what it means? is not yet answered. It may well be that *bachelor* means HUMAN(X) AND ADULT(X) AND MALE(X) AND UNMARRIED(X), but what are we saying about the word *bachelor* when we say that this is what it means? Which brings us back to the original question: What is meaning? That is, what is it for something to have a meaning? We concluded earlier that currently the most promising account of meaning is in terms of use. If this conclusion is correct, the question of what meaning is takes us to pragmatics, the topic of Chapter 12.

Semantic representation: some issues (optional section)

One topic of current research and controversy is the relative importance of lexical decomposition as opposed to inference rules. On the one hand, Katz (1972) and Katz and Nagel (1974) view a substantial portion of the lexicon as susceptible to decomposition, whereas Jackendoff (1972) and Fodor, Fodor, and Garrett (1975), among others, view decomposition as a marginal phenomenon with inference rules being the predominant piece of semantic machinery. To illustrate the pervasiveness of inference rules consider again the fact that (53), *A boy kills a dog,* entails (55a), which has (55b) as its semantic representation:

(55) a. A dog dies.

b. SOME ANIMATE(X) AND CANINE(X) AND (CHANGE TO (NOT-ALIVE(X)))

To infer (55b) from (53) we need first to apply IR 3 to (53) to get (56):

(56) X_1 CAUSE (CHANGE TO (NOT-ALIVE(X_2))) AND SOME CANINE(X_2) AND ANIMATE(X_2)

But to infer (55a) from (53) we still need the principle that causing X to change to being not alive entails that X be not alive. In other words, we need another inference rule:

(IR 5) X_1 CAUSE (CHANGE TO (NOT-ALIVE(X_2))) $\rightarrow$ NOT-ALIVE(X_2)

When (IR 5) applies to (56) it gives (55a) as an entailment. We can see that even with this amount of decomposition, we still need inference rules to account for the entailments of *kill*.

A further challenge to decomposition comes from another quarter, from what are called natural-kind terms. These are words such as *dog, water, gold,* which refer to things (or stuff) that form a "kind," or species, in nature and are governed by particular laws of nature, such as the laws of biology, chemistry, or physics. Some authors—Kripke (1972) and Putnam (1975) are two—have suggested that these sorts of words function semantically in the language very much like proper names and that both proper names and natural-kind terms should receive an historical-chain analysis of their meaning and reference. If that suggestion is correct, then such terms would not be given a meaning, in the traditional sense of a definition, by decomposition. On the historical chain view, something is gold, for example, if it is the same kind of thing, obeying the same physical laws, as the matter originally dubbed *gold* when the word was introduced into the language. If such a view is right (see Schwartz 1977 for a survey discussion), then decomposition is an even more restricted phenomenon than has been supposed.

Exercises

Section 11.1

1. We gave two reasons for a grammar to include a representation of semantic information. What were they? Can you think of another reason?

2. Three examples of speaking nonliterally were given. What were they? Give three more examples, two of which are not declarative sentences.

3. Consider the following dialogue:

a: What chances do I have for a raise?

b: Two, slim and fat.

Does *fat* mean the same thing as *slim* in the language, or is one of these words being used nonliterally? Defend your answer.

*4. Interpret the following sentences. What are the principles of interpretation?

a. Ralph may not be a communist, but he's at least a *pinko*.
b. He traded his hot car for a *cold* one.
c. John is studying sociology and other *soft* sciences.
d. Who *killed* Lake Erie?

*5. Think of five words, write down what you think they mean, then look them up in a good dictionary. Is your idiolect at variance with the dialect called Standard English?

*6. Suppose someone said that a grammar must describe what a *speaker* means in uttering an expression from the language, and that it must do this for every meaningful expression. What problems are there for this proposal?

*7. Entailment relations are transitive: If *cat* → *mammal,* and *mammal* → *animal,* then *cat* → *animal.* Now consider the "part of" relation. Is it transitive? Defend your answer.

a. A second is part of a minute.
A minute is part of an hour.
An hour is part of a day.
Is a second part of an hour? part of a day?
b. The toenail is part of the toe.
The toe is part of the foot.
The foot is part of the leg.
Is the toenail part of the leg?
c. Henry's toe is part of Henry.
Henry is part of the 23rd Battalion.
Is Henry's toe part of the 23rd Battalion?

*8. Consider the following sentences and say what the referring expression refers to:

a. *The chair you are sitting on* sells all over France for $200.
b. *Time Magazine* was bought out by Hearst, so now *it*'s good for wrapping your garbage.

9. Why should a semantic theory be finite?

10. What is it for a semantic theory to be compositional?

Section 11.2
1. What is the Referential Theory of meaning? What is one objection we gave to it?

2. On the Referential Theory of meaning (R), if an expression has a referent it has a meaning. Give at least one example of a kind of expression where this is false.

*3. What is *ambiguity* on the Referential Theory of meaning? How might this semantic property be a problem for a theory (R)? Defend your answer.

4. (a) What is the Mentalist Theory of meaning? (b) What are the two versions of it we discussed? (c) What are the problems with each version?

5. What would *ambiguity* be on the imagist version of the Mentalist Theory of meaning? How might this be a problem for the theory? Defend your answer.

6. What is the Use Theory of meaning? What is its major weakness?

Section 11.3
*1. The words *mother, father, sister,* and *brother* all have religious as well as biological meanings. How would one represent the religious senses of each word?

*2. Do a semantic analysis of the form given in the text for five more kinship terms including *uncle, grandmother,* and *niece.*

3. Given Def. 4, what would the semantic representation of the idiomatic sense of *kick the bucket* be?

4. Find another word like *addled* in Def. 8 which changes its meaning depending on what it is applied to.

5. Are there any more restrictions on the (literal) meaning of *kill* in Def. 10? (Hint: Can the number 2 kill someone?)

*6. The word *kill* has a related figurative sense as in *The bill was killed in Congress.* How would you represent that figurative sense?

7. At the lexical level, how might the nine meaning properties and relations schematized in (31a) be defined? (Hint: Some of these were defined in the text.)

*8. Nothing has been said about *reference* at the lexical level. Does a word like *father* or *chair* or *kill* refer when not a part of a phrase or sentence? What does it refer to? Defend your answer.

9. Work out a derivation of the reading for sentence (54), *A dog kills a boy,* on the model of our derivation in tree 11.3 to tree 11.8.

10. Suppose someone were to claim the following: "Given some combination of phonemes, we can *never* predict the meaning of the combination; given some combination of morphemes, we can sometimes predict the meaning of the combination and sometimes not; given some combination of words into a sentence, if we know the words and their grammatical relations, we can *always* predict the meaning of the sentence." Criticize or defend this claim in terms of evidence based on your knowledge gained from chapters 6–11.

References

Alston, W. (1967) "Meaning," in P. Edwards, ed., *The Encyclopedia of Philosophy,* vol. 5, 233–241, Macmillan, New York.

Bierwisch, M. (1969) "On certain problems of semantic representation," *Foundations of Language,* 5, 153–184.

——— (1970) "Semantics," in J. Lyons, ed., *New Horizons in Linguistics,* Penguin Books, Baltimore.

——— (1971) "On classifying semantic features," in D. Steinberg and L. Jakobovits, eds., *Semantics,* Cambridge University Press, Cambridge, England.

Carnap, R. (1956) *Meaning and Necessity,* University of Chicago Press, Chicago.

Chomsky, N. (1965) *Aspects of the Theory of Syntax,* MIT Press, Cambridge, Mass.

Dillon, G. (1977) *Introduction to Contemporary Linguistic Semantics,* Prentice-Hall, Englewood Cliffs, N.J.

Fodor, J. (1977) *Semantics: Theories of Meaning in Generative Grammar,* Crowell, New York.

Fodor, J., J. A. Fodor, and M. Garrett (1975) "The psychological unreality of semantic representations," *Linguistic Inquiry* 4, 515–531.

Glucksberg, S., and J. Danks (1975) *Experimental Psycholinguistics,* Earlbaum, Hillsdale, New Jersey.

Grice, H. P. (1957) "Meaning," *Philosophical Review* 66, 377–388.

―――― (1968) "Utterer's meaning, sentence-meaning, and word-meaning," *Foundations of Language* 4, 225–242.

―――― (1969) "Utterer's meaning and intentions," *Philosophical Review* 78, 147–177.

Jackendoff, R. (1972) *Semantic Interpretation in Generative Grammar,* MIT Press, Cambridge, Mass.

Katz, J., and J. Fodor (1963) "The structure of a semantic theory," *Language* 39, 170–210.

Katz, J. (1972) *Semantic Theory,* Harper & Row, New York.

Katz, J., and R. Nagel (1974) "Meaning postulates and semantic theory," *Foundations of Language* 2, 311–340.

Kempson, R. (1977) *Semantic Theory,* Cambridge University Press, Cambridge, England.

Kripke, S. (1972) "Naming and necessity," in D. Davidson and G. Harman, eds., *Semantics of Natural Language,* Reidel, Dordrecht, Holland.

Lehrer, A. (1974) *Semantic Fields and Lexical Structure,* North-Holland, Amsterdam, Holland.

Lehrer, K., and A. Lehrer, eds. (1970) *Theory of Meaning,* Prentice-Hall, Englewood Cliffs, N.J.

Lyons, J. (1977) *Semantics,* 2 vols., Cambridge University Press, Cambridge, England.

Miller, G. (1978) "Semantic relations among words," in M. Halle, J. Bresnan, and G. Miller, eds., *Linguistic Theory and Psychological Reality,* MIT Press, Cambridge, Mass.

Putnam, H. (1975) "The meaning of 'meaning'," in K. Gunderson, ed., *Language, Mind and Knowledge,* University of Minnesota Press, Minneapolis.

Schiffer, S. (1972) *Meaning,* Oxford University Press, Oxford, England.

Schwartz, S., ed. (1977) *Naming, Necessity and Natural Kinds,* Cornell University Press, Ithaca, N.Y.

Chapter Twelve

PRAGMATICS: THE STUDY OF LANGUAGE USE AND LINGUISTIC COMMUNICATION

Is Pragmatics Part of a Grammar?

Probably the most pervasive characteristic of human social interaction, so pervasive that we hardly find it remarkable, is that we talk. Sometimes we talk to particular persons, sometimes to anyone who will listen; and when we cannot find anyone to listen, we even talk to ourselves. Although human language fulfills a large variety of functions, from waking someone up in the morning with a cheery *Wake up!* to christening a ship with a solemn *I hereby christen this ship "H.M.S. Britannia,"* we will be focusing here on those uses of language that are instrumental for human communication. But, one might ask, why should a linguist be concerned with language *use* when describing a language? And what are these various uses of language, especially those central to communication? As with semantics, asking such questions begins one's introduction to the subject of pragmatics and attempting to answer them, especially with an informal theory, completes that introduction.

One way of motivating the inclusion of pragmatic information in a grammar is by way of semantics. We suggested earlier that a promising conception of meaning was one in which meaning is determined by use. If use does determine meaning, then the theory of language use will provide the foundations for semantics, so at least that part of pragmatics that concerns itself with meaning and reference will be a part of a grammar.

A second way to motivate the inclusion of pragmatic information in a grammar is by considering the linguistic competence of a fluent speaker. Would we want to say of speakers who did not know any of the kinds of information in (1) that they spoke the English language fluently? We think not.

(1) a. *Hello* is used to greet.

    b. *Goodbye* is used to bid farewell.

    c. The phrase *that desk* can be correctly used by a speaker to refer to some particular desk.

    d. The phrase *is a desk* can be correctly used to characterize any number of desks.

    e. *Pass the salt, please* is used to request some salt.

    f. *How old are you?* is used to ask for someone's age.

    g. *It's raining* is used to state that it is raining.

    h. *I promise I will be there* is used to promise.

12.1 AIMS AND CLAIMS OF PRAGMATICS

From the above list we get a glimpse of the wide variety of possible uses of language, but before we survey these various uses, we must first distinguish between using language *to do* something and using language *in doing* something. It is certainly a very important fact about human beings that they use language *in* much of their thought. It is likely that people could not think some of the thoughts they think, especially abstract thoughts, if they did not have language at their disposal. Central as this fact may be to our cognitive life, it is not central to the pragmatic notion of language use, the use of language to *do* things. When we focus on what people use language to do, we focus on what a person is doing with words in particular situations; we focus on the intentions, purposes, beliefs, and wants that a speaker has in speaking—in performing *speech acts*. Because the study of speech acts is a central concern of pragmatics, we will restrict ourselves to that topic for most of our discussion. We can therefore recast the project of surveying language uses as one of categorizing the nature and variety of speech acts. We will approach the problem of surveying speech acts in stages. First, we will set out the main types of speech acts; second, we will investigate some different ways of performing them; and finally, we will look at some related linguistic phenomena.

Types of Speech Acts

Speech act theorists found no appropriate terminology already available for labeling types of speech acts, so they had to invent one. The terminology we use here comes, in large part, from Austin (1962) and

Searle (1969). According to the theory they have developed, there are four important categories of speech acts, illustrated in figure 12.1.

Utterance acts are simply acts *of* uttering sounds, syllables, words, phrases, and sentences from a language. From a speech act point of view, these are not very interesting acts because an utterance act per se is not communicative; it can be performed by a parrot, tape recorder, or voice synthesizer. The main interest of utterance acts derives from the fact that in performing an utterance act we usually perform either an *illocutionary act* (an act performed *in* uttering something), or a *perlocutionary act* (an act performed *by* uttering something—an act that produces an *effect* on the hearer). It is these latter kinds of acts that interest speech act theorists most.

Austin (1962) characterized the *illocutionary act* as an act performed *in* saying something. For instance, in saying *Ali is the greatest,* one might perform the act of asserting that Ali is the greatest. Some other examples of illocutionary acts:

(2) promising   threatening
    reporting   requesting
    stating   suggesting
    asking   ordering
    telling   proposing

What are some of the important characteristics of illocutionary (as opposed to perlocutionary) acts? First, illocutionary acts can often be successfully performed simply by uttering the right *explicit performative* sentence, with the right intentions and beliefs, and under the right circumstances. For instance, the utterance acts of producing sentences (3a)–(3c) can be performances of the illocutionary acts of ordering, promising, and appointing, respectively.

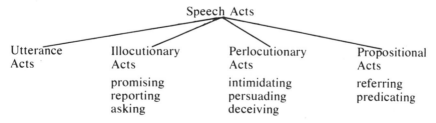

Figure 12.1
Types of speech acts

(3) a. I (hereby) order you to leave.
 b. I (hereby) promise to pay.
 c. I (hereby) appoint you chairman.

Second, illocutionary acts (unlike perlocutionary acts) are central to linguistic communication. Our normal conversations are composed in large part of statements, suggestions, requests, proposals, greetings and the like. When we do perform perlocutionary acts such as persuading or intimidating, we do so by performing illocutionary acts such as stating or threatening.

Third, and most importantly, unlike perlocutionary acts, most illocutionary acts used to communicate have the feature that one performs them successfully simply by getting one's illocutionary intentions recognized. For example, if you say *Ali is the greatest,* and if I recognize your intention to tell me that Ali is the greatest, then you will have succeeded in telling me, and I will have understood you. But if you are attempting to persuade me that Ali is the greatest, it is not sufficient for me just to recognize your intention to persuade me; I must also believe what you said. If Ali says to you, *I'm the greatest,* you will recognize his intention to tell or inform you that he is the greatest, but you will not necessarily be persuaded that he is the greatest. To be persuaded of it you must believe it, and that will probably require watching Ali's fists in action, not just his mouth.

Austin (1962) characterizes *perlocutionary acts* as acts performed *by* saying something. For instance, suppose John believes everything Howard Cosell says; then by saying *Ali is the greatest,* Howard Cosell could convince John that Ali is the greatest. Some typical examples of perlocutionary acts are:

(4) inspiring   persuading
    impressing   deceiving
    embarrassing   misleading
    intimidating   irritating

What are some important characteristics of perlocutionary acts? First, perlocutionary acts (unlike illocutionary acts) are not performed by uttering explicit performative sentences. We do not perform the perlocutionary act of convincing someone that Ali is the greatest by uttering (5):

(5) I (hereby) convince you that Ali is the greatest.

Second, perlocutionary acts seem to involve the *effects* of utterance acts and illocutionary acts on the thoughts, feelings, and actions of the hearer, whereas illocutionary acts do not. Thus, perlocutionary acts can be represented as an illocutionary act of the speaker (*S*) plus its effects on the hearer (*H*):

(6) a. *S* tells + *H* believes . . . = *S* persuades *H* that . . .
    b. *S* tells + *H* intends . . . = *S* persuades *H* to . . .

Illocutionary acts are therefore means to perlocutionary acts, and not the converse. Perlocutionary acts have not been investigated to the extent that illocutionary acts have been, partly because they are not as intimately related to linguistic structure, semantics, and communication as are illocutionary acts. We mention them here mainly to set them aside.

If we look again at illocutionary acts such as asserting, questioning, requesting, and promising, the attentive reader will notice that there can be an overlap in *what* is asserted, questioned, requested. For instance, suppose a speaker utters the following sentences and thereby performs the indicated acts:

(7) a. Borg beat Nastase.   (statement)
    b. Borg beat Nastase?   (question)
    c. Borg, beat Nastase!   (request, demand)

All of the above illocutionary acts are concerned with Borg's beating Nastase, which is called the *propositional content* of the illocutionary act. As (7) illustrates, different types of illocutionary acts can have the same propositional content. Furthermore, each type of illocutionary act can have different propositional contents. For example, the illocutionary act of stating can have a wide variety of propositional contents in that a wide variety of propositions can be stated:

(8) a. Borg beat Nastase. ⎤
                    (statements)
    b. Connors beat Borg.⎦

The simplest type of propositional content is expressed by means of acts of *referring* and *predicating*, wherein a speaker refers to something and then characterizes it. Suppose that a speaker *S* utters the sentence *Borg is tired* and thereby asserts that Borg is tired. In making this assertion, the speaker would also be performing the *propositional acts* of referring to Borg with the name *Borg* and of characterizing him with the predicate *is tired*.

We have now delineated four major types of speech acts: utterance acts, illocutionary acts, perlocutionary acts, and propositional acts—the latter including the subacts of referring and predicating. Although a speaker's purposes in talking may require the performance of any one or more of these types of acts, communication seems centrally bound up with illocutionary acts and propositional acts, and these acts will receive the major portion of our attention. It should not be thought, by the way, that these speech act types cannot be further subdivided in interesting and subtle ways. In section 12.2 we will look at one such attempt.

Ways of Performing Speech Acts

Speech acts in general, and illocutionary acts in particular, can be performed in a variety of ways. The cases we have been discussing so far represent only one of at least six possibilities. To begin with, we will say that an act is *literal* if (roughly speaking) a speaker means what he says. Conversely, we will say that an act is *nonliteral* if a speaker does not mean what his words mean literally. Next, we will say that an act is *indirect* if (roughly speaking) a speaker performs that act by means of performing another speech act. Conversely, we will say that an act is *direct* if it is not indirect, that is, if it is *not* performed by means of performing any other act. What are some examples of these ways of performing speech acts?

Performing Illocutionary Acts

While considering the following examples, keep in mind that many illocutionary acts can be successfully performed but still fail as communication. A speaker may state something but fail to communicate to the hearer for a variety of reasons: the hearer may be asleep, may not know the language, may not know what the words mean. For the illocutionary act to be successful in communicating, the hearer must recognize (identify) the speaker's illocutionary intent—the hearer must identify what it is that the speaker is attempting to do (state, order, promise, and so on). Thus the reason a speaker S says what he says is, for the most part, to enable the hearer to infer S's communicative intentions. As we will see, though, this process of identifying communicative intentions can be either quite direct or indirect and roundabout.

First, consider the performance of literal and direct acts. Typical examples of such acts are utterances of, *I have a headache,* used to report a headache; *Please leave,* used to request someone to leave; and *What time is it?* used to ask someone the time. These sorts of acts are the simplest for a hearer to identify because they involve the minimal amount of inference. With literal and direct acts, knowing the language takes the hearer most of the way toward recognizing what the speaker is up to.

With nonliteral direct acts the matter is a little different. In these cases the hearer H must infer that the speaker S does not mean what his words mean literally, as well as infer what S does mean. Typical examples of nonliteral but direct acts are utterances of *I'd never have guessed,* used (sarcastically) to indicate that something is obvious; *You can say that again,* used (figuratively) to endorse someone's remark; *A pig wouldn't eat this food,* used (as an exaggeration) to condemn the food.

When we turn to indirect acts, the story gets a little more complicated because we have (at least) two acts to contend with—the direct act and the indirect act. There are four possibilities, depending on whether the direct act is literal or not and whether the indirect act is literal or not.

(9) Speech Act$_1$ Speech Act$_2$
   a. literal and direct   +   nonliteral and indirect
   b. literal and direct   +   literal and indirect
   c. nonliteral and direct   +   nonliteral and indirect
   d. nonliteral and direct   +   literal and indirect

Consider two typical examples of (9a)—that is, a literal and direct act associated with a nonliteral and indirect act: utterance of the sentence *I would like some Necco wafers,* used, first, to report a want and, second, to request some Necco wafers; an utterance of *My mouth is parched,* used, first, to report how dry one's mouth is and, second, to request a drink. Note that in each case the second act is nonliteral because in these cases the *speaker* means that the hearer is to do something; but the *sentences* mean, in one case, that the speaker wants a Necco wafer, and, in the other, that the speaker's mouth is dry. (As a test of nonliterality, just ask yourself whether the indirect act would have been literal if it had been direct.)

A typical example of (9b)—that is, a literal and direct act associated with a literal and indirect act—would be an utterance of the sentence *The bull is about to charge,* used, first, to report about a bull and, second, to warn someone of danger. Notice that in this case both the direct and the indirect acts are literal—the speaker means what he says.

A typical example of (9c)—a nonliteral and direct act associated with a nonliteral and indirect act—would be an utterance of the sentence *I'm sure the cat likes you pulling its tail,* used (sarcastically) to point out that the cat does not like having its tail pulled and, second, to request the hearer to stop. Finally, examples of (9d) are controversial and hard to find (see exercises).

This completes our initial survey of ways of performing illocutionary acts. Of the six possibilities summarized in figure 12.2, only category 6 is rare and hard to find; the other five are common and quite important to normal linguistic communication—which would be a good deal less colorful if we were limited to just literal and direct illocutionary acts.

Performing Other Speech Acts (optional section)

Can other kinds of speech acts be performed nonliterally or indirectly? No one has seriously investigated the possibility as yet, but it does seem that some of them can be.

Consider acts of *referring*. To refer nonliterally is to pick out or identify a referent, but not by virtue of meaning what the referring expression means. (On referring expressions, see section 11.1, subsection on "Speaker-reference and linguistic-reference.") In the case of proper names, to refer nonliterally is to pick out a referent by using a name that the referent has not been given. Imagine that Jones believes himself to be Napoleon. We might address him as Napoleon and even

	Speech Act$_1$: Direct	Speech Act$_2$: Indirect
1. I have a headache.	Literal	—
2. A pig wouldn't eat this food.	Nonliteral	—
3. I would like some Necco wafers.	Literal (report)	Nonliteral (request)
4. The bull is about to charge.	Literal (report)	Literal (warning)
5. I'm sure the cat likes you pulling its tail.	Nonliteral (report)	Nonliteral (request)
6. ?	Nonliteral	Literal

Figure 12.2
Ways of performing illocutionary acts

refer to him as Napoleon in speaking to others, yet he is not actually named Napoleon.

What would it be to refer indirectly? It would be to refer to X by referring to Y. Is this possible? Recall that there are at least two subtypes to this problem: where the direct act is literal and where it is nonliteral, instances of the latter being easier to find. Consider cases of figurative language. If a speaker says *The White House announced today*, a normal hearer would infer that the speaker was referring to some person who was speaking for the current administration. Such a speaker would have referred to the spokesman both nonliterally and indirectly.

What would it be to *predicate* nonliterally or indirectly? We have already seen many examples where the referents have the properties or relations expressed by the predicate. If I say *He's a tiger,* intending to attribute to him (whoever *he* refers to) the property of being aggressive, then I have predicated nonliterally (assuming of course that I do not mean, literally, that he is a certain sort of feline).

How about *perlocutionary* acts? Can they be performed nonliterally and indirectly? Since perlocutionary acts are already defined as acts involving the effects of other acts, the most interesting cases are those in which the second, indirect, perlocutionary act is performed by performing some other perlocutionary act. For instance, a speaker might get hearers to leave by boring them or might anger hearers by insulting them.

The notion of a literal (as opposed to a nonliteral) perlocutionary act involves the idea that its illocutionary cause is literal (as opposed to nonliteral). For instance, a speaker may state (illocutionary) something, and by stating something, insult (perlocutionary) the hearer H, and by insulting the hearer, thereby anger H into doing something foolish. Provoking the hearer may well have been the speaker's ultimate objective in uttering the statement. We call the perlocutionary act (in this case the insulting) nonliteral if its illocutionary cause is nonliteral. Insults and flattery are the most common types of nonliteral perlocutionary acts. No speaker who had not adopted a very unusual zoological taxonomy could mean what he says in uttering *You turkey!*

In this section we have looked at a variety of ways in which speech acts might be performed. We have seen that illocutionary acts, propositional acts, and even perlocutionary acts can be performed nonliterally and indirectly.

Other Pragmatic Pheomena (optional section)

Some pragmatic phenomena that have gained prominence in recent linguistic discussions are not directly concerned with the enumeration of types of speech acts, nor with ways of performing them, but rather with relations between the expression uttered and certain aspects of the context of utterance. One of the most widely discussed examples of such phenomena is *pragmatic presupposition*—not to be confused with semantic presupposition discussed in chapter 11.

In the everyday sense of *presuppose,* to presuppose something is to assume something, or to take it for granted in advance, but not to say it. Since assuming something is not normally considered an act but rather a state, presupposing is best viewed as a state and not an act. Related to (pragmatic) presupposing is (pragmatic) *presupposition*: that which is assumed or taken for granted. Clearly, presuppositions are not acts, though they are related to them. This characterization is pretty vague, but the phenomena cited in current linguistics under the label of (pragmatic) presupposition are quite varied, and our characterization has at least the virtue of reflecting a common denominator among many different kinds of cases. To simplify matters, we will identify three main types of phenomena that go by the label of (pragmatic) presupposition in current discussions.

According to one conception, presupposition$_1$, a speaker's assumptions (beliefs) about the speech context are presuppositions. As one author (Lakoff 1970, 175) writes, "Natural language is used for communication in a context, and every time a speaker uses a sentence of his language . . . he is making certain assumptions about that context." Some typical examples of (pragmatic) presupposition$_1$ are the following:

(10) a. Sam realizes that Irv is a Martian.
   b. Sam does not realize that Irv is a Martian.
   c. Irv is a Martian.

(11) a. Sam has stopped beating his wife.
   b. Sam has not stopped beating his wife.
   c. Sam was beating his wife.

In (10) and (11), the (a) and (b) sentences are said to presuppose the truth of the (c) sentence. Notice that on this pragmatic conception of presupposition, as with the semantic notion of presupposition, both a sentence and its negation have the same presupposition.

Another more restrictive notion, (pragmatic) presupposition$_2$, is this: the (pragmatic) presupposition$_2$ of a sentence is the set of conditions that have to be satisfied in order for the intended speech act to be appropriate in the circumstances, or to be felicitous. As one author (Keenan 1971, 49) writes, "Many sentences require that certain culturally defined conditions or contexts be satisfied in order for an utterance of a sentence to be understood . . . these conditions are naturally called presuppositions of the sentence . . . . An utterance of a sentence pragmatically presupposes that its context is appropriate." This view is echoed by another linguist (Fillmore 1971, 276): "By the presuppositional aspects of a speech communication situation, I mean those conditions which must be satisfied in order for a particular illocutionary act to be effectively performed in saying particular sentences." Some typical examples of presupposition$_2$:

(12) a. John accused Harry of writing the letter.
    b. John did not accuse Harry of writing the letter.
    c. There was something blameworthy about writing the letter.

(13) a. John criticized Harry for writing the letter.
    b. John did not criticize Harry for writing the letter.
    c. Harry wrote the letter.

(14) a. Tu es dégoûtant. ("You are disgusting.")
    b. Tu n'est pas dégoûtant. ("You are not disgusting.")
    c. The addressee is an animal or child, is socially inferior to the speaker, or is personally intimate with the speaker.

Again, in each of (12)–(14) it is claimed that the (c) sentence is presupposed by both the (a) sentence and the (b) sentence.

A final notion, (pragmatic) presupposition$_3$, is that of shared background information, which one author (Jackendoff 1972, 230) characterizes as follows: "We will use . . . 'presupposition of a sentence' to denote the information in the sentence that is assumed by the speaker to be shared by him and the hearer." Typical examples of presupposition$_3$ are such sentences as the following:

(15) a. Was it Margaret that Paul married?
    b. Wasn't it Margaret that Paul married?
    c. Paul married someone.

(16) a. Betty remembered to take her medicine.

  b. Betty did not remember to take her medicine.

  c. Betty was supposed to take her medicine.

(17) a. That Sioux Indian he befriended represented the Chief.

  b. That Sioux he befriended did not represent the Chief.

  c. He had befriended a Sioux Indian.

Again, in (15)–(17), the (a) and (b) sentences are said to presuppose the (c) sentence in that the conditions mentioned in (c) must be shared information. It may be disputed whether or not it is useful to apply the term *presupposition* to all of the phenomena just listed, but it cannot be disputed that this data must be explained (or explained away) by an adequate pragmatic theory.

It is sometimes held that certain sentences *invite an inference*, on the part of the hearer, to other sentences, even though the first sentence does not entail the second sentence (see Geis and Zwicky 1971). For example, the (a) sentences in (18) and (19) invite an inference to the (b) sentences.

(18) a. If you *mow* the lawn, I *will* give you five dollars.

  b. If you *don't mow* the lawn, I *won't* give you five dollars.

(19) a. If young girls *or* young boys can compete, it will be a success.

  b. If young girls *and* young boys can compete, it will be a success.

It is often proposed that a pragmatic theory must account for cases of invited inference.

Finally there is the phenomenon of communicating something to the hearer without actually saying it, as when we merely suggest, imply, hint, or insinuate something. A special and interesting class of these phenomena has been explored by Grice (1975) under the label of *conversational implicatures,* so called because they are implied (or as Grice prefers, implicated) by virtue of the fact that the speaker and hearer are cooperatively contributing to a conversation. Grice proposes that conversations are cooperative endeavors where participants may be expected (unless they indicate otherwise) to comply with general principles of cooperation, such as making the appropriate contribution to the conversation. For instance, imagine the following interchange between friends:

(20) a. Questioner: Where is your husband?

  b. Speaker: He is in the living room or the kitchen.

  c. Implication: The speaker does not know which room he is in.

In this case the speaker in saying (20b) implies that (20c) is true, though she does not say that it is. The reason there is this implication is that since the speaker has not indicated noncooperation she may be assumed to be cooperating and so to be giving all of the relevant and requested information. Since the speaker has said (20b) and may be presumed to be cooperative, she has implied (20c). Of course, the speaker may know exactly where her husband is; in that case, she would be misleading the hearer in that she is pretending to cooperate in the conversation but is not really doing so. We will return to this sort of phenomenon in section 12.2.

Goals of a Pragmatic Theory

We will now summarize the minimal requirements on an adequate pragmatic theory.

(21) A pragmatic theory
    a. must contain a classification of speech acts;
    b. must contain analyses and definitions of the various speech acts;
    c. must contain a specification of various uses of expressions: it must say that
    (i) expression e is standardly (literally and directly) used to do X (in context C).
    (ii) expression e has n different uses,
    (iii) expressions e and e' have the same use or uses;
    d. must relate literal and direct language use to such phenomena as
    (i) linguistic structure (semantics, syntax, phonology),
    (ii) the structure of the communication situation, the course of conversations, and social institutions,
    (iii) speaker-meaning, implication, (pragmatic) presupposition, and understanding.

The reader may notice some similarities between the goals of pragmatics and the goals of semantics (section 11.1). For instance, the pragmatic goals mentioned in (c) are the pragmatic analogues of meaning specification, ambiguity, and synonymy, respectively. There are also differences; thus, pragmatic goal (d.iii) explicitly requires an adequate pragmatic theory to mesh with more comprehensive theories of social structure and action. This is a reasonable requirement, since language use is, after all, a kind of action.

At least five disciplines have been interested in pursuing these pragmatic goals over the last ten years: philosophy, linguistics, psychology, sociology, and anthropology. Philosophers have been mainly concerned with categorizing types of speech acts and with defining each category. They have pursued goals (a) and (b). Linguists have been mainly concerned with specifying which expressions in the language have which uses or conditions on uses (where the notions of use have been borrowed mainly from philosophy). In short, linguists have been concerned mainly with goals (c.i), (d.i), and (d.ii). Psychologists have been concerned with the investigation of how information concerning language use is processed, stored, and acquired. Finally, anthropologists and sociologists have been concerned with regularities between language use and social role, as well as the structuring of speech acts into conversations—in short, goal (d.ii). We can see from this that a successful pragmatics will require the cooperation of many disciplines. Here, however, we will be concentrating mainly on linguistic and philosophical concerns. Although we do not have, at present, a pragmatic theory that will meet all of the conditions in (21), we will now sketch a theory that makes an interesting start.

12.2 AN INFORMAL PRAGMATIC THEORY

Usually, our purpose in talking is to communicate, and so any adequate theory of speech acts must give an account of linguistic communication. But we also have other purposes. Sometimes these purposes are perlocutionary—to impress, anger, or flatter our audience. Sometimes our purposes are institutional—to christen a ship, baptize a baby, or fire someone. In the following pages our primary concern will be with a theory of communicative illocutionary acts. However, we should not lose sight of the fact that in the end an adequate general pragmatic theory will have to embrace more than communication.

In chapter 5 we noted what Chomsky calls the creative aspect of language use—our ability to produce and understand novel utterances. Chomsky also points out that human language use can be appropriate to new contexts. How is this possible? Part of the explanation is that natural languages have a *recursive* syntax, wherein words, phrases, and even sentences can reappear in new roles and new relations (see chapter 8). Another part of our account of this creative ability is in terms of semantic *compositionality*, wherein the meaning of complex expressions is determined by their constituents (see chapter 11). But recursive syntax plus compositional semantics does not yet equal full creativity and appropriateness. For instance, a hearer may or may not have heard sentences (22) before.

(22) a. Your wallet or your life.
     b. Move and I'll shoot.

Nonetheless, a normal hearer will realize that in (sincerely and literally) uttering (22a) the speaker is both demanding money and threatening the hearer, and that with (22b) the speaker is warning the hearer *not* to move. Communication here is successful only if the hearer recognizes the speaker's intention to be doing these things; once the hearer does realize that the speaker has these intentions, communication is complete.

How can hearers recognize speakers' communicative intentions, and how can speakers expect them to? One suggestion that has gained wide acceptance is that literal and direct acts are governed by pragmatic rules, and by sharing such rules, speakers and hearers are able to communicate (see Searle 1969). This proposal has the virtue of extending our picture of language as rule-governed beyond the study of structure to the study of function and use. If such a theory could be made to mesh with the present components of a grammar (phonology, syntax, semantics), it would provide a valuable addition to our ability to explain the creative aspect of language use.

Literal and Direct Speech Acts

Recall that the simplest and most straightforward sort of speech act is performed literally and directly. By being literal and direct, a speaker imposes a minimal load on the hearer in understanding the speaker. With nonliteral and indirect acts, more inferring is required on the part of the hearer; breakdowns and misunderstanding can result whenever these extra inferences are required. Thus the simplest kind of case is the literal and direct act. But what does it mean to say that literal and direct acts are rule-governed? What kinds of rules govern such behavior as stating, ordering, asking, and so forth, and how do these rules connect with language? We must distinguish at least two sorts of rules: regulative rules and constitutive rules.

Regulative rules regulate or govern antecedently existing forms of behavior, in the sense that there would be that behavior even if there were no such rules. Consider parking regulations, principles of etiquette, or poolside regulations. In each case (parking one's car, eating, and using a swimming pool) it is clear that the activity would not cease to exist if the rules and regulations were lifted: we would still park our cars, eat, and swim. These activities would be a bit more chaotic, but they would continue to be possible. Usually rules that regulate already existing types of behavior have the form of an imperative, as in (23a), or a conditional imperative, as in (23b):

(23) a. Do *X!* Don't do *X!*
    b. Do *X,* only if *Y.*

Constitutive rules help to establish the existence of a kind of behavior that would not be possible without the rules. Consider chess and tennis. These activities would not exist without the rules that constitute (and define) these games. Although people can move little figures around a board and hit a ball back and forth over a net, one cannot checkmate without certain background rules of chess, nor can one commit a foot fault without certain background rules of tennis. The rules tell participants that, for example, stepping over the baseline on a tennis court constitutes or counts as a foot fault (when one is serving in a game). Thus the form of rules that constitute or define an activity is different from that of regulative rules, which merely regulate behavior. These constitutive rules have the form,

(24) Doing *X counts as* (or *constitutes*) doing *Y*, in context *C.*

Thus in our tennis example putting your foot across the baseline while serving in a game constitutes or counts as committing a foot fault:

(25) Doing *X* (putting one's foot across the baseline) *counts as* doing *Y* (footfaulting), in context *C* (the context of serving in a game).

Illocutionary Acts

We can now turn back to our original problem of explaining literal and direct linguistic communication, armed with this pair of concepts: regulative rules and constitutive rules. Perhaps illocutionary acts such as reporting, requesting, asking, greeting, and so forth, are governed by rules that are in part constitutive. If this is correct, part of learning a language consists in learning rules of the form (26).

(26) Uttering X counts as Y in context C.

Analogously, to learn tennis is to learn that putting one's foot across the baseline counts as a foot fault in the context of serving in a game. If illocutionary acts are constituted by rules such as (26), we can also explain how it is that speakers are able to communicate novel messages to hearers when speaking literally and directly: the speaker and hearer share the language and so they share the rules for performing illocutionary acts.

If an account of literal and direct linguistic communication in terms of rules for performing illocutionary acts is to succeed, we need to exhibit some plausible rules and demonstrate how they can work to effect communication. How does one discover the speech act rules governing literal and direct use of language? A strategy proposed by Searle (1969) that has proved quite effective involves two easy-to-follow steps. First, we set down four kinds of conditions on a given illocutionary act (called felicity conditions) which, if met, guarantee that the act is performed. And, second, from these conditions we extract rules for performing the act.

Promising

As our initial example we take the interesting case of literal and direct promises.

Conditions on promising   Suppose a speaker S says (27a) to a hearer H. We can schematize what S did as (27b):

(27) a. I promise that I will pay you back five dollars.
     b. S promises that he will do act A for H.

Furthermore, let us suppose that there are no impediments to communication: that both S and H are awake, able to speak and hear the language, and so forth. What conditions must be met in order for the speaker to have promised? We will distinguish four kinds of conditions.

First, what is the essential ingredient in a promise—what distinguishes a promise to do something from, say, a prediction that one will do something or just the expression of an intention to do something? The answer seems to be that in promising to do something, one is undertaking an obligation to do that thing. If you predict that you will do something and then do not do it, you are simply wrong and the prediction is false. But if a speaker promises to do something and then does not do it, the promise is not false but broken. This difference in characterizing what happens when the speaker fails to do the thing announced signals a difference in the acts performed. We will record this fact about promising by calling it the *essential condition* on promising:

(28) *Essential Condition*. The speaker S undertakes an obligation to do the act A.

We have just seen that promises can be broken, and of course promises can be made even when the speaker intends to break them. In such cases we consider the speaker still to have promised, but to have promised insincerely. We record this fact about promising by calling it the *sincerity condition* on promising:

(29) *Sincerity Condition*. The speaker S intends to do the act A.

Note that although a promise does not have to be sincere to be a promise, one cannot intend to do something without believing one has the ability to do it. Thus, we still have not exhausted the notion of a promise. Furthermore, we have not yet captured the fact that promises, as opposed to warnings and threats, are believed to be in the hearer's interest. That is, for a speaker S to literally and directly promise to do something, it must be the case that what S promises to do is believed to be in the hearer H's interest. We will record these facts about promising as the *preparatory condition* because it prepares the way for a promise (as opposed to, say, a threat):

(30) *Preparatory Condition*. (i) The speaker S believes that doing act A is in H's best interest, and (ii) S believes that S has the ability to do act A.

Finally, are there any limits on the propositional content of a promise? Can just anything be promised in the same way that just anything can be asserted? The answer is clearly No; not just anything can be promised, and so there are limits to the propositional content of promises. What are they? First, and perhaps most obviously, a speaker can only promise to do some act A in the future. It is nonsense to literally promise to have done some act. How could anyone undertake an obligation to have performed a past action? The reader should not be misled by the fact that we sometimes say things such as (31):

(31) I promise that I did not use your skis.

This use of (31) is not literally a promise to do something; rather, it is a strong assurance that something is the case—it is an emphatic statement. Thus, there seems to be at least one restriction on the predication side of the propositional content of a promise:

(32) *Propositional Content Condition.* The speaker S predicates a future act A.

How about the referential side of propositions? Are there any restrictions on the references the promiser makes? This is slightly more controversial, but it seems that there is a restriction: the speaker must be referring to himself as the person who will do the act A. Even when we say things such as (33), we are undertaking an obligation: the obligation to see to it that John's parallel turns improve:

(33) I promise that John's parallel turns will improve.

In this view, (33) is an elliptical way for the speaker to commit himself to doing what he can to get John to improve his turns. If this is correct, even in these cases the promiser is referring to himself in the propositional act. We can record this fact about promising by elaborating condition (32) as follows:

(34) *Propositional Content Condition (revised).* The speaker S predicates a future act A of himself (S).

This completes our four-part analysis of promising, which can be summarized as follows:

(35) A speaker S (directly) *promises* to do act A for hearer H when the following conditions are met:
a. *Propositional Content.* S predicates a future act A of himself (S).
b. *Preparatory.* S believes that (i) doing A would be in H's best interest and that (ii) S can do A.
c. *Sincerity.* S intends to do act A.
d. *Essential.* S undertakes an obligation to do act A.

These conditions, if met, guarantee that a promise has been made, but we do not as yet have any rules for promising, and extracting such rules for promising is the second stage of our investigation procedure.

Rules for promising Our problem, remember, is to formulate rules for promising, and to formulate them in such a way that if the rules are obeyed the result will be that one promises. Since the conditions in (35) *define* a promise, we can formulate an adequate set of rules for promising simply by converting each condition into a rule. But what kind of rule: regulative or constitutive? The answer is that we need both kinds. We need to capture two facts: (a) expressions for promising are used correctly to promise (literally and directly) only when they are uttered under certain circumstances, and (b) uttering expressions for promising, under those conditions, counts as undertaking an obligation and so counts as promising. There must be a regulative side to the rules for promising as well as a constitutive side. Our problem is to blend these two aspects of promising into a set of rules adequate for promising. How can we do this?

Being both regulative and constitutive, our rules for promising should have the form of both (23) and (26). We want our rules to tell us the *conditions* under which we can utter an expression for promising, and what the utterance of that expression *counts as*. Checking back on the conditions in (35), we see that the essential condition tells us what an utterance counts as insofar as it is a promise, and the others specify conditions that have to be met for the utterance to be correctly produced. Thus the regulative side of promising can be captured in rules that regulate the utterance of expressions for promising, which we will call Utterance Rules (or U-Rules for short). U-Rules limit the utterance of expressions for promising to the first three conditions in (35). To make this clear, we will formulate these conditions as rules (36a)–(36c) for uttering an expression for promising (which we will abbreviate as *Pr*, for *promising*):

(36) a. *Propositional Content Rule*
    Pr is to be uttered only if *A* is a future act predicated of *S*.
    b. *Preparatory Rule*
    Pr is to be uttered only if *S* believes (i) *A* is in *H*'s interest, and (ii) *S* can do *A*.
    c. *Sincerity Rule*
    Pr is to be uttered only if *S* intends to do *A*.
    d. *Essential Rule*
    Uttering *Pr* counts as undertaking an obligation to do *A*.

} U-Rules

} C-Rule

The rule we have listed as (36d) is not regulative but constitutive, because it has the counts-as form (26), and we have called it a C-Rule for Counts-as Rule.

Taken together, the four rules in (36) may be said to constitute or define *promising* in a fashion similar to the way the rules of chess define *checkmate* and the rules of tennis define *foot fault*. Moreover, if both speaker and hearer learn these rules while learning the language, it is easy to see how a speaker's intention to communicate a promise can be recognized by a hearer. Suppose you want to promise something to me, and you know that the expression *Pr* is governed by the rules in (36). Suppose you are also aware that I know the language, and so I also know that *Pr* is governed by the rules in (36). Given this, it is reasonable for you to expect me to recognize your intention to promise in uttering *Pr*, since that is its standard (literal and direct) use in the language. In this way we can see how language can be the vehicle for communication—it includes rules that make the recognition of the speaker's communicative intention possible.

Requesting

The same mode of analysis can be applied to a wide variety of illocutionary acts (see Searle 1969, and exercises). For a final example consider requests. What is it to request something? Of course, there are many ways of requesting, from pleading to commanding, but what is it that these acts all share, as requests? First, it seems essential that in requesting, the speaker is attempting to get the hearer to do something. Second, to request insincerely is to request the hearer *H* to do something one really does not want *H* to do. Thus the sincerity condition on requesting is that the speaker wants the act done. Third, as a preparatory condition on requesting the hearer must be thought capable of performing the requested act. Finally, as far as propositional content goes, requests involve the speaker's predicating a future act of the hearer (not of the speaker, as in promising). Putting these observations together, we get the following four-part analysis of the conditions for requesting, analogous to (35) for promising:

(37) A speaker *S* (directly) *requests* a hearer *H* to do act *A* when the following conditions are met:

a. *Propositional Content*. *S* predicates a future act *A* of the hearer *H*.

b. *Preparatory*. *S* believes *H* is able to do *A*.

c. *Sincerity*. *S* wants *H* to do *A*.

d. *Essential*. *S* is attempting to get *H* to do *A*.

We leave it to the reader to convert these conditions into rules for requesting, as we converted conditions (35) into the rules (36) for promising (see exercises).

Finally, recall that we said earlier that requests could be of quite different kinds, from pleading to ordering. These facts can be systematized within this account simply by varying the conditions and rules on requesting. That is, since they are all species of requests, we can analyze each as a request plus further conditions. For instance, to legitimately *order* someone to do something it is necessary that the speaker have some form of authority over the hearer: a sergeant can order a private, but not conversely; an employer can order an employee to do a job, but not conversely. Also, when ordering someone to do something as opposed to simply requesting it, the speaker is invoking his authority in attempting to get the hearer to do the act. In other words, when ordering the hearer to do something, a speaker attempts to get the hearer to do it by virtue of his authority over the hearer. Thus the four-part analysis of ordering looks just like the four-part analysis of requesting in (37), except that the notion of authority has been added to the preparatory and essential conditions:

(38) A speaker S (directly) *orders* a hearer H to do act A when the following conditions are met:

a. *Propositional Content.* S predicates a future act A of the hearer H.

b. *Preparatory.* (i) S believes H is able to do A, and (ii) S has authority over H.

c. *Sincerity.* S wants H to do A.

d. *Essential.* S is attempting to get H to do A by virtue of S's authority over H.

We leave it as another exercise for the reader to represent other kinds of requests by modifying the basic conditions for requesting given in (37) as we have done for ordering in (38).

Referring (optional section)

Our mode of analysis can be applied to propositional acts such as referring and predicating. We will review only referring here. Recall that in chapter 11 we distinguished between speaker-reference and linguistic-reference, only to put speaker-reference aside. We now want to ask, as we just did with promising, what the conditions are for referring to a particular thing; from these conditions we will again try to extract a set of rules for referring.

As with illocutionary acts, we will assume that there are no impediments to communication, that is, that the speaker and hearer are awake, know the language, and so on. Again, as with illocutionary acts, we first ask what is essential to referring to some particular thing, and the answer seems to be that picking out or identifying something is central to referring. Although to be referring, a speaker does not need to be communicating, normally our purpose in talking is to let the hearer know what we are talking about. This is especially clear in requests, where the hearer must be able to identify the referents in order to comply with the request. For example, in order to carry out the requests in (39), the hearer must at least be able to identify what the speaker is referring to:

(39) a. Take this letter to the president!
     b. Leave my books in my mailbox!
     c. Buy a house on the same street as Richard Nixon!

Thus, we will say that the essential condition on referring to some particular thing is that the speaker pick out, or identify, that thing. As far as we can tell, there is no notion of sincerity associated with reference, so there will be no sincerity condition.

But what about preparatory conditions? It is usually thought that in order for a speaker to refer to something, that thing must exist or have existed. This is not an uncontroversial point, inasmuch as it means that we cannot refer to Pegasus, Sherlock Holmes, and so on. And if we cannot refer to these things (any more than we can catch them) because they do not exist, then how is it that some statements about them seem to be true and some statements false?

(40) a. Sherlock Holmes wore a deerstalker hat. (T)
     b. Sherlock Holmes had three younger brothers. (F)
     c. Pegasus is a flying horse. (T)
     d. Pegasus was sold to a glue factory. (F)

We will not try to solve this problem here; we will simply assume, for the time being, that a thing must exist for a speaker to refer to it.

Finally, if we utter referring expressions that in part pick out or identify something for a hearer, the question arises, How do we do this? Suppose a speaker utters (41a) intending to refer to Gerald Ford:

(41) a. The former president is resting comfortably in the hospital.
     b. Ford is resting comfortably in the hospital.

What makes the utterance of (41a) a reference to Gerald Ford and not
to Richard Nixon? Or again, what makes the utterance of (41b) a
reference to Gerald Ford and not Henry Ford? The answer is that the
speaker had Gerald Ford *in mind* when uttering (41). But now we want
to know what it is to have something in mind. The standard answer is
that one has an object in mind when one has in mind certain facts that
are true just of that object. For instance, when referring to Gerald
Ford, a speaker might have in mind facts such as his succeeding
Richard Nixon in the presidency; his being married to Betty Ford, a
former dancer; and finally, facts about his physical appearance—his
build, his face, and so forth. It is usually such facts as these that pin
down references to particular persons. So part of the preparatory
condition for referring to something consists in having such facts available to identify the referent.

We can now pull together our discussion of reference into the following conditions:

(42) A speaker S (directly) *refers* to something X when the following
     conditions are met:
     a. *Preparatory*. (i) The object X must exist, and (ii) S has some
     facts in mind that are unique to X.
     b. *Essential*. S is identifying or picking out X (to H).

As with the illocutionary act of promising, we can convert these conditions into rules that if followed, will have the consequence that the
speaker refers to something X. Furthermore, if these rules are shared
by speaker and hearer, they will help the hearer to realize both *that* the
speaker is referring, and *to what* the speaker is referring. We let R
represent a referring expression in the language.

(43) a. *Preparatory Rule*
     R is to be uttered only if (i) there exists a thing X ⎫
     to be referred to, and (ii) S has in mind some fact ⎬ U-Rule
     unique to X. ⎭
     b. *Essential Rule*
     The utterance of R counts as identifying or picking ⎫ C-Rule
     out X (to H). ⎭

From this brief discussion, we see that referring can be considered a rule-governed form of behavior, just as promising can be, or chess and tennis. By analyzing referring in terms of rules, we make it explainable in the same terms as other speech acts.

Pragmatic Analysis

We have shown the reader how one might explore the idea that speech acts such as promising, requesting, and referring are rule-governed forms of behavior, and how sharing knowledge of these rules might enable a hearer to identify a speaker's communicative intentions. However, we have left out the final link in the communicative chain: the connection between the rules for performing speech acts, and the expressions that are governed by such rules. If language is to be the bridge between a speaker's communicative intention and a hearer's recognition of that intention, both speaker and hearer must share the knowledge that the expression uttered is governed by rules for performing that communicative act. So far, we have not said much about *which* expressions are governed by which speech act rules; the reason is that as yet not much work has been done on this part of pragmatics. Theorists have been concentrating their efforts on analyzing the various speech acts and setting up systems of categorization rather than on applying these rules to parts of a language. As a consequence much work remains to be done. We have space here only to give the student an idea about how to proceed on this interesting project (see Searle 1969).

Consider again the following expressions taken from the original list in (1):

(44) a. Hello!
     b. Goodbye!
     c. Pass the salt!
     d. How old are you?
     e. I promise I will be there.
     f. I claim it is raining.

We want to explain why these expressions can be vehicles of linguistic communication, and we want to do so in terms of shared rules for performing speech acts. Consequently, the rules must be related to these expressions in some definite way. Moreover, the way the rules are related to these expressions must be such that a recombination of the constituents yields different speech acts. We saw in (7) that the words *Borg*, *Nastase*, and *beat* could be combined into three different expressions used for performing three different speech acts: a statement, a question, and a request or demand. In other words, pragmatics too is *compositional*. How can we account for all of these facts?

We will start with explicit performative sentences such as (44e) and (44f). Clearly, part of each sentence has the function of indicating that if the speaker *S* is speaking literally, then *S* is performing a specific illocutionary act—making a promise in the case of (44e), a claim or statement in the case of (44f). We can account for these facts by first analyzing the sentences into two parts, a part that indicates the *illocutionary* act it is standardly used to perform and a part that indicates the proposition being expressed:

(45) a. [I promise]   [I will be there]

        Promise   *Propositional Content*

   b. [I claim]   [it is raining]

        Claim   *Propositional Content*

We then continue analyzing these expressions until we reach constituents that are the smallest ones having a use in performing speech acts. For instance, the propositional content of (45a) might be further analyzed into the following pragmatic constituents:

(46)   [I]   [will be]   [there]

    Reference   *Predication*   *Reference*

Once the original (complex) expression has been analyzed into its pragmatically primitive constituents, we then specify which speech act rules go with which constituents. For instance, continuing with example (44e), we want our pragmatic theory to say that the parts of the sentence used to indicate that the speaker is promising are governed by the rules for promising, the parts of the sentence used to indicate that the speaker is referring are governed by the rules for referring, and so forth. Since we have already set out rules for such acts as promising (36) and referring (43), this last task is exceptionally easy. Where the rules for promising mention an unspecified expression *Pr* for promising, we can now replace it with a real expression for promising, *I promise that*; and where the rules for referring mention an unspecified expression *R* for referring, we can now replace it with real expressions for referring, *I* and *there*, and so forth, for all pragmatic constituents of the sentence. The result of this process is an analysis of the sentence in terms of the standard uses of its constituents and eventually the standard use of the entire sentence. This process can be diagrammed as in tree 12.1, which indicates that the standard use of sentence (44e) as a whole is to perform the illocutionary act of promising to be there.

We have taken on the most complicated case first, in order to set out as much of the theory as we could. The remaining examples from (44) are handled in a similar fashion. For instance, (44a) and (44b) are analyzed as governed by the rules for greeting and bidding farewell, respectively. Sentences (44c) and (44d) are interesting cases because there is no particular word or phrase in those sentences for the illocutionary rules of questioning and requesting to hook up to. Rather,

Tree 12.1

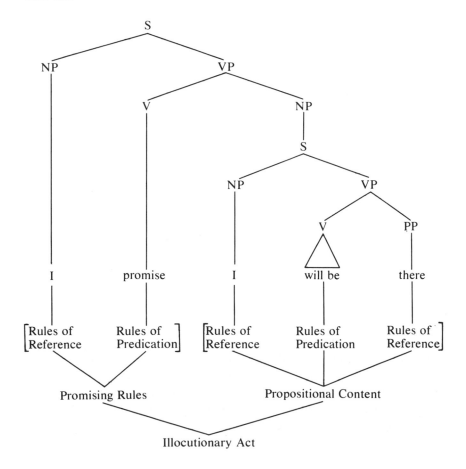

the only clue to what illocutionary act the speaker is intending to perform comes from certain syntactic facts, such as the absence of a subject expression plus a tenseless verb in (44c) and the inverted word order of (44d). How can the illocutionary force of sentences such as these be represented? A number of proposals have been made over the last fifteen years by Katz and Postal (1964), Ross (1970), Sadock (1974), and finally Katz (1977). Each proposal has its problems and limitations, however. Consequently no one is yet quite sure how to handle these sentences—which constitute an interesting area for future research. Most probably, such pragmatic facts are directly related to syntactic structure, which would again illustrate the integration of all aspects of our linguistic ability.

In this section we have shown how some sentences can be analyzed in terms of their pragmatic structure. That is, we have shown how one might break sentences down into pragmatic constituents in such a way that the use of the whole sentence is determined by the uses of its parts and their structural relations (see Harnish, forthcoming, for further discussion). As with syntactic structure and semantic structure, pragmatics too is compositional, and pragmatic compositionality contributes to the explanation of both the creative aspect of language use and its contextual appropriateness. Moreover, by including pragmatic rules in a grammar we can satisfy some of the goals of a pragmatic theory, particularly goals (c) and (d.i) of (21). Of course, this leaves some goals of an adequate pragmatic theory still unreached, though progress is being made toward some of them, particularly the problem of categorizing illocutionary acts, a topic we turn to next.

Categorizing Illocutionary Acts (Optional Section)

Probably the most influential system currently available for categorizing speech acts, especially illocutionary acts, is that proposed by Searle (1975a), who distinguishes five kinds of illocutionary acts in terms of their essential conditions. First, *representatives* represent some state of affairs; typical examples are stating, asserting, explaining, predicting, and classifying. Second, *directives* are acts where the speaker attempts to get the hearer to do something, as in ordering, commanding, requesting, instructing, and pleading. Third, *commissives* commit the speaker to do something, as in promising, vowing, pledging, and offering. Next, *expressives* express a psychological state of the speaker; typical examples are thanking, congratulating, and apologizing. Finally, *declarations* bring extralinguistic states of affairs into existence, as when we declare war, excommunicate, appoint, veto, and so forth. The system is summarized in figure 12.3.

These illocutionary classes may have syntactic correlates in that we use sentences with certain structures to perform certain kinds of illocutionary acts. Consider, for example, the following:

(47) *Representatives*
 a. I verb (that) + sentence
 I predict (that) it will rain.
 I assert that $2 + 2 = 4$.
 b. I Verb NP + NP
 I call that a winner.
 I classify tomatoes as vegetables.

(48) *Directives*
 I verb you + volitional verb (NP)
 I order you to leave (the room).

(49) *Commissives*
 I verb (you) (that) + I volitional verb (NP)
 I promise (you) (that) I will pay (you).

(50) *Expressives*
 I verb you + for VP
 I apologize to you for stepping on your toes.
 I thank you for bringing the flowers.

(51) *Declarations*
 I verb NP + be predicate
 I declare the meeting to be adjourned.

If these observations can be maintained, we would have an indication

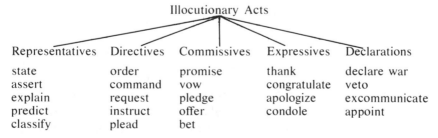

Figure 12.3
Types of illocutionary acts

of a principled connection between syntactic structure and types of illocutionary acts, a connection to be accounted for by a grammar.

More can be said, of course, about this system for categorizing illocutionary acts, and something could be added about competing systems (see Schiffer 1972). Nevertheless, this brief sketch will give the student an idea about how such systems of classification can be constructed as well as a proposal to think about.

Indirect and Nonliteral Illocutionary Acts

In section 12.1, we noted that illocutionary acts could be performed in a variety of ways; the theory we have just presented accounts primarily for literal and direct acts. What about indirect acts? Can the theory be extended to account for these types of communication? The answer is Yes (see Searle 1975b). If we look back at the sorts of examples given for indirect acts and recall the four-part analyses of the illocutionary acts of promising and requesting, we see certain regularities. Consider normal utterances of such sentences as the following:

(52) a. You will be quiet.
    b. Will you be quiet?

(53) a. You can be quiet.
    b. Can you be quiet?

(54) a. I want you to be quiet.
    b. Would I like you to be quiet?

These sentences have the surface form of (a) declaratives and (b) interrogatives, but the utterance of any of them can easily be taken as a request. How is this possible, given that the normal form of a request is an imperative sentence?

A clue to the answer lies in the fact that uttering these sentences and meaning them literally would, in normal circumstances, be contextually inappropriate. We do not normally ask people whether they think they will be quiet or whether they have the ability to be quiet; we request them to be quiet. This suggests that the hearer's cue that the speaker is doing more than performing just the literal and direct act is some principle or rule that can signal an act as indirect. This principle will also give the hearer some clue to the particular indirect act the speaker is performing. Based on (52)–(54) the following Indirect Hypothesis (IH) looks promising:

(IH) Suppose a speaker S utters a declarative or interrogative sentence (such as (52)–(54)) and thereby makes an assertion or asks a question. If that assertion or question would be *contextually inappropriate* were it the *only* act being performed, then the hearer H should infer that the speaker S's assertion or question constitutes the performance of some other illocutionary act. What other act? The act whose condition(s) the utterance asserts or questions.

To see how IH works with examples (52)–(54), recall the conditions we set down on requesting in (37) and notice how each of (52)–(54) asserts or questions one such condition:

(55) a. *Propositional Content Condition.* A future act A is predicated of H.

Sentences (52a) and (52b) conform to IH with respect to the propositional content condition on requests in that (52a) asserts the propositional content condition and (52b) questions it.

b. *Preparatory Condition.* H is able to do A.

Sentences (53a) and (53b) conform to IH with respect to the first preparatory condition on requests in that (53a) asserts it and (53b) questions it.

c. *Sincerity Condition.* S wants H to do A.

Sentences (54a) and (54b) conform to IH with respect to the sincerity condition on requests in that (54a) asserts it and (54b) questions it.

Thus we see how IH can lead the hearer to the speaker's indirect illocutionary act. The same hypothesis (IH) can be applied to other indirect speech acts as well. Consider commissives, such as offering and promising:

(56) a. I'll pay you back.   (promise)
     b. Shall I pay you now?   (offer)

(57) Do you want your money?   (offer)

(58) I intend to pay you back.   (promise)

Turning back to the conditions on promising in (35), the reader can see that these sentences assert or question one such condition (see exercises).

Although IH seems to be on the right track, there are still questions to be answered. For instance, how does a hearer tell (and how can a speaker expect a hearer to tell) when the direct act performed in uttering a sentence is *not* the only act? And how does the hearer tell which illocutionary act (containing the asserted or questioned condition) is the one the speaker is intending to perform indirectly?

The most promising place to turn is to Grice's theory of cooperative conversations. According to Grice (1975) such conversations are governed by a cooperative principle:

(CP) Make your conversational contribution such as is required, at the stage at which it occurs, by the accepted purpose or direction of the talk exchange in which you are engaged.

But what does cooperating amount to? Grice suggests that for stretches of conversation involving mainly transfer of information, cooperating amounts to obeying (if only implicitly) certain *conversational maxims* such as·those given in (59).

(59) *Quantity-1*. Make your contribution as informative as is required (for the current purposes of the conversation).

Quantity-2. Do not make your contribution more informative than is required.

Quality-1. Do not say what you believe to be false.

Quality-2. Do not say that for which you lack adequate evidence.

Relevance. Be relevant.

Manner. Be perspicuous:

a. avoid obscurity of expression;
b. avoid unnecessary ambiguity;
c. be brief (avoid unnecessary prolixity);
d. be orderly.

Clearly, such a list of maxims can be expanded and made more precise. In addition, maxims for types of talk exchange other than transferring information must be formulated to have a complete theory.

Even so, we can use these maxims to answer our questions concerning IH. For instance, consider again the use of sentence (54a), *I want you to be quiet*, to request someone who is being noisy to be quiet. What might the hearer think (and be expected by the speaker to think)? Quite plausibly the hearer would reason as follows, recalling IH:

(60) a. The speaker *S* has said *I want you to be quiet*.

b. If that is all *S* meant, then *S* would have violated the maxim of relevance, since the question of what *S* wants has not arisen.

c. So *S* must have meant to do something more than just report *S*'s desires.

d. *S* has asserted the sincerity condition for requesting me to be quiet.

e. Given that *S* knows that I am being noisy, it would be appropriate and relevant for *S* to be requesting me to be quiet.

f. So, in uttering, *I want you to be quiet, S* is *requesting* me to be quiet.

In this way we can see how maxims of conversation might interact with speech acts in such a way that IH can contribute to explaining indirect speech acts.

Finally, when people speak nonliterally, they expect their audience not to take them as meaning what they say but as meaning something else. As with indirect acts, violation of the maxims of conversation can function to indicate that the speaker is meaning something other than what he says. Consider again the examples of nonliteral acts from section 12.1:

(61) a. I'd never have guessed.
  b. You can say that again.
  c. A pig wouldn't eat this food.

Probably there are circumstances in which each sentence in (61) could be appropriately uttered literally, but in normal contexts such utterances would be flagrantly inappropriate and would violate one or more of the maxims of conversation. For instance, it is common knowledge that a pig will eat virtually anything, and so (61c) is pretty clearly false; or at least it is believed false by people who would use the expression. On the basis of this shared belief, the speaker can expect the hearer *H* to realize that *S* is not speaking literally but is exaggerating.

To some extent these maxims can also help as a guide to what speakers might mean, given that they are not speaking literally. Suppose a speaker *S* after tasting a typical cafeteria lunch, utters (61c). The hearer *H*, given the above shared belief about pigs, will suppose *S* to be speaking nonliterally, but *H* may not yet be sure just what *S* means. Given that the remark is about the food, it is relevant and so conforms to at least the maxim of Relevance. But since the remark violates the maxim of Quality-1, the smallest adjustment *H* has to make to bring *S*'s meaning into alignment with this maxim is to suppose *S* to be claiming that the food is very bad but not claiming it is totally inedible. In this way, the hearer can use (and be expected to use) the maxims as a guide to what a speaker means when speaking nonliterally.

Conclusion

At the end of section 12.1 we surveyed some of the central goals of a pragmatic theory. In section 12.2 we have presented an outline of a theory that represents an attempt to reach some of these goals. For instance, we have developed a theory of standard (literal and direct) use, which, along with syntax and semantics, can explicate the creative aspect of language use in terms of pragmatic rules. On the basis of this theory we have developed both a classification of illocutionary acts and the beginning of a theory of indirect and nonliteral acts within the context of a theory of cooperative conversations.

Of course, we could not have presented a total pragmatic theory in such limited space, and much remains to be done to develop such a theory. Pragmatics is, after all, a comparatively recent discipline; being recent its concepts require substantial discussion and elaboration (see Bach and Harnish, (forthcoming)). Yet it is an exciting field, in part because probably the most pervasive characteristic of human social interaction, so pervasive that we hardly find it remarkable, is that we talk.

Exercises

Section 12.1

1. Either defend or challenge the claim that at least some pragmatic information should be part of a grammar.

*2. What differences in utterance acts are indicated with words such as *whisper* versus *shout*? Think of five more verbs that report utterance acts and that indicate differences in them.

3. Give five verbs indicating *illocutionary* acts to add to the list in (2). Say briefly why each is illocutionary and not perlocutionary.

4. Give five verbs indicating *perlocutionary* acts to add to the list in (4). Say briefly why each is perlocutionary and not illocutionary.

5. What are three differences between illocutionary and perlocutionary acts? Can you think of another, new, difference?

*6. (Difficult) Try to think of an example of a nonliteral but direct act that is the basis for a literal but indirect act. Defend your example, since no clear case has yet been found.

*7. We have said that many insults are nonliteral perlocutionary acts. Can you think of any insults that are literal perlocutionary acts? Defend your examples. (Hint: Consider an utterance such as *You Fascist!*)

*8. Can insults be illocutionary acts (literal and nonliteral)? Defend your answer. (Hint: Can a hearer be insulted by a speaker but not feel offended?)

9. Think of five more examples of direct but nonliteral uses of language from everyday speech; include at least one interrogative sentence and one imperative sentence. (Hint: Consider *How should I know?* and *Go fly a kite!*)

*10. When someone uses the sentence *No man is an island* to deny that people are unaffected by others, is this a case of nonliteral language use? Defend your answer.

11. Give two more cases of examples (9a), (9b), and (9c) of section 12.1. Make at least one of each of them an interrogative or imperative sentence.

12. Give two more examples of conversational implicature.

*13. Which types of language use (types of speech acts) clearly cannot be used to define meaning? Defend your answer.

*14. Which type or types of language use (speech acts) might be used to define meaning? Defend your answer.

Section 12.2

1. Compare and contrast *regulative* rules with *constitutive* rules.

2. Give two more (nonlinguistic) examples of each kind of rule.

*3. (Difficult) section 12.2 is based on the claim that speaking a language is a form of rule-governed intentional behavior. How would you support or challenge this claim?

4. Is the sentence *I promise that I will flunk you if you do not hand in your paper on time* literally used to promise? Defend your answer.

5. Convert the four-part analysis of the conditions for requesting in (37) into rules for requesting.

*6. Do a four-part analysis of conditions and rules for pleading. (Hint: How does pleading differ, as a request, from ordering? Is this difference reflected in your analysis?)

7. Pick two illocutionary acts from list (2) that are not closely related and do a four-part analysis giving (a) the conditions for success and (b) the rules for performing each act.

8. What pragmatic phenomena mentioned in section 12.1 were not accounted for in section 12.2?

*9. How might the theory of indirect speech acts presented in 12.2 account for examples of conversational implicature?

10. Show how sentences (56)–(58) either assert or question some condition on promising.

References

Austin, J. (1962) *How To Do Things With Words*, Harvard University Press, Cambridge, Mass.

Bach, K., and R. Harnish (forthcoming), *Linguistic Communication and Speech Acts*, MIT Press, Cambridge, Mass.

Cole, P., and J. Morgan, eds. (1975) *Syntax and Semantics* vol. 3, Academic Press, New York.

Fillmore, C. (1971) "Verbs of judging: an exercise in semantic description," in C. Fillmore and T. Langendoen, *Linguistic Semantics*.

Fillmore, C., and T. Langendoen, eds. (1971) *Studies in Linguistic Semantics*, Holt, Rinehart & Winston, New York.

Geis, M., and A. Zwicky (1971) "On invited inferences," *Linguistic Inquiry* 2, 561–566.

Grice, H. P. (1975) "Logic and conversation," in P. Cole and J. Morgan, *Syntax and Semantics* vol. 3.

Harnish, R. (forthcoming) "A projection problem for pragmatics," in F. Heny and H. Schnelle, eds., *Syntax and Semantics* vol. 10, Academic Press, New York.

Jackendoff, R. (1972) *Semantic Interpretation in Generative Grammar*, MIT Press, Cambridge, Mass.

Katz, J., and P. Postal (1964) *An Integrated Theory of Linguistic Descriptions*, MIT Press, Cambridge, Mass.

Katz, J. (1977) *Propositional Structure and Illocutionary Force*, Crowell, New York.

Keenan, E. (1971) "Two kinds of presupposition in natural language," in C. Fillmore and T. Langendoen, *Linguistic Semantics*.

Lakoff, G. (1970) "Linguistics and natural logic," *Synthese* 1/2, 151–271.

Ross, J. (1970) "On declarative sentences," in R. Jacobs and P. Rosenbaum, eds., *Readings in English Transformational Grammar*, Ginn & Co., Boston, Mass.

Sadock, J. (1974) *Toward a Linguistic Theory of Speech Acts*, Academic Press, New York.

Schiffer, S. (1972) *Meaning*, Oxford University Press, Oxford, England.

Searle, J. (1969) *Speech Acts*, Cambridge University Press, Cambridge, England.

——— (1975a) "A taxonomy of illocutionary acts," in K. Gunderson, ed., *Language, Mind and Knowledge*, University of Minnesota Press, Minneapolis.

——— (1975b) "Indirect speech acts," in P. Cole and J. Morgan, *Syntax and Semantics*.

Part Three

THE CAPACITY
FOR LANGUAGE:
TWO PERSPECTIVES

INTRODUCTION

Having examined the structure and function of human language, we now turn to two topics having to do with the biological bases of language. First we survey recent research dealing with how language is stored and processed by the human brain. We then examine recent attempts to teach language to chimpanzees, attempts made partly in challenge to the idea that language is unique to the human species. Both of these topics give us a chance to explore issues connected with the *capacity* for language in our species and other species, while giving us a feeling for two areas of research that are of great current interest and significant future potential.

Chapter Thirteen

LANGUAGE AND THE BRAIN

Speaking and understanding our native language is so spontaneous and apparently easy (for most normal individuals), that we are completely unaware of the remarkably complicated tasks carried out by the human brain to make it possible for us to use language so freely and effortlessly. It is interesting and somewhat ironic that until recently, advancement in our understanding of brain functions has come not from the study of normal individuals but largely from the study of individuals with injured brains. Whenever disease or injury affects the left side of the brain, some aspect of the ability to perceive, process, or produce language may be disturbed. Individuals with such brain disease or injury are said to be *aphasic,* and their brain disturbances can give us insight into how the human brain carries out its language-related tasks.

Aphasia is a broad term encompassing numerous syndromes of communicative impairment. Some aphasics labor to speak a single word, whereas others effortlessly produce long, but meaningless, utterances. By studying the effect of brain damage on speech and comprehension, researchers have obtained invaluable clues to the organization of speech and language in the human nervous system. *Neurolinguists* are interested in the correlation between brain damage and speech and language deficits. These language and brain specialists believe that the study of language form and use will reveal principles of brain function, and that the study of brain function may support or refute a linguistic theory.

Of the many questions of interest to neurolinguists, three are fundamental: (1) Where in the brain are speech and language localized? (2)

This chapter was written by Kathryn Bayles, Department of Speech and Hearing Sciences, University of Arizona.

How does the nervous system function to encode and decode speech and language? and (3) Are the components of language—phonology, syntax, semantics—neuroanatomically distinct and therefore vulnerable to separate impairment?

Where is Language Localized in the Brain?

Language: A Left Hemisphere Phenomenon

For over a century scholars have debated the question of speech and language localization within the brain. In the 1860's, scientists known as localizationists speculated that the functioning of specific regions in the brain were responsible for language. Antilocalizationists argued that speech and language were the consequence of the brain functioning as a whole.

In 1861, Paul Broca, a French surgeon and anatomist, described to the Société d'Anthropologie in Paris a patient who in life had had extreme difficulty producing speech. Later, at autopsy, the patient was found to have damage in the posterior inferior part of the *frontal lobe* in the left cerebral hemisphere, now known as Broca's area (see figure 13.1). With the publication of this report Broca became the first indi-

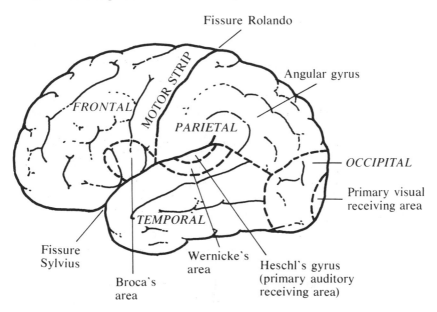

Figure 13.1
Landmarks of the left cerebral hemisphere

vidual to substantiate the claim that damage to a specific area of the brain results in a speech deficit. In 1865, Broca extended his claim about speech localization by reporting that damage to sites in the left cerebral hemisphere produced aphasia, while destruction of corresponding sites in the right hemisphere left linguistic capacities intact.

In 1874, Carl Wernicke, a young German physician, published a monograph describing patients with speech comprehension deficits who had damage (lesions) outside Broca's area, in the left posterior temporal lobe. Wernicke's work strengthened Broca's claim that left hemispheric structures were essential for speech and generated intense interest in the hypothesis that different areas within the left hemisphere fulfill different linguistic functions.

Today scientists agree that specific neuroanatomical structures, generally of the left hemisphere, are vital for speech and language, but debate continues as to which structures are committed to the various linguistic capacities. For most individuals the left cerebral hemisphere is dominant for language, regardless of handedness. Approximately 70 percent of all individuals with damage to the left hemisphere will experience some type of aphasia, as compared with only 1 percent of those with right hemisphere lesions.

Confirmation of left cerebral language dominance has come from many research techniques, one of which was introduced by Wada in 1949. Wada reported that the injection of sodium amytal into the main (carotid) artery on the language dominant side of the brain induced a temporary aphasia. Physicians have subsequently used this technique as a means of determining cerebral dominance in patients facing neurosurgery; in this way, physicians can avoid damaging the language centers during surgery.

Substantially adding to our knowledge of the neurology of language was a report published in 1959 by Wilder Penfield and LaMar Roberts, neurosurgeons at the Montreal Neurological Institute. Penfield and Roberts had been studying the brain as well as treating its infirmities. To provide relief from intractable seizures in patients with epilepsy, Penfield and Roberts surgically removed portions of the brain. Because of the threat of producing aphasia by removing regions subserving speech and language, they used electrical stimulation to map the functions of the exposed brains of their patients.

Electrical current applied to a spot on the brain can sometimes activate involuntary expression of function associated with that brain site. It is also the case that stimulation may interfere with a function being performed by the conscious patient. For example, electrical stimulation applied to areas on one side of the brain associated with motor function, can produce limb twitching, numbness, and movement on the opposite side of the body. Penfield and Roberts discovered that when electrical current was applied to a brain area involved in speech, one of two things occurred: the patient either had trouble talking or uttered a vowel-like cry. However, no patient ever produced an intelligible word as a result of electrical stimulation.

Through the cooperation of hundreds of courageous patients, who remained conscious during surgery, Penfield and Roberts were able to conclude that three areas of the left hemisphere were vital to speech and language: *Broca's area, Wernicke's area,* and *the supplemental motor area* (see figure 13.2).

As evidence accumulated verifying left cerebral speech dominance, researchers sought to discover whether the left hemisphere speech

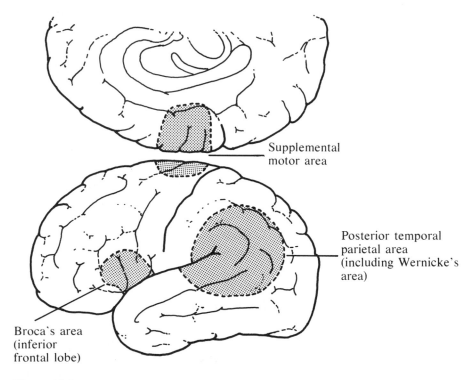

Supplemental
motor area

Posterior temporal
parietal area
(including Wernicke's
area)

Broca's area
(inferior
frontal lobe)

Figure 13.2
Primary cortical areas involved in speech and language function. After Penfield and Roberts 1959.

areas were structurally unique. In 1968, Geschwind and Levitsky were the first to report that a region in the left temporal lobe was larger than the same area on the right in 65 percent of the brains they studied. This area, called the *planum temporal,* has also been found to be larger even in fetal brains, a finding that suggests the readiness of the left hemisphere for language dominance at birth (Wada and Hamm 1975; Witelson and Pallie 1973.)

In order to understand the details of localization theory, it is first necessary to become familiar with some basic concepts about the structure and function of the nervous system.

The Nervous System

The central and peripheral nervous system form an intricate communication network through which the behavior of the body is governed. The brain and spinal cord constitute the central nervous system (CNS) and are linked to the peripheral nervous system by bundles of nerve fibers that extend to all parts of the body. Impulses received from peripheral receptors are sorted, interpreted, and responded to by the CNS.

The basic cellular unit of the nervous system is the *neuron,* of which there are an estimated 12 billion. Each neuron is structurally distinct and composed of (a) a cell body, (b) receptors known as dendrites, and (c) a conductive mechanism, or axon. The dendrites receive input from other neurons and transmit it *to* the cell body, whereas the axon transmits impulses *away from* the cell body. Some nerve fibers transmit sensory information to the CNS, some fibers carry information from the CNS to the limbs and body parts, and others form communicative links between the different parts of the nervous system.

Levels of the Central Nervous System

The central nervous system is hierarchically organized, with higher structures being more complex than lower ones (see figure 13.3). At the lowest level is the spinal cord, which acts as a cable through which streams of neuronal messages between the body and the brain are transmitted. Above the spinal cord is the brain stem, the regulator of such things as breathing, muscle tone, posture, sleep, and body temperature. Lower nervous system structures, such as the spinal cord and lower brain stem, are primarily reflexive and controlled by higher centers. At the highest level of the nervous system are the cerebral hemispheres, responsible for voluntary activity.

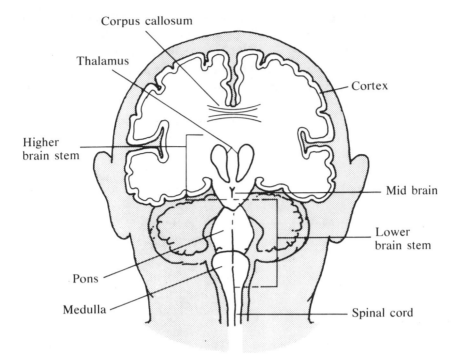

Figure 13.3
Hierarchical arrangement of the central nervous system

The cerebral hemispheres emerge from the higher brain stem and are covered with a convoluted sheath of gray matter, called the *cortex,* which is approximately one-fourth of an inch thick. Within the cortex are approximately 10 billion neurons arranged in at least six layers. The degree of connectivity in this three-dimensional cellular network is almost beyond comprehension. Sholl (1956), a noted neuroanatomist, writes that the cortex contains fields of neurons where a single incoming axon may influence up to 4,000 other neurons.

The Cerebral Cortex: General Characteristics
In outward appearance the two cerebral hemispheres are roughly similar, being composed of convolutions, called *gyri,* and depressions or fissures, known as *sulci.* Certain gyri and sulci serve as landmarks helping to differentiate the boundaries of the four lobes of each hemisphere.

The fissure of Sylvius (see figure 13.1) separates the frontal lobe from the temporal; the fissure of Rolando separates the frontal from the parietal. No fissure separates the parietal and occipital lobes; these two lobes can be distinguished only by microscopic examination of cell structures. Located in the parietal lobe, at the upper end of the fissure of Sylvius, is the cortical area known as the *angular gyrus,* in which functions necessary to speech, reading, and writing are interrelated (see figure 13.1).

Within each hemisphere are areas known to serve specific functions. In front of, and running parallel to, the fissure of Rolando is a strip of cortex, known as the motor strip, which controls fine, highly skilled, voluntary motor movements (see figure 13.1). Sections of the motor strip are related to voluntary movements in particular parts of the body; for example, the facial and laryngeal muscles are represented at the lower end, in close proximity to Broca's area.

Next to Wernicke's area, in the temporal lobe, is *Heschl's gryus,* known also as the primary auditory cortex. When auditory impulses arrive at Heschl's gyrus, a noise is perceived, but meaningful interpretation must be made by the adjacent auditory association area (Wernicke's area). This pattern of cortical organization, consisting of interpretive regions of the cortex lying adjacent to sensory receiving areas, is repeated in the visual cortical system as well as in the system receiving sensations from the body.

Cortical Conduction
The bulk of the cerebral hemispheres, beneath the outer layer of gray matter, is composed of three basic types of nerve fiber tracts that form a neural communication network of astonishing complexity. Association nerve fibers connect different portions of the same hemisphere. Projection fibers connect the cortex with lower portions of the brain and spinal cord, and transverse fibers interconnect the cerebral hemispheres.

Of particular importance to an understanding of speech and language function is a familiarity with the massive transverse fiber tract called the *corpus callosum.* By means of the corpus callosum the two hemispheres are able to communicate with each other in the form of electrical impulses. Eccles (1972) estimated that if one assumes that each of the approximately 200 million nerve fibers constituting the corpus callosum has an average firing capacity of 20 impulses per second, then the corpus callosum can carry the astronomical number of 4 billion impulses per second.

You may wonder why, if speech is localized in the left hemisphere, it is necessary for the cerebral hemispheres to communicate with each other for speech to function normally. The reason is that sensations from the right and left halves of the body go primarily to the contralateral (opposite) hemisphere. If, for example, an object is held in the *left* hand, impulses travel from the left side of the body to the *right* hemisphere, and although the right hemisphere would recognize the object, verbalizing the name of the object would require involvement of the speech center in the left hemisphere.

The importance of the corpus callosum has been made strikingly clear through split-brain research. Gazzaniga and associates studied the effect of disruption of communication between the hemispheres in patients who had had them disconnected surgically by severing the corpus callosum, an operation that is performed to reduce the frequency and severity of incapacitating seizures. Once the cerebral hemispheres are disconnected, there are techniques whereby stimuli can be visually presented to a single hemisphere. When Gazzaniga and Sperry (1967) presented stimuli in the form of written words, letters, and numbers to the left hemisphere alone, patients were able to describe them orally. But information perceived exclusively by the right hemisphere could not be verbalized, either orally or in writing. The right hemisphere was mute.

To investigate the possibility that even though split-brain subjects could not describe visual stimuli presented to their right hemispheres, they nevertheless comprehended them, Gazzaniga and Sperry gave the patients a nonverbal means of responding. For instance, subjects were asked to match a written word with its referent by pointing to the object when it was displayed as one item in a group of assorted items. Under these conditions the right hemisphere was found to be capable of reading letters, short words, and numbers.

To discover whether the right hemisphere could also comprehend spoken words, Gazzaniga and Sperry asked patients to identify words presented auditorily. Because auditory stimuli are received by both sides of the brain, Sperry and Gazzaniga limited the available answers to the right hemisphere. Subjects were instructed to push a button when they saw that one of a set of nouns projected serially to the left visual field (the right hemisphere) matched one previously spoken. Results with split-brain patients showed that the right hemisphere can understand oral (as well as written) language, although the limits of its comprehension have yet to be determined.

Recent research suggests that the right hemisphere may be limited in its linguistic competence. Split-brain subjects have been observed to have difficulty responding appropriately to verbal commands, simple active and passive subject-verb-object sentences, and word sequences when they were presented visually to the right hemisphere. Thus, although the right hemisphere is generally unimpaired in grasping the meaning of single words, it performs poorly with phrases. Perhaps only certain kinds of linguistic stimuli can be comprehended by the right hemisphere. More research is needed to explore its decoding capacities.

How Does the Brain Encode and Decode Speech and Language?

Speech and Language: A Cortical and Subcortical System
What the silence of the isolated right hemisphere has dramatized is that speech is not solely a cortical function. Subcortical fiber tracts as well as gray matter areas deep within the brain—particularly the thalamus —also participate in speech and language.

The thalamus can be conceived of as a great relay station, receiving nerve fiber projections from the cortex and lower nervous system structures and radiating fibers to all parts of the cortex (see figure 13.4).

Emerging as especially important to speech and language function is the left thalamus. Damage to portions of this structure produces involuntary repetition of words and disturbs the patient's ability to name objects. The thalamus is thought to be involved in the focusing of attention by temporarily heightening the receptivity of certain cortical sensory areas. Ojemann and Ward (1971) observed that information presented to patients during left thalamic stimulation was more easily retrieved, both during and after stimulation, than information that had been presented prior to stimulation. They speculated that the thalamus may provide an interaction between language and memory mechanisms.

Neurolinguists are far from being certain as to which neuroanatomical structures are essential to the encoding and decoding of linguistic stimuli, but they agree that speech results from an integrated cortical and subcortical system. An awareness that the neural sensory, motor, and associative mechanisms are interconnected is basic to understanding how the brain functions to encode and decode language.

A simple model can represent our knowledge of the transmission of signals to the language mechanism. In figure 13.5, the dark band between the semicircles (which represent coronal sections of the cerebral

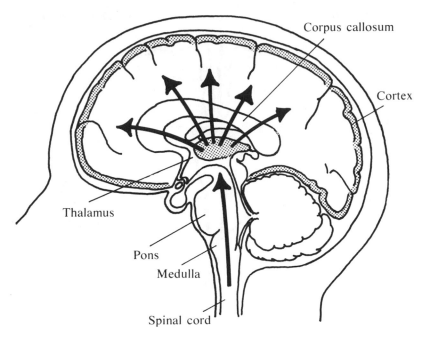

Figure 13.4
Fiber radiations from the thalamus to the cortex

hemispheres) represents the hemispheric connection. Notice that impulses coming from the right side of the body have direct access to the
dominant speech center, whereas those from the left must touch base
with the right hemisphere before passing over the corpus callosum for
processing. The left hemisphere is not dominant, however, for the
processing of *all* auditory signals. Nonspeech environmental sounds do
not have to be passed on to the left hemisphere but are processed
primarily in the right hemisphere. How do we know this?

Evidence from Dichotic Listening Research
By means of a research technique called dichotic listening, we can
analyze the characteristics of incoming stimuli processed by the individual hemispheres. During a dichotic listening task two different
stimuli are presented simultaneously, through earphones, to the left
and right ears. For example, the right ear may be given the word *base*
and the left ear *ball*. The listeners are instructed to say what they hear.
It is fascinating that certain types of stimuli delivered to a particular ear
will be more accurately reported by the listener. This is because the

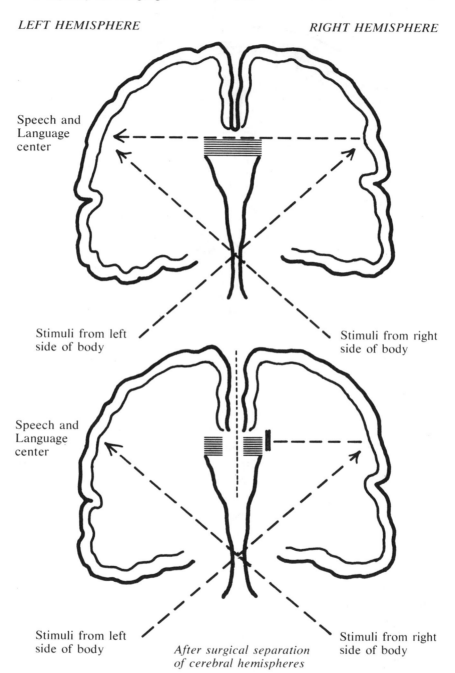

Figure 13.5
Callosal connection

nervous system is capable of scanning incoming stimuli and routing them to that area of the brain specialized for their interpretation. Kimura (1961) was the first to observe that when two digits were presented simultaneously, one to each ear, those to the right ear were more accurately identified by the listener. However, when the listener was known to have the less common right hemispheric dominance for speech, Kimura observed a left ear advantage. In other words the ear having more direct access to the language center had an advantage. Although there is some auditory input to each cortex from the ear on the same side of the body, these uncrossed, or *ipsilateral,* inputs are thought to be suppressed.

The right ear advantage (REA) was originally thought to exist only for linguistically meaningful stimuli, but the same advantage has been found for nonsense syllables, speech played backward, consonant-vowel syllables, and even small units of speech such as fricatives. Intrigued by these findings, investigators have sought to discover those features of speech likely to trigger left hemisphere processing. One hypothesis was that an REA would be found for any sound produced by the vocal tract musculature. Research results have disconfirmed this explanation, for REAs have been found for synthetic speech and Morse code but not for laughing and coughing.

The REA associated with Morse code stimuli suggests that the left hemisphere may be dominant for more than the phonetic structure of language. In fact, the left hemisphere may be dominant for a number of nonlinguistic functions. For example, several investigators have noted that the ability to perform fine judgments of temporal order is a function of the left hemisphere: aphasics perform poorly, compared with controls and subjects with right hemisphere damage, on nonlinguistic tasks requiring temporal order judgments (Brookshire 1972; Swisher and Hirsh 1972). Lackner and Teuber (1973) have proposed that the left hemisphere has an advantage in temporal acuity and, as a consequence, language processing may have been drawn to the left hemisphere since speech is temporally ordered.

Much evidence implies that left hemisphere damage also impairs the ability to program complex motor sequences such as playing a violin. A disorder known as *oral nonverbal apraxia* is commonly associated with left hemisphere damage. DeRenzi (1966, 51) defined the disorder as "the inability to perform voluntary movements with the muscles of the larynx, pharynx, tongue, lips, and cheeks, although automatic movements of the same muscles are preserved." Patients have trouble voluntarily performing simple gestures such as whistling, blowing, clearing the throat, or sticking out the tongue. It has been argued that if the left hemisphere is dominant for programming motor sequences, it is logical that this special ability would be used to program the extremely complex motor sequences associated with speech, which, as pointed out in chapter 6, requires the simultaneous coordination of at least one hundred muscles.

Besides having a superior capacity for processing temporally ordered stimuli and programming complex motor sequences, evidence exists that the left hemisphere is specialized for associative thought. Two notable studies support this hypothesis. DeRenzi and associates (1969) observed that patients with left hemisphere damage performed more poorly than right-lesioned patients in an object matching task. Patients were handed an object and required to match it to one of ten on display in front of them; the held object differed in form and color from its displayed match. The left hemisphere was found to be superior at recognizing the same object in a different form. In the second study, by Faglioni and colleagues (1969), subjects with left hemisphere damage exhibited significantly greater difficulty than both right-damaged individuals and controls in matching a sound, such as a bell, with a picture of its source.

It may be the case, as some investigators theorize, that speech and language function is not cognitively unique but is imposed in the left hemisphere because speech and language functions require the special nonlinguistic capacities of this hemisphere.

Complementary Specialization of the Cerebral Hemispheres

Beware of forming the misconception that the left hemisphere is superior, overall, to the right. Admittedly, this view has been prevalent, but it is one that is changing. The research techniques providing insight into speech and language function have unveiled functions for which the right hemisphere is dominant, particularly those functions requiring spatial ability.

Injury to the right hemisphere can result in visuospatial impairment. An affected individual may have trouble finding his way from one place to another, drawing objects, assembling puzzles, or recognizing faces. Such an individual may disregard anything on the left side of the body, even to the extent that when asked to draw the face of a clock, the patient may squeeze all the numbers in on the right side of the face.

Psychological research suggests that the two hemispheres differ in the manner in which they treat incoming stimuli, the right hemisphere processing stimuli holistically (as wholes) and the left analytically (by parts). For example Kimura (1966) exposed three to ten dots to each visual half-field for 80 msec. Subjects exhibited a left visual field superiority in guessing the number of dots. The brevity of the exposure time prevented subjects from counting the dots, lending support to the notion that the right hemisphere (associated with the left visual field) is superior at grasping the whole without a complete analysis of its parts.

Some musical skills are thought to be right hemisphere dependent. Although musical deficits are likely to exist after damage to the language-dominant (left) hemisphere, people with right hemisphere damage show deficits in discriminating complex sounds, timbres and melodies. In a dichotic listening task, Kimura (1973) played a different melody to each ear simultaneously. Subjects were then asked to pick out these two melodies from among four melodies, each of which was played, individually, to both ears. Normal subjects were able to pick out the melody that had been presented to the left ear (right hemisphere) better than the one presented to the right ear.

Bever (1975) discussed Kimura's findings and suggested that to musically naive subjects the perception of melody is a holistic phenomenon, thereby generating a left ear advantage for those subjects. In his own experiments, however, Bever discovered that musically sophisticated subjects experienced a musical sequence better in the right ear (left hemisphere), because, he argued, they approached the task analytically.

Inasmuch as each cerebral hemisphere has unique functional superiorities (summarized in figure 13.6), it seems inappropriate to refer to the language-dominant left hemisphere as the major one. It is more accurate to conceive of the hemispheres as complementarily specialized. The degree of hemispheric specialization, however, varies among individuals. Right-handed individuals who have a family history of right-handedness will show the greatest hemispheric specialization. Least likely to show hemispheric specialization are left-handed individuals with a family history of left-handedness. Some of these latter individuals are thought to have bilateral representation of basic skills. The possibility of bilateral representation is not surprising when we remember that each hemisphere has the capacity to replicate functions of the other; indeed, one hemisphere may take over for the other when it is injured or removed.

Right-hemisphere language dominance is not uncommon in adults

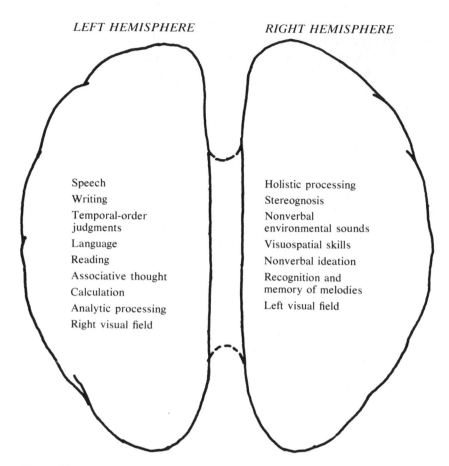

LEFT HEMISPHERE   *RIGHT HEMISPHERE*

Speech
Writing
Temporal-order
judgments
Language
Reading
Associative thought
Calculation
Analytic processing
Right visual field

Holistic processing
Stereognosis
Nonverbal
environmental sounds
Visuospatial skills
Nonverbal ideation
Recognition and
memory of melodies
Left visual field

Figure 13.6
Complementary specialization of cerebral hemispheres

who sustained injury to the left hemisphere early in life. The literature is replete with documented cases of the development of language by the right hemisphere after injury to the left. Nonetheless, the adaptability of the nervous system decreases with age and when left hemisphere injury occurs after puberty, the danger of permanent aphasia is great.

Do the Hemispheres Equally Support the Development of Speech and Language?
Although speech and language function can be taken over by the right hemisphere if necessary, there is evidence that the right hemisphere

does not have the same potential for speech and language specialization as the left has.

Dennis and Whitaker (1976) monitored the development of three children in whom one hemisphere of the brain was surgically removed during infancy (hemispherectomy) to arrest seizures associated with Sturge-Weber-Dimitri syndrome. Of the three children, two (SM and CA) had only the right hemisphere and one (MW) only the left. At the age of ten these children were given psychological and psycholinguistic tests. Intelligence was found to be comparable among the three, as shown in table 13.1. However, other differences emerged. When given a variety of complex verbal commands varying in information and syntactic complexity, only MW, the child with the left hemisphere, was able to maintain proficient performance. Syntactic rather than semantic complexity appeared to impair the performance of SM and CA. By contrast, as might be expected, the isolated left hemisphere (MW) performed more poorly on visuospatial tasks.

Functional asymmetry of the cerebral hemispheres is economical, enabling brain tissue to perform a wider variety of functions than would be possible if each hemisphere were a replicate of the other. On the other hand, the potential of each hemisphere to replicate the functions of the other, in a developing nervous system, provides a prudent backup system. As we conclude the discussion of how the brain functions to encode and decode speech and language, it seems appropriate to pose the question of whether the areas within the left hemisphere speech and language system are functionally divisible into phonologic, semantic, and syntactic subsystems. It is to this question we now turn.

Are Components of Language Neuroanatomically Distinct?

Within the left hemisphere there is neither uniform nor equal representation of linguistic functions. Damage to a small area in the hemisphere does not result in the impairment of *all* linguistic capabilities.

Table 13.1
IQ scores of children in the Dennis and Whitaker study

IQ Test	MW	SM	CA
Verbal	96	94	91
Performance	92	87	108
Full Scale	93	90	99

On the contrary, lesions in different areas of the hemisphere lead to qualitatively distinct aphasia syndromes. A review of the language and speech behaviors associated with the different aphasia syndromes will suggest a crude definition of the boundaries of the various linguistic domains.

Aphasiologists have no uniform criteria for classifying types of aphasia, the consequence of which is considerable terminological diversity. Widely accepted, however, as distinct aphasia syndromes are the following: Broca's aphasia, Wernicke's aphasia, conduction aphasia, and anomia.

Broca's Aphasia
Broca's aphasia, named for Paul Broca, who first described its symptoms, is known also as expressive or motor aphasia. It follows from a lesion in the posterior part of the inferior frontal gyrus, or Broca's area (see figure 13.1). However, according to Mohr (1976) the cluster of symptoms traditionally associated with Broca's aphasia results from a more extensive lesion than the one described by Broca. Ironically, even Broca's own patient had a more diffuse lesion, but Broca focused on the more circumscribed area in the inferior frontal region because of the view of his contemporaries that large strokes always begin as a smaller focus.

The symptoms of Broca's aphasia will seem logical if we note the proximity of Broca's area to the cortical region of the brain controlling the muscles of speech (see figure 13.1). The foremost symptom is the inability of the affected individual to speak fluently. Great effort is required to utter short halting phrases described as telegraphic because of the absence of function words (words like *the, by, but*). Literal *paraphasias*—substitutions, omissions, or distortions of sounds—are both frequent and inconsistent, and when the aphasic is permitted several repetitions of misarticulated phrases, his articulation usually improves.

Bound morphemes such as tense, plural, and comparative markers are frequently missing. Surface word order is usually appropriate, however, and the verbal output makes sense. The characteristics of the spoken speech are mirrored in patients' reading and writing. Although the comprehension of language may not be normal, it is usually good enough for these individuals to grasp the meaning of what they hear. In fact, most Broca's aphasics are painfully aware of their own mistakes. As you read the following samples of utterances produced by Broca's aphasics, remember that there is no way to reproduce on paper the intense effort these persons must make to produce even a few words.

Examiner: Tell me, what did you do before you retired?
Aphasic: Uh, uh, uh, puh, par, partender, no.
Examiner: Carpenter?
Aphasic: (shaking head yes) Carpenter, tuh, tuh, tenty [20] year.
Examiner: Tell me about this picture!
Aphasic: Boy . . . cook . . . cookie . . . took . . . cookie.

Neurolinguists agree that Broca's aphasics have suffered impairment to the phonological system but debate whether the syntactic component of language is impaired. Linguistic observations of aphasic language have a rather recent history compared with clinical studies. More research will be required to settle the issue of whether phonological theory can account for all of the linguistic aberrations displayed by Broca's aphasics when the lesion is confined to the frontal lobe.

Wernicke's Aphasia

Wernicke's aphasia, known also as sensory or receptive aphasia, is the consequence of a lesion in the auditory association cortex of the temporal lobe (see figure 13.1). This area is adjacent to the region that receives auditory stimuli. Predictably, the primary characteristic of this type of aphasia is impairment in the ability to understand spoken and written language. Wernicke's aphasics may suffer a severe loss of understanding even though their hearing is normal. Great variation in symptoms occurs in Wernicke's aphasia.

Fluency is usually not a problem, although interruptions in the flow of speech occur when the patient cannot retrieve a specific word. Often patients speak very rapidly, the content of what they say ranging from mildly inappropriate to complete nonsense, as in the following examples:

Examiner: Do you like it here in Kansas City?
Aphasic: Yes, I am.
Examiner: I'd like to have you tell me something about your problem.
Aphasic: Yes, I ugh can't hill all of my way. I can't talk all of the things I do, and part of the part I can go alright, but I can't tell from the other people. I usually most of my things. I know what can I talk and know what they are but I can't always come back even though I know they should be in, and I know should something eely I should know what I'm doing . . .

Circumlocutions are numerous: the aphasic talks in circles about an object he is unable to name, as when a patient says *what you drink* for *water*. Patients with word retrieval deficits overuse empty words like *thing* and *one*. Language alterations in the form of word substitutions may be numerous. At times the substitution bears a relation to the intended word, as when someone says *slipper* for *shoe* or *corn flakes* for *cereal*. At other times there is no apparent connection between the intended and substituted words. In extreme cases, patients use unrecognizable words called neologisms.

For patients with severe comprehension deficits the prognosis for recovery is poorer than for Broca's aphasics, who have better comprehension. Aphasiologists speculate that Wernicke's aphasics have damaged feedback systems, limiting their ability to monitor what they say and thus limiting their ability to correct themselves.

Whereas Broca's aphasia is primarily a deficit in the phonological component of language, Wernicke's aphasia affects the semantic and syntactic components. The Sylvian fissure separating Broca's and Wernicke's areas may represent a neuroanatomical boundary separating the phonological from the syntactic and semantic components at the cortical level. It must be pointed out, however, that Broca's and Wernicke's areas are connected subcortically by a bundle of nerve fibers called the *arcuate fasciculus*. This may serve as a transmission line carrying signals received in the auditory reception cortex to the auditory association cortex for interpretation and, subsequently, to the speech production cortex for verbalization. Should the arcuate fasciculus be damaged, the affected individual would be expected to have difficulty repeating what he had heard. And that is exactly what does happen in conduction aphasia.

Conduction Aphasia
Conduction aphasia follows from localized lesions in the temporoparietal regions that serve to synthesize meaning and form. All avenues of expression are affected. Spontaneous speech is fluent but circumlocutory and inadequately structured. Similar defects are found in spontaneous writing. Reading aloud is difficult, and repeating is severely disturbed. Comprehension of oral and written material is normal or only mildly affected.

Conduction aphasics can be differentiated from Broca's aphasics by their fluent spontaneous speech; Broca's aphasics find spontaneous speech harder than repetition. Conduction aphasics are like Wernicke's aphasics in that they are fluent, but unlike Wernicke's they have good speech comprehension. Conduction aphasia is not a problem of receptive or expressive mechanisms as much as it is a problem of the transmission between the two.

Anomia

In classic anomia the patient has difficulty finding words, both during the flow of speech and in naming on confrontation. That is, when presented with a stimulus object, the individual is unable to retrieve its name. Yet when these individuals are offered the correct name of the stimulus item, they instantly recognize it. Further, they can usually select the correct name from a group of names.

Comprehension and repetition of speech are normal, and speech is fluent although filled with circumlocutions. The following selected responses made by anomic aphasics aptly illustrate word finding difficulties.

Examiner: Who is the president of the United States?
Aphasic: I can't say his name. I know the man, but I can't come out and say . . . I'm very sorry, I just can't come out and say. I just can't write it to me now.
Examiner: Can you tell me a girl's name?
Aphasic: Of a girl's name, by mean, by which weight, I mean how old or young?
Examiner: On what do we sleep?
Aphasic: Of the week, er, of the night, oh from about 10:00, about 11:00 o'clock at night until about uh 7:00 in the morning.

The brain lesions associated with classical anomia involve the dominant angular gyrus (see figure 13.1), that area of the brain thought to be necessary for the formation of association between the sensory modalities.

To sum up, the different forms of aphasia show that representation of linguistic functions in the left hemisphere is by no means uniform or equal. We have seen that lesions in different areas of the left hemisphere lead to distinct aphasia syndromes. Future research on these distinctions is certain to be both interesting and important.

Exercises

1. Many technical terms appeared in this chapter. Compose a definition for each of the following:

a. aphasia
b. neurolinguistics
c. corpus callosum
d. temporal lobe
e. neuron
f. Broca's area

g. Wernicke's area
h. dichotic listening
i. ipsilateral
j. arcuate fasciculus
k. anomia
l. cortex

2. In what cortical regions are speech and language thought to be localized?

3. What is the corpus callosum, and how is it relevant to speech and language function?

4. Describe one research technique that has provided neurolinguists with information as to where speech and language are localized in the brain.

5. Suppose you were holding a pencil in your left hand and you wished to describe it. Discuss the chain of events occurring in the nervous system that would enable you to describe the pencil.

6. Discuss the complementary specialization of the cerebral hemispheres.

*7. Why is it thought that speech and language function may not be cognitively unique?

References

Bever, T. (1975) "Cerebral asymmetries in humans due to differentiation of two incompatible processes: holistic and analytic," in D. Aaronson and R. Rieber, eds., *Developmental Psycholinguistics and Communication Disorders,* New York Academy of Sciences, vol. 263, p. 251.

Brookshire, R. (1972) "Visual and auditory sequencing by aphasic subjects," *Journal of Communication Disorders* 5, 259–269.

Dennis, M., and H. Whitaker (1976) "Hemispheric equipotentiality and language acquisition," in *Language Development and Neurological Theory,* Brock University Conference, May 1975, Academic Press, New York.

DeRenzi, E., A. Pieczuro, and L. Vignolo (1966) "Oral apraxia and aphasia," *Cortex* 2, 50–73.

DeRenzi, E., G. Scotti, and H. Spinnler (1969) "Perceptual and associative disorders and visual recognition," *Neurology* 19, 634–642.

Eccles, J. (1972) *The Understanding of the Brain,* McGraw-Hill, New York.

Faglioni, P., H. Spinnler, and L. Vignolo (1969) "Contrasting behavior of right and left hemisphere-damaged patients on a discriminative and a semantic task of auditory recognition," *Cortex* 5, 366–389.

Gazzaniga, M., J. Bogen, and R. Sperry (1963) "Laterality effects in somesthesis following cerebral commissurotomy in man," *Neuropsychologia* 1, 209–215.

Gazzaniga, M., and R. Sperry (1967) "Language after section of the cerebral commisures," *Brain* 90, 131–148.

Geschwind, N., and W. Levitsky (1968) "Human brain: left–right asymmetries in temporal speech region," *Science* 161, 186–187.

Geschwind, N. (1972) "Language and the Brain," *Scientific American* 226, 76–83.

Kimura, D. (1961) "Cerebral dominance and the perception of verbal stimuli," *Canadian Journal of Psychology* 15, 166–171.

——— (1966) "Dual functional asymmetry of the brain in visual perception," *Neuropsychologia* 4, 275–285.

——— (1973) "The asymmetry of the human brain," *Scientific American*, March, 70–78.

Lackner, J., and H. Teuber (1973) "Alterations in auditory fusion thresholds after cerebral injury in man," *Neuropsychologia* 11, 409–415.

Levy, R. (1977) "The question of electrophysiological asymmetries preceding speech," in Haiganoosh Whitaker and Harry Whitaker, eds., *Studies in Neurolinguistics and Psycholinguistics,* Academic Press, New York.

McAdam, D., and H. Whitaker (1971a) "Language production: electroencephalographic localization in the normal human brain," *Science* 172, 499–502.

——— (1971b) "Electrocortical localization of language production," *Science* 174, 1359–1360.

Mohr, J. (1976) "Broca's area and Broca's aphasia," in Haiganoosh Whitaker and Harry Whitaker, eds., *Studies in Neurolinguistics and Psycholinguistics,* Academic Press, New York.

Ojemann, G., and A. Ward, Jr. (1971) "Speech representation in ventrolateral thalamus," *Brain* 94, 669–680.

Penfield, W., and L. Roberts (1959) *Speech and Brain Mechanisms,* Princeton University Press, Princeton, N.J.

Sholl, D. (1956) *The Organization of the Cerebral Cortex,* Wiley, New York.

Swisher, L., and I. Hirsh (1972) "Brain damage and the ordering of two temporally successive stimuli," *Neuropsychologia* 10, 137–152.

Wada, J., R. Clarke, and A. Hamm (1975) "Cerebral hemispheric asymmetry in humans," *Arhives of Neurology* 32, 239–246.

Wada, J. (1949) "A new method for the determination of the side of cerebral speech dominance: A preliminary report on the intracarotid injection of sodium aymtal in man," *Medical Biology* (Tokyo) 14, 221–222.

Witelson, S., and W. Pallie (1973) "Left hemisphere specialization for language in the newborn: neuroanatomical evidence of asymmetry," *Brain* 96, 641–646.

Chapter Fourteen

CAN CHIMPANZEES
LEARN LANGUAGE?

Anyone concerned with the study of human nature and human capacities must somehow come to grips with the fact that all normal humans acquire language, whereas acquisition of even its barest rudiments is quite beyond the capacities of an otherwise intelligent ape.
—N. Chomsky, *Language and Mind*

We have concentrated so far on natural systems of communication for both animals and humans, natural in the sense that these systems develop spontaneously and normally without outside intervention. We have raised questions with respect to the structure, use, processing, and acquisition of these systems. It is both interesting and helpful to compare these natural communication systems with systems that are not natural to the species learning them. Table 14.1 shows some examples of natural and nonnatural communication systems. Our purpose here is not to settle questions about the existence or nature of nonhuman language use, but rather to give readers enough data and direct them to enough references to allow them to critically assess these issues in light of our discussions of language structure and use in part II. Are chimpanzees able to use language the way humans do? The following sections should help the reader decide.

Washoe

In June 1966, Alan and Beatrice Gardner began a project that was to have immediate popular appeal, if not immediate academic acceptance. Their project was to teach a young (approximately one-year-old) female chimpanzee to communicate in American Sign Language (ASL). Although their avowed purpose was to probe "the extent to which another species might be able to use human language" (1969,

Table 14.1
Communication systems

	Human	Nonhuman
Natural	English Chinese Navajo	Bird vocalizations Bee dance Primate calls
Nonnatural	Fortran (computer language) Symbolic logic	Washoe's signs Sarah's tokens

664), it is evident that they were challenging claims such as the one we have quoted from Chomsky. As might well be expected, the success of the project quickly became a hotly debated issue. The popular press concluded almost immediately that Washoe was able to converse in ASL and articles began appearing with titles such as "First Message from the Planet of the Apes." This kind of reaction put the skeptic in a position comparable, in the public mind, with that of seventeenth-century defenders of the uniqueness of man, who argued that "brutes" (animals), unlike man, have no souls. It is unfortunate that the skeptic was placed in this position, because the Gardners' project is interesting and important enough to deserve serious intellectual consideration, and such consideration requires that we carefully scrutinize all claims about linguistic proficiency of chimps. We will review Washoe's basic accomplishments, inviting readers to consider for themselves some of the central questions raised by these studies (see exercises).

The problem of teaching a member of another species a human language presents the investigator with two fundamental preliminary decisions: what species to pick, and what language to use. The Gardners' choice in these matters was inspired.

Why a Chimp?
First and foremost, chimpanzees are among the most intelligent creatures of the animal world. When one combines this with the fact that they are notoriously imitative and quite sociable with their human cousins, one gets a promising picture of a prospective language learner. Chimps have other important characteristics as well. They are manually dexterous, are sociable with members of their own species, and grow to a convenient size through a sequence of phases that are comparable to those in human development as shown in figure 14.1. (Recall that as recently as 1900, human life expectancy in the United States was only 47 years.) These latter characteristics are important in

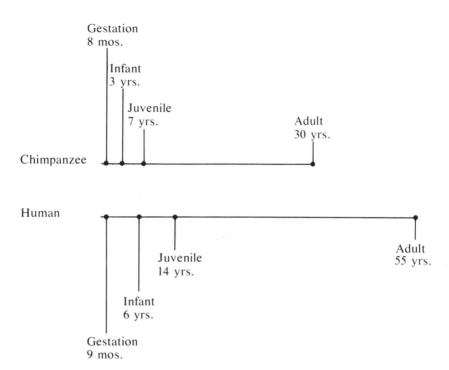

Figure 14.1
Primate age spans

that they allow the possibility of investigating communication among members of the species as well as allowing comparison of the acquisition of language with that of a normal human child.

Why American Sign Language?

Attempts to teach chimps *spoken* English have not been at all encouraging. For instance, Keith and Catherine Hayes (1951) attempted to teach spoken English to a chimp named Vicki. They raised Vicki like a human child, in an optimal home environment. Yet after six years of training, Vicki's speaking vocabulary was barely four words: *mama, papa, cup,* and *up.* The main problem seemed to be that a chimp's vocal apparatus is not suited to the production of many human speech sounds. Recalling the dexterous and imitative nature of chimps (who will occasionally gesture spontaneously to humans), the Gardners hit upon the idea of using a gestural language as the test system. A number of gestural systems of communication are available, but American Sign Language (ASL) was a natural choice for a number of reasons. Most important, it is a system used naturally by many people; it therefore affords a good basis of comparison for such things as acquisition rate, proficiency, and comprehension. It is also a system with structure comparable in many ways to spoken human languages. Finally, there is an iconic aspect to many signs that may be of some value at early stages of instruction. We will see examples of this iconicity in Washoe's acquisition of the signs for *bib, flower,* and *leash.* (These signs and others we will discuss are described in table 14.3.)

Teaching and Learning

Washoe's Learning Conditions
Unlike Vicki (the Hayes's chimp), Washoe was not raised in the home like a child. She was not raised in a conventional laboratory, either. Most of her time with the Gardners was spent in a two-and-a-half room house trailer supplied with the usual trappings of human life and surrounded by a pleasant yard, 5000 square feet in area. Washoe spent her nights alone, but during the day she was provided with an environment that was as stimulating as possible for learning ASL. She never lacked an ASL communicant, and there was opportunity for plenty of conversation, much play, and many outings. It will be easier to follow Washoe's progress with the chronology of events provided in table 14.2.

How Washoe Learned
Since the goal of the Gardners' experiment with Washoe was to assess the extent of her ability to learn ASL and not to test any particular theory of learning, virtually any teaching method thought to work was tried on occasion. In spite of this variation, the Gardners were still able to keep track of how Washoe learned at least some of her signs.

Just as human children do a great deal of verbal babbling, so chimps produce a certain amount of manual babbling, that is, natural and spontaneous gesturing. The Gardners thought that some of these natural gestures might form the basis of meaningful signs. But this hope was thwarted: probably only one of Washoe's signs was based on her natural gestures (the sign for *funny*) and this sign proved to be unstable. Babbling shades easily into invention, and it is possible to describe Washoe's acquisition of signs for *come/gimme* and *hurry* either as modified babbling or as invention. However, the Gardners describe a less controversial example of an invented sign when they write,

Table 14.2
Washoe chronology

Date	Event
1965 (c. June)	Washoe was born in the wild
1966 (June)	Is brought to Nevada and begins training
1966 (December)	Has acquired her first 4 signs
1967 (April)	Signs her first combinations
1967 (July)	Has acquired her first 13 signs
1968 (April)	Has acquired her first 34 signs
1969 (c. June)	Has acquired 85 signs; end of first three years of training
1970	Is sent to the Institute for Primate Studies in Norman, Oklahoma
1975	Is reported to have 160 signs

Sometimes we could not find an ASL equivalent for an English word in any of our manuals of ASL and no informant was available to supplement the manuals. In these cases we would adapt a sign of ASL for the purpose. The sign for *bib* was one of these cases and we chose to use the ASL sign for *napkin* or *wiper* to refer to bibs as well. This sign is made by touching the mouth region with an open hand and a wiping movement. During Month 18 Washoe had begun to use this sign appropriately for bibs, but it was still unreliable. One evening at dinner time, a human companion was holding up a bib and asking her to name it. Washoe tried *come-gimme* and *please,* but did not seem to be able to remember the *bib* sign that we had taught her. Then, she did something very interesting. With the index fingers of both hands she drew an outline of a bib on her chest—starting from behind her neck where a bib should be tied, moving her index fingers down along the outer edge of her chest, and bringing them together again just above her navel.

We could see that Washoe's invented sign for *bib* was at least as good as ours, and both were inventions. At the next meeting of the human participants in the project, we discussed the possibility of adopting Washoe's invention as an alternative to ours, but decided against it. The purpose of the project was, after all, to see if Washoe could learn a human system of two-way communication, and not to see if human beings could learn a system devised by an infant chimpanzee. We continued to insist on the *napkin-wiper* sign for bibs, until this became a reliable item in Washoe's repertoire. Five months later, when we were presenting films on Washoe's signing to fluent signers at the California School for the Deaf in Berkeley, we learned that drawing an outline of a bib on the chest with both index fingers is the correct sign for *bib* (1971, 39).

As a further possible case of innovation, Washoe was later reported (in Oklahoma) to have signed *water bird* for swans, though her attendant used the sign for *duck*.

Some signs were acquired by imitation. For instance, *sweet, flower, toothbrush,* and *smoke*. On the other hand, *more* and *open* were selectively shaped from gestures that were similar in some respect to these signs.

Finally, *tickle* and many other signs were the result of guidance (also called molding). In these cases, Washoe's hand was formed or molded into the proper shape and then brought through the motion required for the sign.

What evidence was there that Washoe was using these signs, especially the nouns, in the same way that human ASL signers do? That is, what evidence was there that Washoe was really learning the semantics of ASL? Not much has been reported on the results of various tests that were run on Washoe's vocabulary. In one experiment (1971, § VII) Washoe was shown three different exemplars—miniatures or photographs—of each of 33 different common objects, presented one at a time, in a box. She was asked to identify what was in the box and her first sign was recorded as the answer. She scored 53 out of the 99 correct answers on both test and retest, where chance would predict less than 3 correct. Even where there was error, the error was often reasonable in that she would give a sign for another member of the same category (for example, *brush* for *comb* or *cat* for *dog*). The Gardners also make the following interesting observation:

A particularly striking case of the information that can be obtained from errors occurred with the exemplars for the items *bird, cat, cow, dog,* and *ride*. For obvious reasons we could not put live animals in the boxes. Yet, we did not want to use two-dimensional photographs as the only illustrations for these items. Our solution was to use both photographs and miniature figurines, including toys. (In the case of *ride*, at the time of this test Washoe did not have a separate sign for automobile, so a toy automobile served as a valid exemplar.) Pooling the data of both the original session and the retest of the 99-trial test, there were 30 trials in which an exemplar of one of these items was presented. In 14 of these trials, the exemplar was a three-dimensional miniature and Washoe made the correct sign on only 3 of these trials. However, on 5 of the 11 trials in which she made an error, the error made was the sign for *baby*. In contrast, for the 16 trials in which the exemplar was a photograph, Washoe named the exemplar correctly on 8 trials. Of the 8 errors that she made for the photographs, only once did she make the sign for *baby*. Among the remaining 73 errors that Washoe made in these two sessions, the sign for *baby* only occurred on 3 trials (1971, 160).

To this the Gardners add:

The consistencies in Washoe's responses could not have been based on the absolute sizes of the exemplars that we used. In the photographs of animals, wagons, and automobiles there were no comparison objects to provide cues to relative size, yet Washoe could name them correctly although the figures were often smaller than the three-dimensional miniatures that she called *baby*. On the other hand, photographs of dolls and human babies, which also contained no comparison objects, were all correctly named (1971, 161).

These experiments may indicate that an important feature of human language acquisition is present in Washoe's case—the generalization of the use of a sign from its original referent to new cases. The sign for *key* is a case in point:

A great many cupboards and doors in Washoe's quarters have been kept secure by small padlocks that can all be opened by the same simple key. Because she was immature and awkward, Washoe had great difficulty in learning to use these keys and locks. Because we wanted her to improve her manual dexterity, we let her practice with these keys until she could open the locks quite easily (then we had to hide the keys). Washoe soon transferred this skill to all manner of locks and keys, including ignition keys. At about the same time, we taught her the sign for "key," using the original padlock keys as a referent. Washoe came to use this sign both to name keys that were presented to her and to ask for the keys to various locks when no key was in sight. She readily transferred the sign to all varieties of keys and locks (1971, 162).

It has also been noted in studies of child language acquisition that children will sometimes undergeneralize a word, and will, for example, use *dog* to refer only to one particular dog. Similar observations have been made with other signing chimps:

Lucy was presented with twenty-four different fruits and vegetables. Over a period of four days she was asked what the fruits and vegetables were in order to gather baseline data for the responses to these items. The signs she had in her vocabulary that were food-related signs were: *food, fruit, drink, candy,* and *banana*. She used *food, fruit,* and *drink* in a generic manner, whereas *banana* was specific to bananas. After the four days of baseline data the sign *berry* was taught to her using a cherry as an exemplar. She was presented with the fruits and vegetables for eight more days in order to determine whether the *berry* sign would generalize to the other berry-like items, or whether it would remain highly specific to cherries as the *banana* sign is specific to bananas. The *berry* sign remained specific to the cherries. After day eight she was taught the *berry* sign using a blackberry as an exemplar. She called the blackberry *berry* for two days and then returned to using *fruit* or *food* to describe it; *berry* was not only specific to cherry but there seemed to be a resistance to using the sign for other items (Fouts 1975, 381).

What Washoe Learned: Her Idiolect

Vocabulary   Although it has been reported that by 1975 Washoe had a vocabulary of at least 160 signs (Fouts 1975), the most detailed report of her vocabulary is by Gardner and Gardner (1975), who describe Washoe's first 85 signs in the order of acquisition. These signs passed the test of being used spontaneously and appropriately on 15 consecutive days. Table 14.3 lists some of these signs.

So far we have discussed only Washoe's vocabulary, but a vocabulary does not make a language. What evidence is there that her sign code has compositional structure?

Compositionality and Syntax   We have maintained that part of the essence of a human language is its compositional structure, and we would be inclined to say that Washoe has learned a human language only insofar as her idiolect reflects compositionality. It is therefore unfortunate that so little is known about this important aspect of her achievement.

As Washoe's chronology indicates, her first combinations such as *gimme sweet* and *come open* were observed after about 10 months of training. Over the next 26 months she was observed to make 294 different two-sign combinations. By the spring of 1968, after about two years of training, Washoe was using appropriately four- and five-sign combinations such as *you me go out* and *you me go out hurry*. Nonetheless, even such appropriate use does not settle the question of the syntax and semantics of Washoe's idiolect. It does not tell us whether her sentences have any structure (see chapter 8), nor does it tell us whether her semantics is in any way dependent on syntactic structure (let alone tell us in what *way* the semantics is dependent on the syntax).

More recently, the Gardners have attempted to establish that in Washoe's idiolect the signs are grouped into such categories as proper names, common nouns, pronouns, modifiers, verbs, and locatives (Gardner and Gardner 1975). However, the evidence for this categori-

Table 14.3
Signs used reliably by Washoe within three years of beginning of training
(27 out of total of 85)

Gloss	Usage
1. Come-gimme	Requesting a person or an animal to approach; also asking for objects out of reach; typically combined: *Come tickle, Gimme sweet*
2. More	For continuation or repetition; typically combined: *More go, More sweet gimme*
3. Up	Designating the location of objects or persons who are above Washoe; for a change in location from a lower to a higher place
4. Sweet	Sweet food and drinks; often combined: *Sweet drink, Sweet fruit*
5. Open	Opening doors, containers, and faucets
6. Tickle (Touch)	Tickling games
7. Go	Locomotion, especially when walking hand-in-hand with a person; being carried or being pulled in her toy wagon (Washoe usually indicated the direction of movement desired)
8. Out	Designating the location of persons or objects; for a change in location, as in going outdoors or removing objects from a container
9. Hurry	For getting things done quickly, such as an approach or the serving of a meal; typically combined: *Open hurry, Blanket hurry*
10. Toothbrush	Toothbrushes; the act of brushing teeth
11. Funny	An epithet for herself and certain persons; also when playing games such as tickling and chasing, and occasionally when being pursued after mischief
12. Flower	Flowers
13. Dog	Dogs and barking

Form		
Place where sign is made (P)	Configuration of active hand (C)	Movement (M)
The space in front of body	Relaxed hand, palm up	Wrist or fingers bend toward signer
Fingertips	Relaxed hand, palm toward signer	Fingertips of C contact P
The space above body	Flat hand, fingertips up	Pointing upward
Tongue	Index and second finger, extended from spread hand, fingertips toward signer	Contact
Index finger edges of hands	Relaxed hands, palm down	The hands contact, then separate with a rotating movement
Back of hand	Index finger hooked and extended	C is drawn across P
The space in front of body	Relaxed hand	Away from signer
Palm of curved hand	Relaxed hand, palm toward signer, fingertips down	C contacts P and is drawn upward
The space in front of body at shoulder height	Spread hand, bent at wrist	Vigorous shaking
Teeth	Index finger extended, side toward signer	Back and forth
Nose	Index finger extended	Contact (Washoe added a distinctive sound component to this sign by snorting while contacting nose)
Nose	Curved hand, palm toward signer	Fingertips of C contact P
Thigh	Flat hand, palm down	Repeated contact

Table 14.3

Gloss	Usage
14. You	Designating her companion; typically combined: *You drink, You Susan, You tickle Washoe*
15. Wiper (Napkin)	Bibs, washcloths, facial tissues, and handkerchiefs
16. Brush (Rub)	Hairbrushes, paintbrushes, whisk brooms; for being brushed
17. Me	Designating herself; typically combined: *Me drink, Me Washoe, Tickle me*
18. Roger	Roger S. Fouts, research assistant
19. Washoe	Chimpanzee Washoe, research subject
20. Càt	Cats and meowing
21. Key	Keys and locks
22. Baby	Human infants, dolls, and figurines, including those representing animals
23. Bird	Birds and birdcalls
24. Comb	Combs, combing and grooming
25. Smoke	Cigarettes, cigarette packages, matches, and matchboxes; smoking
26. Cow	Ungulates, and mooing
27. Car	Automobiles

Source: Gardner and Gardner 1975

Form		
Place where sign is made (P)	Configuration of active hand (C)	Movement (M)
Chest of her companion	Index finger extended	Contact
Mouth region	Flat hand, palm toward signer	Contact, usually followed by upward or sideways wiping motion
Back of hand	Compact hand, palm down	C is drawn back and forth over P repeatedly
Middle of chest	Index finger extended	Contact
Ear	Thumb and index finger together	Grasp then pull P
Ear	Relaxed hand, fingertips up	Forward, brushing P
Cheek	Thumb and index finger together	Grasp then pull to the side
Palm of hand	Index finger hooked and extended	Contact and rotate
Elbows	Curved hands	Arms cross and C grasps P, both hands active
Lips	Thumb and index finger together pointing toward P	Repeated grasping
Top, then side of head	Curved hand, palm toward P	C is drawn along P
Lips	Index and second finger extended from spread hand, palm toward signer	Contact
Brow ridge	Thumb extended	Contact
The space in front of body	Compact hands	Forearms are extended, then hands move up and down alternately, several inches distance maintained between hands

zation comes mainly from comparing Washoe's question-and-answer sequences with those of young children; such comparison leaves open a number of issues that might call the conclusions into question. In particular, this procedure assumes that one can really motivate these syntactic categories in the analysis of child language, and that is not obviously the case, because many of the tests are semantic and pragmatic.

For now, we must conclude that the existence of syntax and compositionality in Washoe's sign code is still an open question.

Chimp and Child

Part of the attractiveness of ASL as a language to teach Washoe was that it is a human language and thus it might be possible to compare Washoe's progress against that made by children. We know of no detailed comparison of Washoe and deaf children acquiring ASL, but the Gardners (1971) have compared her two-sign combinations with the earliest two-word utterances of hearing children, as shown in table 14.4.

As can be seen, the two schemes resemble each other closely.

Table 14.4
Parallel descriptive schemes for the earliest combinations by children and Washoe

Brown's (1970) scheme for children	
Types	Examples
Attributive: Ad + N	big train, red book
Possessive: N + N	Adam checker, mommy lunch
N + V	walk street, go store
Locative: N + N	sweater chair, book table
Agent–Action: N + V	Adam put, Eve read
Action–Object: V + N	put book, hit ball
Agent–Object: N + N	mommy sock, mommy lunch

Source: Thorpe 1974, from Gardner and Gardner 1971

Curiously, though, there are no reports of Washoe spontaneously asking questions, and this distinguishes her in one important respect from the normal child.

Conclusions about Washoe

What is one to conclude about Washoe's linguistic ability? Does she use ASL? Has she learned to communicate in a human language? These are extremely difficult questions to answer. We think it is important to keep a number of things in mind when coming to any conclusion, even a tentative one. On the one hand, chimps are quite clever, and care should be taken not to be too impressed by their ability to figure out complicated ways of getting what they want. On the other hand, our standards for determining language acquisition should not be so high that by the same standard human children could not be said to learn their language. It is important that any comparison include data on the acquisition of ASL by deaf children who are otherwise normal. Finally, since it is Washoe's idiolect that is under investigation, more must be known about its syntax and the syntax of ASL (on the latter, see Klima and Bellugi, 1978).

Scheme for Washoe	
Types	Examples
Object–Attributable	drink red, comb black
Agent–Attribute	Washoe sorry, Naomi good
Agent–Object	clothes Mrs. G., you hat
Object–Attribute	baby mine, clothes yours
Action–Location	go in, look out
Action–Object	go flower, pants tickle
Object–Location	baby down, in hat
Agent–Action	Roger tickle, you drink
Action–Object	tickle Washoe, open blanket
Appeal–Action	please tickle, hug hurry
Appeal–Object	gimme flower, more fruit

Sarah

It is clear from recent research that with the appropriate amount of training, chimps can learn small lists of individual vocabulary items, as Washoe did with signs. This, after all, is consistent with what we know about natural primate communication systems, which consist of fixed lists of individual vocabulary items in the form of discrete calls (see chapter 4). As we have already noted in connection with Washoe, before one can make the claim that a chimp has learned a language comparable to human language, one must show that it reflects compositionality. Can a chimpanzee string vocabulary items together in linear order in a compositional way? To put it another way, can a chimp make structured sentences? (Recall that linear order of elements is not enough to establish compositionality: bird songs are made up of sequences of individual discrete notes, but the individual notes have no meaning in isolation, nor is the song as a whole a compositional function of its parts.) As we have seen, compelling data on whether Washoe's language is compositional is lacking.

However, Ann and David Premack, in their work with a chimp named Sarah, have explicitly made the claim that Sarah not only learned vocabulary items but, further, that she at least understood structured sentences, even if she did not spontaneously produce them. This is an interesting claim, and we will examine the evidence for it.

Beginning in 1966, the Premacks and their associates taught Sarah to use a small set of plastic chips on a magnetic board; the chips were of various sizes, shapes, and colors, and each chip stood for a different vocabulary item. Sarah's training was based on conventional conditioning techniques, as illustrated by the manner in which Sarah learned the term *banana* (Premack and Premack 1972, 95):

The trainer began the process . . . by placing a slice of banana between himself and Sarah. The chimpanzee, which was then about five years old, was allowed to eat the tasty morsel while the trainer looked on affectionately. After the transaction had become routine, a language element consisting of a pink plastic square was placed close to Sarah while the slice of banana was moved beyond her reach. To obtain the fruit Sarah now had to put the plastic piece on a "language board" on the side of her cage. (The board was magnetic and the plastic square was backed with a thin piece of steel so that it would stick.) After Sarah had learned this routine the fruit was changed to an apple and she had to place a blue plastic word for apple on the board. Later several other fruits, the verb "give" and the plastic words that named each of them were introduced.

In this way, Sarah was able to associate certain objects and actions with individual chips, which formed the words, as it were, of her artificial language. She was able to write and understand simple instructions on her magnetic board. When she wrote *give apple,* a piece of apple was given to her; when she wrote *wash apple,* the trainer washed an apple in a bowl of water; and so on.

So far, this does not show that Sarah is using her language in a compositional way, since the instruction with two chips *give apple* might simply be a single unanalyzable message used by Sarah when she wants an apple. However, the Premacks (1972, 98) present the following evidence to substantiate their claim that Sarah could comprehend structured sentences:

To test Sarah's sentence comprehension she was taught to correctly follow these written instructions: "Sarah insert apple pail," "Sarah insert banana pail," "Sarah insert apple dish" and "Sarah insert banana dish." Next instructions were combined in a one-line vertical sequence ("Sarah insert apple pail Sarah insert banana dish"). The chimpanzee responded appropriately. Then the second "Sarah" and the second verb "insert" were deleted to yield the compound sentence: "Sarah insert apple pail banana dish." Sarah followed the complicated instructions at her usual level of accuracy.

The test with the compound sentence is of considerable importance, because it provides the answer to whether or not Sarah could understand the notion of constituent structure: the hierarchical organization of a sentence. The correct interpretation of the compound sentence was "Sarah put the apple in the pail and the banana in the dish." To take the correct actions Sarah must understand that "apple" and "pail" go together but not "pail" and "banana," even though the terms appear side by side. Moreover, she must understand that the verb "insert" is at a higher level of organization and refers to both "apple" and "banana." Finally, Sarah must understand that she, as the head noun, must carry out all the actions. If Sarah were capable only of linking words in a simple chain, she would never be able to interpret the compound sentence with its deletions. The fact is that she interprets them correctly. If a child were to carry out the instructions in the same way, we would not hesitate to say that he recognizes the various levels of sentence organization: that the subject dominates the predicate and the verb in the predicate dominates the objects.

The Premacks, then, take as their crucial evidence the fact that Sarah interpreted the "compound sentence" correctly. Presented with *Sarah insert apple pail banana dish,* she correctly placed the apple in the pail and the banana in the dish, and she did not carry out some other action—say, to place all three items (apple, pail, banana) on the dish. The claim, then, is that Sarah understood that the linear sentence sequence *apple pail banana dish* was structured roughly as *(apple-in-pail) AND (banana-in-dish)*. This, in effect, is to claim that Sarah's chip language is structured and compositional.

The Premacks' claim is a strong one. It would be quite striking if true, and for this reason we must be very careful in evaluating the evidence. Does the evidence we have presented support the claim that Sarah could comprehend structured sentences? We will not attempt to settle this question here, for readers are now in a position to judge for themselves how "human" Sarah's language can be said to be. After a careful reading of the Premacks' article, the reader is invited to ponder some questions: Could we use a compound sentence to instruct Sarah to carry out novel actions, instead of actions that she had been previously trained to carry out? In other words, is Sarah able to comprehend a novel message? Further, structural ambiguity is an important aspect of human language structure—what would it mean for Sarah's chip language to be structurally ambiguous? That is, what various actions might Sarah carry out when faced with the sequence *apple, pail, banana, dish* that would suggest that Sarah is able to assign different groupings (structures) to strings of items? These questions will surely have to be dealt with in assessing the claim that Sarah's language is structured and compositional.

Chimp to Chimp Communication

Recall that one desirable quality of chimps as potential language learners is their sociability with others of their species. This makes it feasible to attempt to answer a number of further questions concerning chimps who have been taught even the rudiments of a human language. For instance: (1) Are there individual differences between chimps learning sign language? (2) Can and will chimps communicate with other signing chimps? (3) Can and will chimps teach each other to sign? The reports are still too incomplete (Fouts 1975) or anecdotal (Linden 1976) for one to feel confident about them, but there are glimmers of answers.

To investigate the first question, Fouts (1973) taught two male and two female chimps ten signs each and recorded the amount of time it took each to learn the signs. Each chimp was then tested in a box experiment, similar to the one already reported, and the results con-

Table 14.5
Acquisition times and accuracy of four chimpanzees for ten signs

	Minutes to acquisition (mean)	Correct responses (percentage)
Cindy	79.7	26.39
Booee	54.3	58.33
Thelma	159.1	59.72
Bruno	136.4	90.28

tinue to indicate considerable individual variation, this time in accuracy, as shown in table 14.5.

As to the second question, investigations concerning communication *among* chimps are currently under way. In the preliminary findings, signing between chimps seems confined to such situations as mutual comforting, eating, and general play activities. But there are some complications, as Fouts ruefully notes (1975, 380):

The food eating situation has turned out to be somewhat of a one-way ASL communication because neither of the two males seems to want to share food with the other. For example, when one of the two chimpanzees has a desired fruit or drink, the other chimpanzee will sign such combinations as *gimme fruit* or *gimme drink*. Generally, when the chimpanzee with the desired food sees this request, he runs off with his prized possession.

It is still too early to answer the third question, whether chimps can and will teach each other to sign, and we must await the results of future research. But the first necessary steps have been taken. After living and signing with human beings, Washoe is now settled in a colony with other chimps. What will happen? When we recall the Koshima Island macaques who established a food-washing tradition among themselves (see chapter 4), we have some grounds for hoping that chimps will teach other chimps to sign. At the moment, we can only wait and watch.

In this book we have studied natural animal communication systems as well as (natural) human language. We now have an excellent opportunity to integrate these areas in evaluating the work that has been done on the artificial languages of chimps. Thus, in ending this book we have posed a set of questions that readers can use as a beginning for their own exploration of language and communication.

Exercises

*1. Why might Washoe have called miniatures, but not pictures, *baby*? (Could *baby* also mean to Washoe "small example of"?)

2. What evidence is there that Washoe produces and understands ASL?

*3. Design an experiment (a thought experiment) that could show, to your satisfaction, whether Washoe can use ASL as a human does.

4. Recall, from chapter 8, four important aspects of syntactic structure. What evidence is there that Washoe's idiolect has syntactic structure?

*5. What semantic similarities and differences are there between Washoe's sign language and natural spoken languages? Can we attribute *meaning* to Washoe's code?

*6. What pragmatic similarities and differences are there between Washoe's signing and human speech? Is Washoe's signing stimulus-free and contextually appropriate?

*7. What are some similarities and some differences between the way Washoe was instructed in sign language and the way normal children learn their first language?

*8. Suppose Washoe were to successfully pass a suitable language use test. What would this tell us about the answers to such questions as:
(a) Is the capacity for language acquisition innate?
(b) Is the capacity for language acquisition specific to the human species?
(c) Is the capacity for language acquisition innate in the human species?

*9. Give a nonstructural explanation for Sarah's behavior with the string *apple pail banana dish*. (Hint: Suppose she simply goes from top to bottom, putting an item into the container mentioned next.)

*10. Why might a task such as stacking distinct blocks be better than placing fruit in containers as a test of Sarah's comprehension of structure?

*11. Discuss the communication systems of Sarah and Washoe in terms of the theories listed on the chart picturing the structure of human language given in the Note to the Student at the beginning of this book.

References

Brown, R. (1970) "The first sentences of child and chimpanzee," in *Selected Psycholinguistics Papers*, Free Press, New York.

Fouts, R. (1972) "The use of guidance in teaching sign language to a chimpanzee," *Journal of Comparative and Physiological Psychology*, 80, 515–522.

——— (1973) "Acquisition and testing of gestural signs in four young chimpanzees," *Science* 180, 978–980.

——— (1974) "Language: origins, definition and chimpanzees," *Journal of Human Evolution* 3, 475–482.

————— (1975) "Capacity for language in great apes," in R. Tuttle, ed., *Socioecology and Psychology of Primates*, Mouton, The Hague.

Gardner, B., and R. Gardner (1971) "Two way communication with an infant chimpanzee," in Schreier and Stollnitz, ed., *Behavior of Non-Human Primates*, Academic Press, New York.

Gardner, R., and B. Gardner (1969) "Teaching sign language to a chimpanzee," *Science* 165, 664–672.

————— (1975) "Evidence for sentence constituents in early utterances of child and chimpanzee," *Journal of Experimental Psychology* 104, 244–267.

Hayes, C. (1951) *The Ape in Our House*, Harper & Row, New York.

Klima, E., and U. Bellugi (1978) *The Signs of Language*, Harvard University Press, Cambridge, Mass.

Linden, E. (1976) *Apes, Men and Language*, Pelican Books, Baltimore, Maryland.

Premack, A., and D. Premack (1972) "Teaching language to an ape," *Scientific American* 227, 92–99.

Thorpe, W. H. (1974) *Animal Nature and Human Nature*, Doubleday, Garden City, New York.

INDEX